PAST PERFORMANCE HANDBOOK

Applying Commercial Practices to Federal Procurement

SECOND EDITION

PAST PERFORMANCE HANDBOOK

Applying Commercial Practices to Federal Procurement

SECOND EDITION

Joseph W. Beausoleil

MANAGEMENTCONCEPTS

MANAGEMENTCONCEPTS
8230 Leesburg Pike, Suite 800
Vienna, VA 22182
(703) 790-9595
Fax: (703) 790-1371
www.managementconcepts.com

Printed in the United States of America

Library of Congress Cataloging-in-Publication Data

Beausoleil, Joseph W.
Past performance handbook : applying commercial practices to federal procurement / Joseph W. Beausoleil. — 2nd ed.
p. cm.
Prev. ed. authored by Peter S. Cole and Joseph W. Beausoleil.
ISBN 978-1-56726-280-3
1. Public contracts—United States. 2. Letting of contracts—United States—Decision making. 3. Performance standards. 4. Contracting out—United States. I. Cole, Peter S. Past performance handbook. II. Title.
HD3861.U6C655 2010
352.4'390973—dc22

2010013854

10 9 8 7 6 5 4 3 2 1

ABOUT THE AUTHOR

Joseph W. Beausoleil served as an advisor to the U.S. Agency for International Development in implementing past performance requirements that resulted from the Federal Acquisition Streamlining Act of 1994. He developed the agency's procedures for evaluating past performance information and contractor performance. He has had extensive experience offering past performance training to contracting and technical officers. As the agency's liaison with the Office of Federal Procurement Policy, Mr. Beausoleil participated in interagency working groups in developing the sample report form used to evaluate contractor performance and rewriting the best practices guide for past performance.

Mr. Beausoleil has a PhD in Management from the University of California for Advanced Studies and an MA in Economics from UCLA. He now resides with his wife in Estero, Florida. His email address is jbeausolei@aol.com.

In memory of

Peter S. Cole
1936–2008

CONTENTS

PREFACE TO THE SECOND EDITION

Evaluating contractor performance and using the evaluation results to make future award decisions in competitive acquisitions has been a difficult practice to implement across the federal government. The original edition of this handbook identified two necessary conditions for success. One was that agency procedures used to evaluate contractor performance must focus on the same assessment areas and use similar rating scales. The other was that past performance information obtained through the evaluations had to be accessible to source selection officials from a single source.

The second condition has been met. No longer do source selection officials have to obtain access to each agency's past performance database to obtain a copy of the evaluation information on one of the agency's contractors. One system for maintaining and making accessible all contractor performance reports—the Past Performance Information Retrieval System (PPIRS)—is now in place. The first condition, however, has been only partially achieved. All agencies have procedures for evaluating contractor performance, but the agencies lack uniformity among their assessment areas and rating scales. The lack of uniformity limits the usefulness of the information in PPIRS. This revised edition of the *Past Performance Handbook* proposes a way to standardize the assessment areas and rating scales without affecting the evaluation system particular to any agency or designed for a particular product or service line.

In spite of the developments to systems of collecting and maintaining performance information, the Government Accountability Office reports that less than a third of required contracts are being evaluated. The underlying problem seems to be relying on only the contracting officer to conduct the evaluations. The evaluation of contractor performance is a responsibility shared with the acquisition team, which includes not just government employees but also the contractors providing the product or service. For this reason, this second edition focuses on making the various team members aware of their roles and providing them with the tools they need.

Contracting officers and contractors will find something of interest in every chapter. The first chapter is directed primarily to contracting officers and the last chapter, to contractors. Source selection officials should focus on the material in Chapters 2 through 6 before taking on the responsibility of evaluating proposals. Officials from technical and program offices, when serving as contracting officer representatives (CORs) or as contracting officer technical representatives (COTRs), should concentrate on the material in Chapters 7 through 12.

If contracting officers evaluated every contract and order, they would greatly simplify the source selection process and awards would be made to the most qualified offerors. I hope that the *Past Performance Handbook* will serve as a practical resource for those participating in the evaluation of contractor performance and for those using the evaluation results in source selection.

Joseph W. Beausoleil
July 2010

ACKNOWLEDGMENTS

I had enormous help writing this second edition of the *Past Performance Handbook*. First, I must recognize the late Peter S. Cole, coauthor of the first edition, whose guidance on using past performance information in source selection is as valid today as it was eight years ago. Peter's experience as a Navy procurement officer and as a consultant and trainer in government contracting provided valuable insight and knowledge.

I want to also acknowledge Thomas L. McGovern, a partner with Hogan & Hartson LLP, and Timothy D. Palmer, a former general counsel with Lockheed Martin Systems Integration, who wrote the original Chapter 13 on legal issues in past performance. They emphasized the importance of Government Accountability Office (GAO) decisions in informing federal contractors of their legal rights and in guiding agency procurement officials in future procurements.

I am particularly grateful to Lawrence W. Byrnes, former Dean of Education at Florida Gulf Coast University, for providing insights on how to achieve my goal of convincing the procurement community that evaluating contractor performance and using past performance information in source selection are interdependent. In other words, objective performance evaluations produce constructive past performance information for use in selecting the best qualified offerors.

My appreciation goes to GAO for the many decisions cited in the text and abridged in Appendix B. The GAO also provided data to support the claim that to make past performance information consistent and useful throughout the government, we must first standardize evaluation criteria and rating scales in evaluating contractor performance.

Many thanks also to Management Concepts for inviting me to prepare this second edition, supporting the effort, and allowing me to use the invaluable research tool, the *FAR Update Service*.

Most of all, thanks to my wife, Patricia, who has been my sounding board and has such a gentle way of letting me know when I need to change something.

CHAPTER 1

EVALUATING PAST PERFORMANCE

"By increasing attention to contractor performance on in-process contracts and ensuring that past performance data is readily available for source selection teams, agencies are reaping two benefits: (1) better current performance because of the active dialog between the contractor and the government; and (2) better ability to select high quality contractors. . . ." OFPP[1]

The evaluation of past performance is not a new concept. It has been a long-established requirement that an offeror's past performance be examined as part of the responsibility determination made just before contract award.[2] Relatively new, however, are the requirements to consider an offeror's past performance as an evaluation factor for source selection[3] and to evaluate a contractor's performance annually and upon completion of a contract or order.[4]

The requirement to use past performance as an evaluation factor in source selection was initiated by the Federal Acquisition Streamlining Act of 1994, which called for greater use of commercial practices in government procurement. In the private sector, good performers are rewarded with new business. Using past performance information in source selection, however, necessitates the availability of past performance information. Thus, the periodic evaluation of contractor performance is also required.

RELATED BUT DIFFERENT EVALUATIONS

Although the evaluation of an offeror's past performance information for source selection and the evaluation of a contractor's performance in executing a contract are related, they are very different kinds of evaluations. They have different purposes, are done at different times, and rely on different information sources. These two evaluations are linked, however, because they use the same evaluation criteria. Thus, the results of contractor performance evaluations provide the input—past performance information—for source selection evaluations.

Source Selection Evaluations

Purpose—The purpose of source selection evaluations is to assess the offeror's ability to perform the prospective contract based on the offeror's past performance on comparable contracts and then match it to the assessed ability of competing offerors as indicated by their past performance. An offeror's past performance on other contracts is a good indicator of how well it might perform on future contracts. It can be a significant factor in the determination of the competitive range or in the source selection decision if the award is made without discussions. The evaluation results also can be a significant factor in tradeoff decisions and in the final source selection.

Timing—Evaluating past performance information for source selection is a solicitation activity primarily performed before establishing the competitive range or making an award without discussions. An offeror's past performance also may be considered when making the source selection decision.

Information Sources—Information about an offeror's performance on past contracts is obtained from contract references provided by the offeror, information gleaned from agency records or from third parties, and reports on contractor performance evaluations conducted by the contracting agency or other agencies.

Contractor Performance Evaluations

Purpose—The purpose of contractor performance evaluations is to obtain past performance information for use in source selection. The evaluations also motivate contractors to optimum performance because the results of the evaluation—past performance information—might be used in future award decisions.

Timing—Contractor performance evaluations must be conducted at the time the work under the contract or order is completed. In addition, interim evaluations must be conducted on contracts and orders exceeding one year.

Information Sources—Contractor performance evaluations are based on input from the acquisition team, which always includes representatives from the contracting and technical offices and, when appropriate, end users. The acquisition team also includes the financial, legal, audit, and other personnel involved with the contract, as well as the contractor that is furnishing the supplies or services.

SAME EVALUATION CRITERIA

Evaluation criteria are based on the same four assessment areas: quality of product or service, timeliness, cost control, and business relations. The first three of the areas—quality, timeliness, and cost control—are concerned with how well the contractor complied with the specific contractual requirements. The fourth assessment area, business relations, relates to the working relationship between the contractor and the government, as well as the contractor's management in delivering the product or service.

In source selection, the evaluation criteria should be tailored to the specific elements of quality, timeliness, cost control, and/or business relations that are considered critical to successful completion of the proposed contract. The criteria (i.e., factors and significant subfactors) are stated in the request for proposals (RFP).[5] In contractor performance evaluations, the criteria are the requirements specified in the contract regarding quality, timeliness, and cost control, along with generally accepted professional standards for relating to the government and managing a contract.

MEASURABLE PERFORMANCE STANDARDS

The requirement to evaluate a contractor's performance changes the way performance standards are written. In the past, performance standards were considered adequate if they served as the basis for a judgment regarding the acceptance or rejection of the contractor's performance in furnishing a service or supply. Now, performance standards should facilitate a judgment regarding how well the contractor performed all aspects of contract execution, not just delivering the end results. This change places an added responsibility on the government to establish measurable performance standards that will enable an assessment, and not merely an acceptance or rejection, of a contractor's performance.

The purpose of contractor performance evaluations is to provide past performance information for source selection. The more accurate and objective the past performance information, the more useful the information will be in source selection. The information will be accurate and objective to the extent that the evaluation was based on measurable performance standards.

Generally, it is not difficult to establish measurable performance standards for acquisitions that are expressed in terms of physical characteristics (e.g., construction and supply contracts). The physical characteristics—the description or specifications—contain measurable standards against which a contractor's performance can be evaluated accurately and objectively.

Acquisitions that are expressed in terms of functions to be performed or performance required are a different story. The performance standards must be tailored to the instant acquisition, and their measurability varies depending on the nature of the acquisition. Using performance-based acquisition methods,[6] however, ensures that the performance standards are expressed to the highest degree of measurability for the instant acquisition. These methods include (1) expressing the requirements in terms of the results required and (2) establishing, to the extent practicable, measurable performance standards with respect to quality, timeliness, and quantity.

In summary, if the requirements are expressed in terms of physical characteristics, the performance standards are measurable and the contractor performance evaluation can result in an accurate and objective assessment of the contractor's performance. If the requirements are expressed in terms of functions to be performed or performance required, the accuracy and objectivity of the evaluation of contractor performance depend on the extent to which the government was able to establish measurable performance standards. Thus, the usefulness (i.e., the accuracy and objectivity) of past performance information in the source selection depends on the measurability of the performance standards used in the contract.

ESTABLISHING THE BASIS FOR EVALUATION IN THE SOLICITATION AND CONTRACT

The basis for past performance evaluations for source selection is established in the solicitation. The basis for contractor performance evaluations is established in the contract.

Evaluation Basis for Source Selection

When using the uniform contract format,[7] the past performance evaluation criteria used for source selection are stated in the RFP's Section M, *Evaluation Factors for Award.* Section M refers to the evaluation criteria as factors and significant subfactors. They must represent the key areas of importance and emphasis to be considered in the source selection decision and support meaningful comparison and discrimination between competing proposals. The rating method need not be disclosed, only the general approach for evaluating past performance information. The RFP must also state the relative importance of the non-cost evaluation factors in relation to cost or price.

Note that when acquiring commercial items,[8] a different contract format applies. Instructions to offerors on submitting past performance information are provided in solicitation provision FAR 52.212-1, and the past performance evaluation criteria are incorporated into solicitation provision FAR 52.212-2.

Evaluation Basis for Contractor Performance Evaluations

Performance standards are found in various parts of the contract. For example, in the uniform contract format, the performance standards are in Section C, *Description/Specifications/Statement of Work;* Section E, *Inspection and Acceptance;* Section F, *Deliveries or Performance;* and Section I, *Contract Clauses.* If the acquisition is for a commercial item, the performance standards are contained in the schedule of supplies/services (block 20 of the SF 1449) and in contract clauses 52.212-4 and 52.212-5.

Performance standards may be explicit, i.e., specifically stated in the contract, or implicit, i.e., implied in generally accepted professional or business practices regarding relations with the government. The contractor performance evaluation is an overall assessment of how well the contractor met its contractual commitment; it is not restricted to specifically identified evaluation criteria, as is the case with the evaluation for source selection.

The results of contractor performance evaluations are the best source of past performance information for use in source selection. The accuracy and objectivity of the past performance information depend on the measurability of the performance standards used in evaluating the contractor. The more measurable the performance standards, the more accurate and objective the past performance information. The more accurate and objective the past performance information, the more useful it will be in future award decisions.

PRE-AWARD AND POST-AWARD ACTIVITIES

Because the evaluation of past performance information in source selection and the evaluation of a contractor's performance on current or completed contracts are two very different kinds of evaluations, each has its own policies and procedures. This book treats the evaluations separately. Source selection evaluations are a pre-award activity and are treated first in Chapters 2 through 6. Contractor performance evaluations, a post-award activity, are addressed in Chapters 7 through 12. The final chapter addresses legal rights that contractors can invoke to ensure fair evaluation of their past performance.

Note that disputes have arisen regarding the interpretation of past performance regulations. Such disputes are usually resolved through a formal bid protest filed with the Government Accountability Office (GAO) or the Court of Federal Claims. The resulting decision resolves the immediate protest on past performance. More important, however, these decisions, when considered as a body of law, fill in the "gaps" in the regulations and thereby serve both to inform federal contractors concerning their legal rights and to guide agency procurement officials' actions in connection with future procurements.

GAO, in particular, has fostered consistent practices among agencies by issuing numerous decisions that provide guidance as to how the regulations should work in practice. At times, to support the discussion of past performance regulations, examples from GAO decisions are used in this handbook. The examples are presented in summary form, i.e., the issue and the rationale for the decision. Those who would like more information can find an abridged version of the GAO decision in Appendix B.

NOTES

1. Office of Federal Procurement Policy, *Best Practices for Collecting and Using Current and Past Performance Information,* May 2000, p. 1.
2. FAR 9.104-3(b). "*Satisfactory performance record.* A prospective contractor that is or recently has been seriously deficient in contract performance shall be presumed to be nonresponsible, unless the contracting officer determines that the circumstances were properly beyond the contractor's control, or that the contractor has taken appropriate corrective action. Past failure to apply sufficient tenacity and perseverance to perform acceptably is strong evidence of nonresponsibility. Failure to meet the quality requirements of the contract is a significant factor to consider in determining satisfactory performance. The contracting officer shall consider the number of contracts involved and the extent of deficient performance in each contract when making this determination. If the pending contract requires a subcontracting plan pursuant to Subpart 19.7, The Small Business Subcontracting Program, the contracting officer shall also consider the prospective contractor's compliance with subcontracting plans under recent contracts."
3. FAR 15.304(c)(3)(i). "Except as set forth in paragraph (c)(3)(iii) of this section, past performance shall be evaluated in all source selections for negotiated competitive acquisitions expected to exceed the simplified acquisition threshold. (ii) For solicitations involving bundling that offer a significant opportunity for subcontracting, the contracting officer must include a factor to evaluate past performance indicating the extent to which the offeror attained applicable goals for small business participation under contracts that required subcontracting plans (15 U.S.C. 637(d)(4)(G)(Ii)). (iii) Past performance need not be evaluated if the contracting officer documents the reason past performance is not an appropriate evaluation factor for the acquisition."
4. FAR 42.1502. "Policy

   "(a) Past performance evaluations shall be prepared as specified in paragraphs (b) through (g) of this section at the time the work under the contract or order is completed. In addition, interim evaluations shall be prepared as specified by the agencies to provide current information for source selection purposes, for contracts or orders with a period of performance, including options, exceeding one year. These evaluations are generally for the entity, division, or unit that performed the contract or order. The content of the evaluations should be tailored to the size, content, and complexity of the contractual requirements.

"(b) Except as provided in paragraphs (e), (f) and (h) of this section, agencies shall prepare an evaluation of contractor performance for each contract that exceeds the simplified acquisition threshold.

"(c) Agencies shall prepare an evaluation of contractor performance for each order that exceeds the simplified acquisition threshold placed against a Federal Supply Schedule contract, or under a task order contract or a delivery order contract awarded by another agency (i.e. Governmentwide acquisition contract or multi-agency contract). This evaluation shall not consider the requirements under paragraph (g) of this section.

"(d) For single-agency task order and delivery order contracts, the contracting officer may require performance evaluations for each order in excess of the simplified acquisition threshold when such evaluations would produce more useful past performance information for source selection officials than that contained in the overall contract evaluation (e.g., when the scope of the basic contract is very broad and the nature of individual orders could be significantly different). This evaluation need not consider the requirements under paragraph (g) of this section unless the contracting officer deems it appropriate.

"(e) Past performance evaluations shall be prepared for each construction contract of $550,000 or more, and for each construction contract terminated for default regardless of contract value. Past performance evaluation may also be prepared for construction contracts below $550,000. (f) Past performance evaluations shall be prepared for each architect-engineer services contract of $30,000 or more, and for each architect-engineer services contract that is terminated for default regardless of contract value. Past performance evaluations may also be prepared for architect-engineer services contracts below $30,000. (g) Past performance evaluations shall include an assessment of contractor performance against, and efforts to achieve, the goals identified in the small business subcontracting plan when the contract includes the clause at 52.219-9, Small Business Subcontracting Plan.

"(h) Agencies shall not evaluate performance for contracts awarded under Subpart 8.7."

5. FAR 15.304(b). "Evaluation factors and significant subfactors must— (1) Represent the key areas of importance and emphasis to be considered in the source selection decision: and (2) Support meaningful comparison and discrimination between and among competing proposals."
6. FAR 37.102. "Policy

   "(a) Performance-based acquisition (see Subpart 37.6) is the preferred method for acquiring services (Public Law 106-398, section 821). When acquiring services, including those acquired under supply contracts or orders, agencies must—

   "(1) Use performance-based acquisition methods to the maximum extent practicable, except for— (i) Architect-engineer services acquired in accordance with 40 U.S.C. 1101 et seq.; (ii) Construction (see Part 36); (iii) Utility services (see Part 41); or (iv) Services that are incidental to supply purchases; and

"(2) Use the following order of precedence (Public Law 106-398, section 821(a)); (i) A firm-fixed price performance-based contract or task order. (ii) A performance-based contract or task order that is not firm-fixed price. (iii) A contract or task order that is not performance-based."

7. FAR 15.204-1.
8. FAR 12.303. "Contract format. Solicitations and contracts for the acquisition of commercial items prepared using this Part 12 shall be assembled, to the maximum extent practicable, using the following format: (a) Standard Form (SF) 1449; …"

CHAPTER 2

PRE-AWARD: USING PAST PERFORMANCE AS AN EVALUATION FACTOR

"... [P]ast performance shall be evaluated in all source selection for negotiated acquisitions expected to exceed the simplified acquisition threshold." FAR[1]

This chapter provides guidance to government personnel in preparing a request for proposals (RFP) when past performance is used as an evaluation factor in source selection. The evaluation process has not changed. Past performance has been and remains one of the six non-cost evaluation factors cited in the FAR that may be used to assess the quality of an offeror's proposal. What has changed is the requirement to use past performance as an evaluation factor or significant subfactor in source selection.[2]

To comply with that requirement, contracting officers should answer the following questions before preparing the RFP:

- Which evaluation factors would be most appropriate?
- Is there a reasonable explanation for not using past performance as an evaluation factor?
- What is the relative importance of the evaluation factors selected?
- What will be evaluated as past performance?
- How will past performance be described in the RFP?
- How will past performance be rated or scored?

The following sections will address these areas, suggest how they might be handled, discuss some of the problems that might be encountered, and propose solutions.

EVALUATION FACTORS

Before deciding whether and how to use past performance as an evaluation factor, the contracting officer should consider what other factors might be important in the instant acquisition. The FAR identifies seven areas that are considered in source selection decisions. In addition to cost or price, which must be considered in every source selection, there are six non-cost evaluation factors: past performance, compliance with solicitation requirements, technical excellence, management capability, personnel qualifications, and prior experience.[3]

Cost or Price

Cost or price is a mandatory evaluation factor in all procurements. Although cost or price need not be the most important factor, no award is valid unless cost or price has been considered in some fashion during the source selection process.[4]

Past Performance

Past performance is used to evaluate how well the offeror performed the same or similar effort on past or current contracts or orders and how that past performance is likely to affect the current effort. The evaluation should consider the currency and relevance of an offeror's past performance, the source and validity of the past performance information received, the context of the data, and the general trend of the offeror's past performance.

The use of past performance as an evaluation factor is required by the FAR for all procurements in excess of the simplified acquisition threshold,[5] except when the contracting officer documents the contract file to indicate why using past performance as an evaluation factor is not appropriate for the acquisition.[6]

Compliance with Solicitation Requirements

When compliance with solicitation requirements is used as an evaluation factor, the offeror must demonstrate that the proposed product or service meets the requirements of the solicitation. Generally, compliance with solicitation requirements is used in fixed-price acquisitions in which the requirements are not complex and the technical and management aspects are not likely to be factors in discriminating among the potential offerors.

Compliance with solicitation requirements is appropriate to use when the prime consideration, besides price, is that the offeror's proposal demonstrates that all the mandatory solicitation requirements will be met, as might be the case with fixed-price construction contracts or contracts for the manufacture or provision of standard supplies, equipment, or services. It is also appropriate in solicitations in which the award will be made to the lowest-priced, technically acceptable proposal. In such cases, technical excellence is not a factor; the only requirement is that the proposal demonstrate that it meets the minimum standard for compliance with the solicitation requirements. All proposals that meet the minimum standards (i.e., are acceptable) are then competed on the basis of the proposed prices.

Technical Excellence

Technical excellence has to do with evaluating the quality of an offeror's technical proposal in terms of meeting the contractual requirements. The proposal is evaluated considering such things as technical understanding, as demonstrated by the offeror's analysis of the requirement; technical approach, as demonstrated by the techniques or methodology to be employed; and technical planning, as demonstrated by the scheduling and sequencing of the planned effort. Overall, the technical evaluation must consider the feasibility of the technical proposal, the probability of technical success, and the offeror's ability to do what is proposed within the contractual time frames.

Technical excellence is most appropriate when the requirement is unique or complex and the government needs to see how the competing offerors propose to meet the technical requirements of the RFP. Its use is also appropriate when there are a number of different ways to meet the technical requirements and the government wants to select the best technical approach.

Generally, technical excellence is used as an evaluation factor if the government determines that (1) it must evaluate how the offerors propose to meet the contract requirements, (2) the differences in the technical proposals will be a discriminating factor in the evaluation, and (3) there is likely to be a need to discuss aspects of the technical proposals with the offerors in the competitive range.

Management Capability

Management capability involves the evaluation of how well an offeror's proposal demonstrates that the offeror can effectively manage all aspects of contract performance. The proposal is evaluated according to (1) how well the management plan demonstrates that the work effort will be managed effectively and establishes well-defined lines of authority, responsibility, and communication; (2) how well management techniques are established to facilitate the early identification and resolution of problems and a prompt response to changes; (3) the extent to which the staffing represents an appropriate level and labor mix and reflects the technical input and ability for successful and timely contract performance; and, as appropriate, (4) the offeror's ability to react to workload fluctuations.

Using management as an evaluation factor is most appropriate for large, complex requirements when how the work is staffed and managed could be a major factor in the success or failure of the contract effort, such as in systems acquisition, research and development, technical support services, bundled contracts, and other complex acquisitions. Evaluating management issues is less important in standard, noncomplex acquisitions, such as acquiring commercial items and standard supplies or services. Management capability also may be used as a subfactor to the technical excellence evaluation factor.

Management capability is probably an overused evaluation factor. Often it is automatically coupled with the technical excellence evaluation factor. Except for the large, complex efforts noted above, how an offeror proposes to manage its contractual effort is not necessarily a discriminating factor in an evaluation. However, even when other management aspects are not particularly important, how an offeror proposes to staff the work effort could be a discriminating factor.

Basically, staffing is evaluated to determine if the offeror is proposing adequate staffing. The evaluation should also consider, however, how the offeror proposes to manage its staffing, considering such things as staffing distribution, staffing for standard and peak workload conditions, cross-utilization, personnel turnover, and retention plans. Staffing, rather than management, might be used as a primary evaluation factor when acquiring complex technical support services or in other acquisitions in which how an offeror proposes to manage its staffing effort could be a discriminating factor.

It should be noted that proposed staffing is inherent to assessing the offeror's understanding of the requirement. Staffing could also be used as a subfactor to the technical excellence evaluation factor.

Personnel Qualifications

Personnel qualifications (often called key personnel) involve evaluating the availability, competency, pertinent education, and related experience of an offeror's proposed key personnel with respect to their potential contribution to successful contract performance. Personnel qualifications are evaluated on the basis of information provided by the offeror regarding each individual's qualifications and commitment to work on the proposed contract.

Personnel qualifications often are used in evaluating proposals for research and development, information technology services, technical and other complex support services, and other requirements in which the qualifications of proposed key personnel are vital to the success of contract performance and would be a discriminating factor in the evaluation. Personnel qualifications may be used as a primary evaluation factor or as a subfactor under technical excellence, management capability, or staffing.

The use of personnel qualifications as an evaluation factor has been the subject of numerous protests. Generally, protests in this area can be minimized if the

RFP (1) identifies the key positions so that the offeror can provide specific names and résumés, (2) identifies the minimum qualifications required of the personnel proposed to fill these positions so that the offeror can provide the appropriate qualification information, (3) identifies the documentation required (such as résumés and letters of commitment) to support the offeror's identification of such personnel, and (4) warns that it is the offeror's responsibility to ensure that the proposed key personnel are available and committed to perform under the contract throughout the acquisition process and to propose new personnel should the originally proposed personnel become unavailable.

Prior Experience

Prior experience (often referred to as corporate experience) involves the evaluation of an offeror's knowledge based on its work on past and current contracts of the same or similar nature. It is related to whether the offeror has done such work before, not to how well it performed the work. Prior experience is evaluated on the basis of information provided by the offeror (and verified as necessary) that identifies specific past or current contracts demonstrating the offeror's involvement with work relevant to the current procurement.

Prior experience is typically evaluated in terms of the number of years of general or specialized experience or the number of comparable or relevant contracts. Prior experience also can be evaluated in terms of the experience of an offeror's senior technical or management personnel, subcontractors, or other members of a joint venture.

Prior experience is important when the government needs some assurance that the offeror has performed the required work. The degree of importance depends on the size and complexity of the required work effort. Prior experience is an indicator of an offeror's ability to complete a complex effort that involves many personnel and multiple work units and requires interfacing both inside and outside the corporate structure. In large efforts, the existence of prior experience often provides some assurance that corporate memory will be retained.

Prior experience may be less important on smaller efforts that involve only a few personnel because the retention of corporate experience is less assured if only a few personnel were involved in the contract. Prior experience is, after all, little more than the corporate memory of the persons currently working for the offeror. The fact that an offeror previously performed the same or similar work is not necessarily a qualifying factor if the key experienced personnel who performed the work are no longer employed by the offeror.

When prior experience is used as an evaluation factor, the RFP should permit offerors to show how the innovative use of their products or services or of subcontractors or joint venture partners will enable the offeror to meet the contractual requirements.

SELECTING EVALUATION FACTORS

When selecting the evaluation factors and significant subfactors to use in a competitively negotiated procurement, certain conditions must be met. The contracting officer (1) must tailor the evaluation factors and subfactors to the needs of the specific procurement, (2) must use only those evaluation factors and subfactors that support meaningful comparison and discrimination between and among competing proposals, (3) should limit the number of evaluation factors, and (4) must always include cost or price and address quality by considering one or more non-cost evaluation factors.

Tailor the Evaluation Factors to the Procurement

Evaluation factors must be tailored to the requirement being procured.[7] The relationship between the evaluation factors and the statement of work (SOW) and other contractual requirements should be clear. The evaluation scheme should include only those evaluation factors and significant subfactors that represent the key areas of importance and emphasis to be considered in the source selection decision. In a competitive acquisition, the evaluation factors (as well as the SOW requirements) cannot be designed so that only one offeror can meet the requirements. It should be noted that, with the exception of cost or price (which is always required) and past performance (which is required when appropriate), the evaluation factors cited in the FAR are not required for all procurements and are not the only criteria that may be used. Any factors appropriate to the evaluation may be used.

Ensure That the Evaluation Factors Discriminate among Offerors

Evaluation factors and significant subfactors must support meaningful comparison and discrimination among the competing proposals.[8] They must reflect that which is most important in determining which offeror can perform the contract successfully and which, when considering cost or price, offers the best value. Using evaluation factors that are likely to result in similar evaluation results is not effective. Select the factors and subfactors that are most likely to point out the differences rather than the similarities between the proposals. Keep in mind that the purpose of the evaluation is first to identify the most highly rated proposals (for the competitive range determination) and then to determine which of the competitive proposals offers the best value (for source selection). This cannot be done effectively unless the evaluation criteria provide the basis for identifying the differences, and the respective value of those differences, among the competing proposals.

Limit the Number of Evaluation Factors

Keep the number of different evaluation factors and subfactors to a minimum. Do not try to evaluate every facet of an offeror's proposal. Limit the factors and subfactors to only those most important to the success of the procurement. Proposal scoring often becomes diluted if there are a large number of evaluation factors and subfactors. The overall scores tend to level off and become roughly equal, making it difficult to distinguish between and rank the relative worth of the competing proposals and to select the proposal offering the best value. Usually, using more than three primary factors and a similar number of subfactors will have a leveling effect.

Always Include Cost or Price and Quality

All procurements must include cost or price as an evaluation factor, although it need not be the most important factor. Cost or price does not even need to be weighted or scored, but it must be considered in the source selection because an evaluation scheme in which cost or price is not considered in some fashion can be successfully protested.

Quality also must be addressed in some fashion. As noted earlier, quality may be expressed in terms of such non-cost evaluation factors as past performance, compliance with solicitation requirements, technical excellence, management capability, personnel qualifications, prior experience, or any other non-cost factor appropriate to the procurement. Past performance must be used in acquisitions that exceed the simplified acquisition threshold unless the contracting officer documents a decision that the use of past performance is not appropriate.

Before addressing the decision to use past performance as an evaluation factor, a few words about the other non-cost evaluation factors are in order. Prior to the current emphasis on the use of past performance in the evaluation, the standard primary evaluation factors were technical excellence, management capability, and prior experience. Often these were used automatically, with personnel qualifications as a subfactor to either technical excellence or management capability when appropriate. Compliance with solicitation requirements was used when the acquisition did not require the evaluation of technical excellence and management capability. Past performance was used as an evaluation factor, but its use was uncommon.

Now that the FAR requires the use of past performance, we are seeing some variances in evaluation schemes, particularly with fixed-price contracts. Agencies now look more critically at using non-cost evaluation factors. Some agencies are soliciting on the basis of price and past performance as the only evaluation factors when acquiring standard supplies or services. Other agencies, when appropriate, are substituting past performance for the technical and management evaluation factors when they have determined that how an offeror has performed in the past is a better indicator of how it will perform in the future than the promises made in technical and management proposals.

DETERMINING WHETHER TO USE PAST PERFORMANCE AS AN EVALUATION FACTOR

Despite the emphasis on using past performance in competitive evaluations, keep in mind that the final decision is up to the contracting officer. The contracting officer must determine whether using past performance as an evaluation factor is appropriate and, if so, how it should be used. If past performance is not used in the evaluation, however, the contracting officer must document the reason why in the contract file.

Using past performance as an evaluation factor should depend on the significance of past performance as a discriminator in the current procurement. It cannot be assumed automatically that past performance is an important factor without first considering whether it is needed to discriminate among offerors. For example, if all potential offerors are good performers, the evaluation of past performance might not enhance the evaluation process. If the acquisition is a once-in-a-generation acquisition, there will not likely be any significant past performance to evaluate (assuming that there is no sufficiently similar effort).

The effective use of past performance also can be diminished when a number of new firms with no performance history are competing or when the acquisition is for a new item or service that has no germane performance history. The rationale for not using past performance as an evaluation factor should indicate the circumstances of the procurement that preclude using past performance as a discriminating factor and state that, because past performance will not be a significant discriminator, it should not be used in the evaluation.

Generally, past performance can be used in most acquisitions either as a primary evaluation factor or as a significant subfactor. For example, if previous contracts for the same or similar items or services have a history of performance problems, past performance, as an indicator of performance risk, is a very important criterion and should be used as a primary evaluation factor. Past performance is also an effective evaluation factor in the repetitive acquisition of standard supplies or services when there are many competing offerors and a significant performance history.

Past performance also is significant if strict conformance with the specifications and delivery times is critical to the program the procurement supports. For example, the acquisition of military clothing requires strict conformance to the specifications and delivery schedule. This field is very competitive, and the evaluation of past performance helps limit the competition to proven suppliers. Past performance also is important in the acquisition of supplies and equipment when the required items are sensitive and complex devices and the proven ability to produce the items successfully in conformance to specifications and to make timely delivery are critical to selecting the successful offeror.

The evaluation of past performance is also applicable to services, such as technical support services, when the proven ability to respond successfully to complex technical requirements is critical to source selection, or even standard services, such as janitorial services, where successful past performance is an important indicator of an offeror's likely future performance.

Past performance also can be evaluated separately from the standard non-cost evaluation factors as a performance risk factor, in which the risk of successful performance is evaluated through assessing risk and determining the likelihood that instances of poor past performance (or superior past performance) will be repeated in the prospective contract.

Performance risk should not be confused with proposal risk. Proposal risk is an assessment of the likelihood that the proposed technical and management approach will be successful, based solely on the contents of an offeror's technical and management proposals. Performance risk evaluation is based on information such as the agency's personal knowledge, customer surveys, past performance questionnaire replies, and reports in the Past Performance Information Retrieval System (PPIRS).[9] Performance risk assessment is not restricted to the information contained in the proposal.

DETERMINING THE RELATIVE IMPORTANCE OF PAST PERFORMANCE AS AN EVALUATION FACTOR

To submit accurate and realistic proposals, offerors must understand the criteria against which their proposals will be evaluated. Therefore, the evaluation factors and significant subfactors and their relative importance must be set forth in the RFP in a manner that clearly expresses their value and interrelationships.

Determining the Relative Importance of Evaluation Factors

Once the evaluation factors and subfactors to be used have been identified, the relative importance of each should be determined based on an assessment of the value of each factor to the overall evaluation.[10] This is usually done by determining first the relative importance of each primary evaluation factor and then the relative importance of each subfactor to its associated primary factor.

To determine relative importance, you must first review the solicitation requirements to decide what it is that you need to know from each offeror to determine the worth of the offeror's proposal. The things you need to know are represented by the evaluation factors (e.g., technical excellence, management capability, prior experience, past performance), and the relative importance of each factor depends on how important each is to the identification of those offerors to be included in the competitive range and the eventual source selection.

Evaluation factors are listed in the RFP in descending order of importance, and their relative importance is set forth either in a narrative (if the relationships are simple and easy to understand and there are not many factors) or by publishing the specific evaluation weights in the RFP. The primary purposes of describing the relative importance of the evaluation factors and subfactors are (1) to ensure that offerors address the issues represented by the evaluation factors with the appropriate emphasis and (2) to ensure that offerors understand how their proposals will be evaluated.

Determining the Relative Importance of Past Performance

When past performance is used as a primary evaluation factor, it should be weighted at 25 percent or more, or at least equal in significance to the other non-cost evaluation factors. This ensures that significant consideration is given to past performance. A very low weighting might reduce the overall perception of how important good contract performance is as an element of the source selection process.

Note, however, that the importance of past performance as an evaluation factor must be based on its importance in determining which proposal offers the best value, which in turn depends on a number of varying factors, all relating to the current acquisition and not to a policy statement or general guidance. The overall requirement must be assessed carefully, first to determine which evaluation factors to use and then to determine the relative importance of each. Automatically assigning past performance some predetermined evaluation weight would be a poor practice.

When used, past performance usually is one of the primary evaluation factors, but not necessarily the most important. Technical excellence and management capability factors provide insight into how the offeror proposes to perform the current requirement. The prior experience factor indicates the offeror's knowledge of the subject matter. When the requirement is large and complex, specific technical expertise is required. There are different ways to accomplish the requirement, and how an offeror proposes to do the work and its technical and management expertise could be critical discriminators in the evaluation. In such instances, past performance might be of lesser importance in the evaluation scheme.

There are times, however, when technical excellence or management capability factors might not be significant to the source selection. For example, in the procurement of continuing services (particularly when using performance-based acquisition contracting), how a contractor plans to perform or manage the contract might not be as significant as its track record in performing the same or similar services.

When the performance of services is standardized, as in commercial or commercial-like services, the competitors typically will be alike in their technical and management approaches. If their technical and management proposals were to be evaluated, it is likely that they would be rated as roughly equal, in effect rendering technical and management capabilities ineffective as discriminators. In such instances, substituting past performance for the technical excellence or management capability evaluation factors rather than adding past performance as another evaluation factor would make the evaluation more effective. A number of agencies, when acquiring standard supplies or services on a fixed-price basis, have found that using past performance and price as the only evaluation factors is an effective and efficient approach.

Distinguishing between Past Performance and Prior Experience

The evaluation of past performance and of prior experience is similar in that both use the same database—previous contracts for the same or similar effort. They differ in the way the previous contracts are evaluated. Prior experience is used to evaluate whether the offeror has performed such work in the past. Past performance is used to evaluate how well the offeror has performed the same or similar past or current contracts. Therefore, past performance is a better indicator of future performance. Prior experience demonstrates that the offeror is capable of performing the proposed contract.

Because past performance and prior experience use the same database, only one or the other should be used in the same source selection. Past performance is a required non-cost evaluation factor. If the contracting officer determines that past performance is not appropriate in the instant solicitation, prior experience may be considered. Using both prior experience and past performance can dilute the importance of past performance, as shown by the GAO decision in *Si-Nor, Inc.*, B-282064; B-282064.2, May 25, 1999, summarized in Example 2.1.

Example 2.1—Relative importance of past performance can be diluted by adding prior experience.

Issue: In a fixed-price solicitation for refuse collection and disposal services, proposals were to be evaluated based on (1) past performance/experience and (2) price/cost, which were to be approximately equal in weight. Past performance and experience were also to be approximately equal in weight. Award was to be made on a best-value basis. Si-Nor protested on the basis that Eagle's higher performance rating did not warrant payment of an $858,636.80 premium.

Resolution: The award decision was successfully protested because the reasonableness of the tradeoff decision was not adequately documented. Of interest here, however, is the perhaps unintended consequences of the evaluation scheme as explained by the Comptroller General in a footnote to his decision. Since past performance/experience and price/cost were to be given approximately equal weight, each was worth approximately 50 percent of the overall rating; since, within past performance/experience, each of the two component[s] was approximately equal, past performance was worth approximately 25 percent of the overall rating.

By adding prior experience as equal in importance to past performance, the relative importance of past performance was diminished, which would make a tradeoff favoring superior past performance difficult to support.

For an abridged version of GAO's decision in *Si-Nor, Inc.*, see Appendix B, Example 2.1.

The problem noted in Example 2.1 could have been avoided by using either past performance or prior experience. If past performance is appropriate, it must be used. As noted above, both evaluation factors use the same database—past or current contracts of the same or similar nature and scope as the requirements of the instant solicitation.

Same or Similar Efforts

It is critical that the contracts identified by the offeror be for the same or similar efforts. After all, an evaluation of past performance should be made using relevant past effort. How else can you relate an offeror's past performance to its likely performance on the prospective contract? The GAO decision in *Power Connector, Inc.*, B-286875, B-286875.2, January 14, 2001, summarized in Example 2.2, demonstrates the need for relevancy.

Example 2.2—Basing evaluation on contracts most relevant to solicitation.

Issue: In a Federal Bureau of Prisons UNICOR solicitation for a best-value award of a fixed-price, indefinite-quantity contract for leather to be used in manufacturing work gloves, the solicitation cited three evaluation factors in a descending order of importance—past performance, compliance with technical specifications, and price.

Power Connector, Inc. (PCI) listed four past performance references—two for leather contracts and two for communications components contracts. After concluding that the communications components contracts were not similar to the current leather requirement, the contracting officer checked UNICOR's database and found that PCI had a current contract to supply leather to UNICOR. Because she viewed this contract as similar to the solicited requirement, she used it as the third reference instead of the communications components contracts. Based on the ratings for these three contracts—one excellent, two good—the contracting officer evaluated PCI as overall good for past performance.

After another firm received the award, PCI protested, asserting, among other issues, that the contracting officer had improperly failed to consider the two communications components contract references. PCI claimed that had those contracts been considered, PCI would have received all excellent ratings and would have been in line for award.

Resolution: The GAO determined that:

In evaluating past performance, an agency has discretion to determine the scope of the vendors' performance history to be considered, provided that it evaluates all submissions on the same basis and consistent with the solicitation.[11] *An agency may base its evaluation on contracts it believes are most relevant to the solicitation,[12] it has discretion to consider information other than that provided by the vendors,[13] and need not consider all references a vendor submits.[14]*

UNICOR's actions fall within the above standard. The contracting officer sought to identify the most relevant contracts for purposes of assessing PCI's past performance and, in doing so, considered a relevant contract not listed in PCI's quotation and disregarded two listed contracts which were not similar to the current requirement. This was reasonable, and well within the agency's discretion. Moreover, although we think the logic of evaluating similar contracts to assess past performance is obvious, the RFQ requirement that firms provide references for "similar" contracts put PCI and the other vendors on notice that the agency wanted to evaluate similar contracts; thus, the agency's reliance on PCI's ongoing leather contract was fully consistent with the evaluation scheme.

For an abridged version of the GAO decision in *Power Connector, Inc.*, see Appendix B, Example 2.2.

Distinguishing between Past Performance as a Responsibility Factor and Past Performance as an Evaluation Factor

Using past performance as a responsibility factor must be distinguished from using it as an evaluation factor to ensure that both are handled properly.

FAR Subpart 9.1 requires that all contracts be awarded to responsible contractors and establishes the responsibility standards that must be met. Past performance is one of the responsibility standards. FAR 9.104-3(b) requires the use of past performance in making determinations of responsibility, stating that "[a] prospective contractor that is or recently has been seriously deficient in contract performance shall be presumed to be non-responsible, unless the contracting officer determines that the circumstances were properly beyond the contractor's control, or that the contractor has taken appropriate corrective action. Past failure to apply sufficient tenacity and perseverance to perform acceptably is strong evidence of non-responsibility. Failure to meet the quality requirements of the contract is a significant factor to consider in determining satisfactory performance."

Distinguishing between past performance as a responsibility factor and past performance as an evaluation factor is necessary because determining responsibility and evaluating proposals are two distinct and separate functions. They are performed for different purposes at different times by different people during the procurement process.

As an evaluation factor, past performance is evaluated for purposes of source selection in competitively negotiated acquisitions. All evaluation factors are evaluated by the application of specific criteria set forth in the RFP, through a comparative assessment that establishes the relative value of each proposal and the relative ranking of each offeror. Past performance is evaluated during the initial evaluation for the establishment of the competitive range and later during the final evaluation to establish which proposal represents the best value to the government.

It should be noted that in a comparative assessment, a failure to meet the minimum requirements of an evaluation factor does not in itself require automatic rejection of a proposal. It simply results in a lower assessment or score. A technical evaluation team performs this evaluation.

Responsibility factors are assessed in all acquisitions to determine whether a proposed contractor is a responsible business able to perform the contract. Past performance is one of a number of responsibility factors that are assessed by the application of specific responsibility standards established in the FAR. This assessment is made on a pass/fail basis, and a failure to meet the minimum requirements of any responsibility standard requires rejection of the proposal. A contractor is either responsible or not responsible; there is no middle ground. The contracting officer performs this assessment after completion of the final evaluation and immediately before award.

The need to distinguish between past performance as a responsibility factor and past performance as an evaluation factor lies in how failures are handled if a small business is involved. If a small business firm fails to meet the responsibility standards and is determined to be not responsible, the matter must be referred to the Small Business Administration (SBA), which may issue a Certificate of Competency (COC) declaring that the firm is a responsible business concern. If the SBA does not issue a COC, the firm's proposal must be rejected.

If, however, a small business firm's proposal is downgraded under past performance during a comparative assessment (evaluation) of all proposals, the matter is not reviewable by the SBA because, as noted earlier, a failure to meet the minimum requirements of an evaluation factor does not require automatic rejection of a proposal but simply results in a lower assessment or score. The SBA's authority extends only to matters of non-responsibility and does not encompass matters involving comparative assessments.

Using past performance as an evaluation factor is not a substitute for assessing past performance in the responsibility determination. Past performance is an established responsibility factor and must be considered in a determination of responsibility. Therefore, if past performance is used as an evaluation factor, it could be evaluated twice—first, as part of the assessment of the value of an offeror's proposal in comparison to the proposals of other offerors and second, to determine whether the offeror's past performance meets the minimum standards of responsibility.

Generally, however, if past performance is an evaluation factor, an offeror whose past performance is such that it would be considered non-responsible would not remain in the competition long enough for a responsibility determination. Only the most highly rated offerors are included in the competitive range, and an offeror's significantly deficient performance record will, in most cases, lower the offeror's score enough to result in proposal rejection during the initial proposal evaluation. However, there are always exceptions to the rules, and knowing the difference between using past performance as an evaluation factor and using it in a responsibility determination before issuing the RFP will help avoid mistakes that can be protested successfully.

WHAT IS EVALUATED AS PAST PERFORMANCE

A contractor's actions executed under previously awarded contracts are relevant past performance information. That information is categorized under four areas—quality of product or service, timeliness, cost control, and business relations. The first three assessment areas relate to the contractor's compliance with contractual requirements. The fourth concerns the contractor's relationship with the acquisition team and some of the other requirements of the contract not related to quality, timeliness, or cost control. Each assessment area contains specific elements, as can be seen from the following:

- **Quality of Product or Service**—This area includes a contractor's performance in making sure that the product or service conforms to contractual specifications or standards of good workmanship.
- **Timeliness**—This area has to do with a contractor's reliability. It encompasses the contractor's adherence to contract schedules, such as milestones, delivery dates for interim or final products, or reporting requirements.
- **Cost Control**—This area is concerned with a contractor's performance with respect to forecasting costs, controlling costs, submitting reasonably priced change proposals, and providing current, accurate, and complete billings. It is applicable only to cost reimbursement, time and materials, and labor-hour contracts.

- **Business Relations**—This area involves an assessment of the contractor's business management philosophy and practice that includes both the external relations of the contractor with the government's acquisition team and the internal relations with its own staff and subcontractors.

DETERMINING HOW THE RFP WILL ADDRESS PAST PERFORMANCE

It is important that the RFP clearly explain how past performance will be evaluated. Section L, Instructions, Conditions, and Other Statements to Offerors, asks for a list of current and past contracts that demonstrate performance relevant to the solicitation requirements. In Section M, Evaluation Factors for Award, the past performance factor and/or subfactors must be tailored to the acquisition.

Tailor Past Performance Factor and Subfactors to the Acquisition

Whether past performance is used as one factor or as one or more significant subfactors, it "must (1) represent the key performance criteria of the statement of work and (2) support meaningful comparisons and discrimination between and among competing proposals."[15]

Past performance may be described by a narrative listing one or more of the key performance criteria (e.g., quality of product or service, timeliness, cost control), or it can be described by identifying each key criterion separately (i.e., one or more significant past performance subfactors). The difference lies in the amount of information that must be provided. If the key areas of importance or emphasis are listed as subfactors, each must be clearly described and its relative importance indicated. If a narrative approach is used, only the relative importance of the primary past performance factor need be identified.

The important thing to remember is that the description of the past performance factor or significant subfactors must be tailored to the requirement. The description must be such that offerors will clearly understand the areas of importance and emphasis that they should address in their proposals.

Indicate How Past Performance Will Be Evaluated

In addition to identifying the past performance areas to be evaluated, the RFP should state that an offeror's past performance will be evaluated to assess its relative merit with respect to the current requirement and then as compared to that of competing offerors. The RFP should indicate that the evaluation will be based on current and past performance information furnished by the offeror as well as information from other available sources, such as other government agencies, suppliers, subcontractors, or customers of the offeror. The RFP should also state that offerors without a record of relevant past performance or those for whom information on past performance is not available will not be evaluated favorably or unfavorably on past performance but will be given a neutral rating.

If past performance will be evaluated separately from the other technical evaluation factors, as a performance risk factor, this should be specifically noted along with an explanation of the evaluation criteria to be used.

The evaluation must be conducted as set forth in the RFP. If the RFP indicates that certain areas will be evaluated and certain methods will be used, the evaluators may not deviate from this unless the RFP is first amended to show the changes and offerors are given an opportunity to revise their proposals accordingly. A failure to evaluate in accordance with the RFP can result in a successful protest.

When describing past performance in Section M of the RFP, the more subfactors used, the more complicated the evaluation will be because each subfactor listed in the RFP must be evaluated. Therefore, the number of past performance evaluation subfactors should be kept to a minimum, using only those that would be significant to the performance of the proposed contract. Or, the past performance factor might be described as containing those areas otherwise used as subfactors.

Indicate the Documentation Required

In the proposal preparation instructions (RFP Section L), the information that the offeror should submit as past performance information is identified. Offerors are required to list current and past contracts (which may be federal, state, or local government or private contracts) for the same or similar work.[16] To ensure that the listed contracts are properly identified (e.g., contract number, dollar value, dates, contracting party, description of the work effort, contact telephone number), it is recommended that a form similar to the sample in Appendix C be included with the instructions.[17] State that it is important that the work under each referenced contract be relevant to the proposed effort. Inform the offerors that some, but not necessarily all, of the references will be checked to assess the quality of the contractor performance.

Indicate that offerors may describe the quality of their performance on the referenced contracts and may (or must, as appropriate) also provide information on predecessor companies, key personnel who have relevant experience, or subcontractors that will perform major or critical aspects of the requirement, when such information is relevant to the instant acquisition.

It is important to require offerors to identify any performance difficulties in the referenced contracts and to discuss the corrective action taken. The offeror should provide evidence that it was able to identify the cause of the problems and demonstrate that the problems were resolved. Tell the offerors that if past problems are not fully addressed, it will be assumed that they still exist and the proposal will be evaluated accordingly.

You also should indicate that offerors may provide information on awards or commendations that they may have received regarding work on referenced contracts. These are positive indicators of an offeror's past performance and could significantly affect the evaluation.

DETERMINING HOW PAST PERFORMANCE WILL BE RATED OR SCORED IN THE EVALUATION

Before issuing the RFP, consider how offerors' past performance will be rated or scored. In the initial evaluation, each offeror's proposal is evaluated based on the factors and significant subfactors stated in the RFP. The evaluation facilitates developing an initial rating and ranking the proposals for the contracting officer's use in establishing the competitive range. Although some comparative assessment may be done when establishing the competitive range, the primary emphasis is on assessing how well the offeror met the past performance evaluation criteria.

In the final evaluation for source selection, an offeror's past performance is primarily assessed on a comparative basis with the competing offerors to determine which proposal offers the best value. Tradeoffs between past performance and other non-cost evaluation factors, or between past performance and price, are often determinative in the source selection decision.

When the contract will be awarded without discussions, an offeror's past performance is first evaluated based on the RFP's evaluation criteria and then comparatively assessed (with tradeoffs as necessary) with the competing offerors to provide a basis for the award decision.

There are two ways to rate past performance information: (1) with respect to the quality of performance in meeting past contractual requirements and (2) with respect to the degree of performance risk.

Rating the Quality of Past Performance

The rating system for source selection should be compatible with the rating system used to evaluate contracts on completion of performance in compliance with FAR 42.1502. This is logical considering that the purpose of those evaluations is to provide past performance information in source selection. Using a compatible rating system alleviates the need to correlate the principal source of past performance information, i.e., past performance reports.

The rating system recommended by the Office of Federal Procurement Policy (OFPP) has five adjectival ratings—Excellent, Very Good, Satisfactory, Marginal, and Unsatisfactory—with a definition assigned to each rating. For offerors with no past performance history, a neutral rating is given. In effect, a range of scores with the middle score equivalent to meeting the requirement or norm allows the evaluators to measure the extent to which the contractor has exceeded or fallen below the requirement or norm.

A numerical value may be assigned to each of the above ratings. It should be noted, however, that assigning numerical scores to such a varied informational base conveys a preciseness that might be misleading. The numerical scores are only guides for the evaluators and cannot be used as the basis for decisions. Decisions are made on the basis of the narrative explanations supporting the scores or rating assigned.

Color coding also may be used. It provides a broad evaluation range, and the absence of numbers eliminates the implied preciseness of numerical scoring.

Whether numerical scoring or color coding is used, documenting an evaluation using only the wording of the definitions provided for each score or rating does not constitute adequately explaining the scores assigned. A narrative explanation that is related to the specific proposal is required. It must relate the problems (or strengths) found in the past performance information to the rating assigned and its definition.

Develop Narrative Before Scoring

Two problems are associated with both numerical scoring and color-coding systems: (1) although both systems work well in identifying poor proposals (for the competitive range determination), they do not work as well in distinguishing the best of the most highly rated proposals (for the source selection decision); and (2) there is a tendency to concentrate more on the rating categories than on the required narrative evaluation. In a properly conducted evaluation, the narrative evaluation should be developed before assigning any numerical ratings or color codes. Comptroller General decisions offer ample evidence, however, that the documentation in this area is not as good as it should be. Competitive range and source selection decisions must be based on the narrative and not the adjectival, numerical, or color-coded rating.

Rating the Degree of Performance Risk

Evaluating past performance separately as performance risk is probably the most effective way to evaluate past performance. The evaluation of past performance is essentially an assessment of the risk of successful performance based on an offeror's past performance history. The evaluation of performance risk uses broad ranges, such as high, moderate, and low risk, and requires a risk analysis rather than detailed scoring. The risk analysis relates the strengths or weaknesses of the offeror's past performance to the likelihood of successful performance on the prospective contract. Using broad ranges is more effective primarily because trying to rate prospective performance more closely is not realistic. A quotation from a Comptroller General decision amplifies this point:[18]

> *Past performance instills confidence that a company will probably do well but does not, in and of itself, guarantee that a company will do well, whereas, poor performance is a good indicator of performance risk.*

When used, the evaluation of past performance in terms of performance risk should be kept simple, particularly for fixed-price contracts. Generally, there is no need to use multiple evaluation ratings because the degree of risk, particularly at the high and low ends, is not particularly important in distinguishing one proposal from another.

Remember that scoring systems are only guides to evaluation decisions. The actual decisions must be based on the narratives developed during the evaluation, which should provide the basis for distinguishing the differences between the proposals, particularly with respect to supporting tradeoff and source selection decisions.

NOTES

1. FAR 15.304(c)(3)(i). "Except as set forth in paragraph (c)(3)(iii) of this section, past performance shall be evaluated in all source selections for negotiated competitive acquisitions expected to exceed the simplified acquisition threshold."
2. Ibid.
3. FAR 15.304(c)(2). "The quality of the product or service shall be addressed in every source selection through consideration of one or more non-cost evaluation factors such

as past performance, compliance with solicitation requirements, technical excellence, management capability, personnel qualifications, and prior experience, and ..."

4. FAR 15.304(c)(1). "Price or cost to the Government shall be evaluated in every source selection …"
5. FAR 2.101. "Definitions. … 'Simplified acquisition threshold' means $100,000, except for acquisitions of supplies or services that, as determined by the head of the agency, are to be used to support a contingency operation or to facilitate defense against or recovery from nuclear, biological, chemical, or radiological attack (41 U.S.C. 428a), the term means—(1) $250,000 for any contract to be awarded and performed, or purchase to be made, inside the United States; and (2) $1 million for any contract to be awarded and performed, or purchase to be made, outside the United States."
6. FAR 15.304(c)(3)(iii). "Past performance need not be evaluated if the contracting officer documents the reason past performance is not an appropriate evaluation factor for the acquisition."
7. FAR 15.304(a). "The award decision is based on evaluation factors and significant subfactors that are tailored to the acquisition."
8. FAR 15.304(b). "Evaluation factors and significant subfactors must—(1) Represent the key areas of importance and emphasis to be considered in the source selection decision: and (2) Support meaningful comparison and discrimination between and among competing proposals."
9. FAR 13.106-2(b)(3)(ii). "[Evaluation] [m]ay be based on one or more of the following: (A) The contracting officer's knowledge of and previous experience with the supply or service being acquired; (B) Customer surveys, and past performance questionnaire replies; (C) The Governmentwide Past Performance Information Retrieval System (PPIRS) at www.ppirs.gov, or (D) Any other reasonable basis."
10. FAR 15.304(d). "All factors and significant subfactors that will affect contract award and their relative importance shall be stated clearly in the solicitation. The rating method need not be disclosed in the solicitation. The general approach for evaluating past performance information shall be described."
11. *OMV Medical, Inc.; Saratoga Medical Center, Inc.*, B-281387 et al., 2/3/99, 99-1 CPD ¶52 at 4.
12. *USATREX Int'l, Inc.*, B-275592; B-275592.2, 3/6/97, 98-1 CPD ¶99 at 4; *Braswell Services Group, Inc.*, B-278921.2, 6/17/98, 98-2 CPD ¶10 at 6.
13. *TEAM Support Services, Inc.*, B-279379.2, 6/22/98, 98-1 CPD ¶167 at 6.
14. *Advanced Data Concepts, Inc.*, B-277801.4, 6/1/98, 98-1 CPD ¶145 at 10.
15. FAR 15.304(b)(1) and (2).
16. FAR 15.305(a)(2)(ii). "The solicitation shall describe the approach for evaluating past performance, including evaluating offerors with no relevant performance history, and shall provide offerors an opportunity to identify past or current contracts (including Federal, State, and local government and private) for efforts similar to the Government requirement. The solicitation shall also authorize offerors to provide information on problems encountered on the identified contracts and the offeror's corrective actions.

The Government shall consider this information, as well as information obtained from any other sources, when evaluating the offeror's past performance. The source selection authority shall determine the relevance of similar past performance information."

17. Another sample form is found in Department of Defense, *A Guide to Collection and Use of Past Performance Information*, Version 3, May 2003, p. 42.
18. *Keane Federal Systems, Inc.*, B-280595, 10/23/98, GCR 110,440.

CHAPTER 3

PRE-AWARD: OBTAINING PAST PERFORMANCE INFORMATION

"The solicitation ... shall provide offerors an opportunity to identify past or current contracts ... for efforts similar to the Government requirement." FAR[1]

This chapter has two parts—one directed at government personnel and the other directed at contractor personnel. The first part addresses those things government personnel should do when obtaining past performance information for evaluation purposes in a competitive acquisition. The second part is directed at contractor personnel who will be involved in providing past performance information in response to a government solicitation.

FOR THE GOVERNMENT

Government personnel should direct their attention to the following areas when obtaining past performance information:

- How to obtain past performance information
- Verifying offeror's information
- Conducting reference checks
- Asking the right questions.

Obtaining Past Performance Information

The solicitation provides offerors with the opportunity to identify past or current federal, state, local government, and private contracts for the same or similar work.[2] Each contract listed should include the name of the contracting entity, contract number, dollar value, date of award and completion, a description of the work, and the name, phone number, and email address of at least one contact.

In addition, the RFP should encourage offerors to provide information on problems encountered on the identified contracts and the corrective action taken. Offerors should be allowed to provide information on predecessor companies, key personnel, and subcontractors that will perform major or critical aspects of the requirement when such information is relevant to the instant acquisition.

Particular attention should be given to how the offeror is to provide references. If you do not indicate the number of references to be provided, the number is up to the offerors. Some might provide a large number, and some might provide only a few. This might prove to be a problem when evaluating past performance.

OFPP guidance[3] suggests that offerors be required to provide references for five to ten relevant contracts, not more than three years old, to establish their past performance qualifications. There are, however, practical considerations that affect the number of references or the currency of those references, such as the following:

- The solicitation should not ask for more references than you are prepared to check. If you expect a large number of responses, five to ten references from each offeror might exceed your ability to check them all. Although the Comptroller General has ruled that the source selection authority is not required to check all references, offerors will expect that any reference provided will be checked. Failure to check all references might generate protests. The agency will win the protest but lose a great deal of time responding to it.
- Asking for five to ten references might adversely affect small businesses or newly formed businesses that have not had an opportunity to perform the requisite number of contracts that are the same as or similar to the work required. Even large businesses might have trouble in this area if the prospective contract is for supplies or services that are unique, innovative, or simply not often acquired. The number of references required should be realistic in relation to the kind of work required by the prospective contract. One way to avoid problems in this area is to ask for a minimum number of references and indicate that if more than the minimum number are provided, the government reserves the right to determine how many and which of those references will be checked. The minimum number should be that which the evaluation resources available can check efficiently.
- Generally, the listed contracts should have been completed within a three-year period. The time period may be expanded for supplies or services not frequently acquired. When establishing a time period, consideration should be given to whether there have been changes in technology or methodology that might affect the relevance of older contracts. The time period should be realistic for the kinds of supplies or services being required.

Verifying Offeror's Information

While the other non-cost evaluation factors (e.g., technical excellence, management capability) are evaluated based on the information provided in the proposals, past performance is evaluated primarily on the findings of the reference checks done on the contracts listed by the offeror. The exception is that the solicitation authorizes the offeror to provide information on problems encountered and corrective actions taken on the contracts listed in the proposal. Any information on problems and corrective action must be verified when contacting the references provided.

Conducting Reference Checks

Reference checks are done only for listed contracts that meet the relevancy and currency test. However, if a federal contract listed by the offeror has been evaluated as required by FAR Subpart 42.15, there is no need to contact the reference listed in the solicitation. It is simply a matter of accessing the report card from the Past Performance Information Retrieval System (PPIRS).

Checking only the references provided by the offeror usually is not adequate because the offeror might not identify past contracts that had serious performance deficiencies. The agency's contract database should be searched because agencies are obligated to consider past performance information that is readily available. In addition, the Federal Procurement Data System–Next Generation (FPDS-NG)[4] provides information on all federal government procurement actions. FPDS-NG uses ezSearch, a text-based search engine that allows users to enter any element of a contract they are interested in (e.g., vendor name, agency name, dollar amount, scope). It is available to registered government users at www.fpds.gov.

Private-sector sources, such as subcontractors, suppliers, financial institutions, and commercial customers, may also be used if they can be identified (market survey information might be helpful here). When using private-sector sources, documentation should support any comments used in the evaluation. Documentation is particularly important when adverse comments are involved.

Surveys of end users might be useful if you can identify the appropriate end users. End users, however, are often difficult to identify for a specific contract. Generally, end user surveys are practicable only for supplies or services that were shipped or provided directly to the end users and can be connected to a specific contractor.

The purpose of a reference check is to obtain performance information with respect to the past performance factor and/or significant subfactors as described in the solicitation. Contact is made with the person or persons identified by the offeror for each of the current or past contracts listed in the proposal.

The initial contact should be made by telephone to explain the purpose of the inquiry. In some instances, it might be possible to conduct an interview by telephone. If for some reason a telephone interview is not possible, a questionnaire can be forwarded for the contact to complete.

One challenge with questionnaires is getting useful information. Getting a negative response (which is of greater interest) might be more of a problem than getting a positive response because the responder must expend more time and effort to explain why the offeror's past performance was deficient. You cannot accept "yes" or "no" responses to your questions when the response indicates poor performance; explanations are required.

An allegation of poor performance, particularly when in conflict with information from other sources, should be examined closely to determine the accuracy of the allegation. If it is accurate, is it likely to affect performance under the proposed contract?

Getting a positive response is not difficult, but for the response to be useful, it needs to be explained. The explanation will be important when distinguishing the quality of one offeror's past performance from that of another offeror.

Asking the Right Questions

The source selection authority should develop a list of questions to assess the offeror's performance regarding the quality of the product or service, timeliness, cost control, and business relations. It is suggested that the first question be a general assessment of the offeror's performance. This would be followed by specific questions tailored to the prospective acquisition. That is, the questions should focus on particular aspects of the four assessment areas that are of importance or emphasized in the prospective acquisition. The final question should concern problems encountered and the offeror's corrective action. The questions should be short and simple like the following examples:

1. If you had a choice, would you contract with this contractor again? If no, why not? If yes, does the contractor's performance have any particular performance strong points?
2. Did the products or services meet contractual requirements, particularly with respect to the quality provided?
3. Did the contractor make contractual and administrative deliveries on time? If not, why not, and what specific delivery dates were not met?
4. Did the contractor complete the effort within the budget? If not, were the cost growth or other cost control problems due to contractor inefficiency

or lack of expertise? (NOTE—These questions do not apply to fixed-price contracts.)

5. Was the award amount or delivery schedule changed? If so, was the contractor cooperative and responsive in carrying out the changes?
6. Did the contractor demonstrate business-like concern for the customer?
7. If there were problems, did the contractor act promptly to resolve them? How effective was the contractor's corrective action?

FOR THE OFFERORS

This section is directed primarily at contractor personnel who will be involved in preparing the proposal in response to a government solicitation. It covers:

- General considerations
- Describing past performance in a proposal
- Planning for contract performance.

General Considerations

An offeror should pay close attention to Sections L and M of the RFP. Section L indicates specific past performance information that the offeror is to submit in the proposal.[5] Section M describes the evaluation criteria that will be used to rate the offeror's past performance.[6]

Section L asks offerors to identify past or current contracts similar to the RFP's requirement. Section L also authorizes offerors to provide information on problems encountered on the identified contracts and the offeror's corrective actions. It may specify a number or range of contracts to be identified, further elaborate on its definition of "similar" contracts or relevancy, and set currency limitations.

Section M describes the past performance factor and/or subfactors that will be used in the acquisition. The factor and/or subfactors are the performance criteria that will be used by the source selection authority in evaluating the offeror's past performance information.

Contractors should develop a strategy to deal with the increased emphasis given to past performance as a source selection factor. Such a strategy would involve how to submit past performance information in the proposal, respond to negative past performance reports during the evaluation of proposals (addressed in Chapter 5), identify actions to take during contract performance (addressed in Chapter 9), respond to the annual and final past performance evaluations (addressed in Chapter 10), and use past performance information to the contractor's competitive advantage (addressed in Chapter 13).

Preparing the Proposal

The offeror should check the solicitation closely to ensure that the proposal responds to all the solicitation requirements, particularly with respect to past performance information. The offeror bears the responsibility to provide enough information to enable the government to evaluate its proposal. A failure to comply with all solicitation requirements will result in the downgrading and possible rejection of the proposal, as shown in the GAO decision in *Menendez-Donnel & Associates,* B-286599, January 16, 2001, which is summarized in Example 3.1.

Example 3.1—Failure to comply with RFP instructions (#1).

Issue: The RFP required offerors to provide information on three prior similar contracts for the prime contractor and each key subcontractor. The protestor's proposal failed to provide information for its key subcontractor, claiming that a neutral rating should have been assigned.

Resolution: The Comptroller General denied the protest, stating:

Since an agency's evaluation is dependent upon the information furnished in a proposal, it is the offeror's burden to submit an adequately written proposal for the agency to evaluate, especially where, as here, the offeror is specifically on notice that the agency intends to make award based on initial proposals without discussions. An agency may reject a proposal for informational deficiencies that prevent the agency from fully evaluating the proposal.[7]

We note that, since the record confirms that the prior contracts MDA listed to establish its past performance were not similar to the current requirement, the agency reasonably determined that MDA's prior contracts did not provide a basis for assessing the firm's past performance. However, it appears this aspect of MDA's past performance warranted a neutral, rather than an unacceptable rating; under FAR 15.305(a)(2)(iv), where an offeror does not have a record of relevant past performance, the offeror may not be evaluated either favorably or unfavorably. On the other hand, even if this were the case, and even if we also agreed with MDA that the agency should have clarified its experience or obtained additional information from its own records, as discussed below, GSA reasonably rated the proposal unacceptable based on MDA's failure to establish adequate experience and past performance for its subcontractors and key employees.

To the extent MDA contends that GSA was required to assign a neutral rating to its proposal based on the absence of information relating to its key subcontractors, we disagree. Although FAR 15.305(a)(2)(iv) requires an agency to assign a neutral rating where past performance information is not "available," here, the protester's proposal represented that its proposed subcontractors are engaged in projects that would illustrate their performance capability. The information thus was available, but MDA chose not to present the information in its proposal, in direct contravention of the terms of the RFP. In our view, an offeror cannot simply choose to withhold past performance information—and thereby obtain a neutral rating—where the solicitation expressly requires that the information be furnished, and where the information is readily available to the offeror.

For an abridged version of the GAO decision in *Menendez-Donnel & Associates*, see Appendix B, Example 3.1.

Example 3.1 presents several points of interest to an offeror preparing to submit a proposal to the government. First and foremost, if the RFP requires the submission of certain information, the information must be submitted in complete detail, as set forth in the RFP. This is particularly true with respect to past performance information because the government must be able to verify this information with the contracting entities involved. In this case, MDA chose not to provide the required information about its key subcontractors. While a neutral rating is appropriate where past performance information is not available, the required information was, in fact, readily available to MDA. Therefore, because subcontracting was a major consideration in this evaluation, the failure to provide the required information was enough to find the proposal technically unacceptable.

The importance of complying with RFP requirements is again demonstrated by the GAO decision in *Boland Well Systems, Inc.*, B-287030, March 7, 2001, which is summarized in Example 3.2.

Example 3.2—Failure to comply with RFP instructions (#2).

Issue: Boland Well Systems, Inc., alleged that the Air Force did not properly consider its past performance. Boland received a "neutral/unknown confidence" rating based on its failure to submit in its proposal evidence that it had performed contracts relevant to the solicited effort.

Resolution: The Comptroller General denied the protest, stating:

Boland submitted the overall low price. While the ratings Boland received from its references ranged from satisfactory to very good, all of the responses involved contracts that were for landscaping projects that were valued at significantly less than the government estimate. Since Boland's prior contracts for landscaping work showed no relevance to the gate replacement work required by the solicitation, Boland's proposal received a rating of neutral/unknown confidence. Award was made to another offeror who had a slightly higher price but had received a past performance rating of exceptional/high confidence.

The record shows that the prior contracts listed by Boland to establish past performance were all landscaping projects. In our view, the agency reasonably concluded that the landscaping contracts were not relevant to the current requirement for gate replacements. In sum, Boland simply did not provide in its proposal or at any time during the conduct of the procurement evidence establishing that the company had relevant past performance. In accordance with the solicitation, the agency performed a performance/price tradeoff and determined that the higher priced proposal of IRD, which had a better performance risk rating than the protester, represented the best value to the government.

For an abridged version of the GAO decision in *Boland Well Systems, Inc.,* see Appendix B, Example 3.2.

Offerors must pay attention to what the RFP says about the information that must be provided with respect to past performance. Here the RFP clearly stated that award would be made based on a performance/price tradeoff and that offerors were required to submit detailed past performance information on contracts that were relevant to the proposed effort. A failure to submit relevant information would result in a neutral/unknown confidence rating. The past performance evaluation must be conducted as set forth in the RFP and based on the information required by the RFP. Boland had failed to provide relevant information, and it received the appropriate rating.

The fact that the requirement was not complex and that the simplicity of the effort should have been given considerable weight was not germane to the agency's decision. Based on the RFP requirements, Boland should have noted this lack of experience in its proposal and explained how it still had the ability to perform the requirement. Boland would probably not have received the award in any event because of the past performance/price tradeoff. Its slightly lower price would not have offset its lack of experience against the awardee's exceptional past performance rating on the same type of work.

If the solicitation does not clearly define these factors, the offeror should obtain clarification from the contracting officer before the time set for receipt of proposals. This is particularly important if it appears that prior experience and past performance have been combined into a single evaluation factor and whether they will be evaluated separately or together is not clear. If this issue is not cleared up before the time set for the receipt of proposals, the offeror cannot complain (protest) about it later.

Generally, the solicitation should indicate how many referenced contracts are required. It is not a good idea to provide more referenced contracts than required unless the RFP cites only a minimum requirement. Be aware, however, that the government is not required to check all the referenced contracts listed.

The government may use other sources (e.g., agency records, the records of other agencies, contractor performance reports, queries to suppliers or other business contacts) to check past performance, so not referencing a problem contract does not ensure that the contract problems will not come up. If there were problems with a referenced contract, the offeror should identify the problems and explain the corrective action taken. This is necessary to show that previous problems will not recur.

If the past performance of a subcontractor is pertinent, such as when a subcontractor will perform a significant part of the contract work, the offeror may use information about the subcontractor's past performance but must explain the relationship and how this information applies to the prospective contract.

A newly formed firm or a firm lacking relevant performance history may cite the past performance of its key personnel on other contracts as a substitute for the firm's lack of past performance history. However, the proposal must show how such personnel contributed to the success of the referenced contracts and how the referenced contracts relate to the prospective effort.

The past performance of other firms may be cited if they are team members or affiliates, but only if they will be significantly involved in the performance of the prospective contract. It is important to explain the relationship (shared management, workforce, facilities, or other resources that would affect contract performance) in order to demonstrate the extent of the other firm's involvement.

If previous work has resulted in awards or letters of commendation, reference should be made to them in the proposal. Such information can make a difference in the evaluation of past performance, particularly in tradeoff determinations and the final source selection.

What is contained in the initial proposal may be the only chance an offeror gets to explain past problems, particularly if award is to be made without discussions. When award is to be made without discussions, the government may (but is not required to) provide an opportunity to the offeror to clarify "adverse past performance information to which it has not previously had an opportunity to respond."[8] Generally, unless there is a reason to question the validity of the past performance information, the government chooses not to permit clarification. It is best, therefore, to explain past problems fully in your initial proposal submission.

If discussions are to be held, the government is required to permit offerors to address adverse past performance information to which the offeror has not previously had an opportunity to respond if the past performance information is a determining factor preventing the offeror from being placed in the competitive range. Note, however, that in a comparative assessment, past performance might not be the most heavily weighted evaluation factor. Where past performance problems only contributed to, but were not necessarily the determining factor in, a low overall rating, the government may not be required to permit the offeror to rebut the past performance evaluation, particularly if the past performance information was not adverse but simply not as highly rated as that of other offerors—all the more reason to ensure that the proposal provides clear, concise, candid, and complete past performance information.

It should be noted here that the phrase "adverse past performance information to which the offeror has not previously had an opportunity to respond"[9] generally excludes instances where a contractor has been afforded an opportunity to comment on the evaluation of its contract performance. The opportunity is given to a contractor prior to the preparation of a final contractor performance evaluation. Contractors would be well advised to retain any correspondence relating to such evaluations and be prepared to explain in the initial proposal how any past problems have been corrected and will not recur under the prospective contract.

Contracts that have been evaluated in accordance with FAR 42.15 are submitted to PPIRS and are available to all agencies. Those contracts, whether referenced in the proposal or not, are easily accessible when needed in source selection. Unlike the contracts listed without performance evaluations, a reference check has to be done. Many times there is no response to those requests. GAO's decision in *Guam Shipyard,* B-311321; B-311321.2, June 9, 2008, summarized in Example 3.3, shows how the evaluation of an offeror's proposal may depend on one performance evaluation record accessed from PPIRS.

Example 3.3—PPIRS accessible to all agencies.

Issue: Guam Shipyard (Guam) protested the reasonableness of the agency's evaluation of proposals and award made to Gulf Copper, which received a higher past performance rating but offered a higher price than Guam.

Resolution: Guam's proposal was evaluated as marginal based on an unfavorable Contract Performance Assessment Report (CPAR) in PPIRS. This was the only past performance information considered by the source selection evaluators team. Guam referenced two other contracts in its proposal, but neither contact responded to the agency's request for information.

The CPAR concerned an ongoing Guam contract with the Navy for similar work. Guam had not provided information on problems with this current contract when it listed the contract in the proposal, nor had Guam rebutted the allegations of poor performance when it had the opportunity to do so before the CPAR was finalized.

The GAO denied the protest, stating:

An agency is only required to use reasonable effort to contact an offeror's references, and is not required to make multiple attempts to contact a firm's past performance references. Here, the agency points out that the past performance reference listed by the protester failed to respond to the agency's email inquiry for relevant survey information. While Guam suggests that proof of the reference's receipt of the email message is necessary to show a reasonable attempt at contacting the reference, the firm provides no support for its contention. Rather, in light of the RFP's emphasis on the importance of the offeror providing reliable contact information (including, as was used here, email addresses) and ensuring cooperation from its references, we think the agency's email inquiry was an adequate effort to contact the reference; the failure of the reference to respond does not show that the agency's effort was inadequate (particularly in view of Guam's apparent failure to ensure, or, at a minimum, encourage its reference to cooperate) or that the past performance evaluation was improper.

For an abridged version of the GAO decision in *Guam Shipyard,* see Appendix B, Example 3.3.

The best way to counter negative past performance information already in PPIRS is for the offeror to demonstrate that it learned from the experience and knows how to deal with the problem. If a contractor had performance problems on a contract, the contractor should take advantage of the opportunity to comment on any adverse performance before the evaluation report is finalized. The comments must explain the specific corrective actions taken or the reasons why the performance was not satisfactory. Generalized comments or vague promises are not acceptable. A response at the time of the performance evaluation might be the offeror's only chance to respond to a negative evaluation because the government is not obligated to permit further comments in a later acquisition.

Any government communication during contract performance about less-than-satisfactory performance should receive a prompt and complete response. Offerors should retain such communications because they might be needed for future proposals to demonstrate how problems were corrected. This is particularly important when the RFP indicates that award will be made without discussions. Note, however, that the comments must stand alone; additional non-contemporaneous comments or justifications may be submitted but will probably be accorded little weight.

Planning for Contract Performance

Past performance will play an ever-increasing role in a contractor's ability to win future contracts. Although not part of the proposal, contract planning should consider what administrative actions should be taken to improve future evaluations of past performance.

If there are problems during contract performance and there is disagreement about factual matters, contemporaneous records of the problem are often determinative. One way to defend a position is to keep an internal record or log of performance problems and what was done to correct them, particularly of any event or activity that the government might view unfavorably.

Because the government might not always reveal to the contractor what it considers to be problems, it is wise to keep a contemporaneous record of all contract activity. This includes delays, conformance problems, contract changes, and any disagreements with government representatives. Contractors should record the event, the participants, the problem, and what action was or will be taken. The record should be kept up-to-date, particularly with respect to prospective actions and the final results. The contractor should, however, check with legal counsel to determine how to do this if the proposed contract will include FAR clause 52.215-2, *Audit and Records—Negotiation.* This clause gives the government the right to examine certain records, and legal counsel will want some input as to how, or whether, such records are kept.

It is a good practice to keep a record of performance feedback from government representatives during contract execution. If the feedback is not in writing, at least make a note of the feedback for your records. Recording positive feedback is particularly important because such information usually will be considered a strong point in the evaluation of past performance. Negative feedback also should be recorded to ensure that action is taken to resolve the problem.

Contractors also might consider developing a past performance file or database similar to that of government agencies. This would involve developing a past performance questionnaire and requesting that the contracting agency complete it at the end of contract performance. The contractor then can use copies of the completed questionnaires as past performance information for future procurements. This has the advantage of providing contemporaneous past performance information that might counter different information provided by the agency in response to a later past performance questionnaire by a different procuring agency.

Such a file would have proved useful to FC Construction Company[10] in its protest. An agency either erroneously or intentionally misrepresented telephonic responses to queries about FC's past performance. FC alleged that the responses rated its performance higher than that recorded by the agency. FC's protest on this point was denied when it was unable to produce the individuals in question for a GAO conference. FC would not have had this problem if it could have produced contemporaneous documentation of its past performance.

As noted earlier, all federal agencies are required to complete a contractor performance report at the end of contract performance and provide a copy to the contractor. A contractor's request for the completion of a past performance questionnaire would be a subtle reminder to the contracting agency of the requirement to perform an evaluation on completion of activities.

During contract performance, a contractor should respond quickly and positively to government requirements or inquiries. The government is the customer. A contractor should not construe this as a surrender of its contract rights but as a show of respect for the customer.

If problems arise during contract performance, they need to be addressed immediately. If the government finds fault with contract performance and is correct, the problem should be fixed promptly. If the government is not correct, an explanation of why the government's position is incorrect should be accompanied by suggestions on how the misunderstanding might be resolved. When addressing performance problems, specifics, not generalizations, are needed. Such correspondence may be particularly helpful when addressing past performance problems in future proposals.

Despite the need to be cooperative and sensitive to the customer's needs, the contractor should not surrender its contractual rights, such as making contract claims, questioning specifications, or requesting contract changes. The Comptroller General has ruled that such actions cannot be cited as adverse past performance during the evaluation of past performance.

It is virtually impossible to have contract performance that is completely problem-free. Contract problems can be minimized, however, through effective communication with the government. Doing so has become even more important with the increasing importance of past performance evaluations in awarding future contracts.

Responding to adverse past performance information is critical, whether it comes up during the solicitation process or at the end of contract performance. Generally, a contractor will get only one chance to respond. The response to such information must be clear, concise, and, most of all, convincing. The fact that a contractor does not agree with the adverse findings is not sufficient. It is a contractor's responsibility to successfully rebut adverse past performance information, and the agency's perception of adverse past performance will prevail if a contractor fails to respond fully to the adverse information.

Chapter 5 discusses responding to adverse past performance information during the solicitation process in greater detail.

NOTES

1. FAR Subpart 15.3–Source Selection.
2. FAR 15.305(a)(2)(ii). "The solicitation shall describe the approach for evaluating past performance, including evaluating offerors with no relevant performance history, and shall provide offerors an opportunity to identify past or current contracts (including Federal, State, and local government and private) for efforts similar to the Government requirement. The solicitation shall also authorize offerors to provide information on problems encountered on the identified contracts and the offeror's corrective actions. The Government shall consider this information, as well as information obtained from any other sources, when evaluating the offeror's past performance. The source selection authority shall determine the relevance of similar past performance information."
3. Office of Federal Procurement Policy, *Best Practices for Collecting and Using Current and Past Performance Information,* May 2000, p. 18.
4. See FAR Subpart 4.6–Contract Reporting.
5. FAR 15.204-5(b). "*Section L, Instructions, conditions, and notices to offerors or respondents.* Insert in this section solicitation provisions and other information and instructions not required elsewhere to guide offerors or respondents in preparing proposals or responses to request for information. Prospective offerors or respondents may be instructed to submit proposals or information in a specific format or severable parts to facilitate evaluation…"
6. FAR 15.204-5(c). "*Section M, Evaluation factors for award.* Identify all significant factors and any significant subfactors that will be considered in awarding the contract and their relative Importance (see 15.304(d)). The contracting officer shall insert one of the phrases in 15.304(e)."
7. *Phantom Products, Inc.,* B-283882, 12/30/99, 2000 CPD ¶7 at 4.
8. FAR 15.306(d)(3). "At a minimum, the contracting officer must, subject to paragraphs (d)(5) and (e) of this section and 15.307(a), indicate to, or discuss with, each offeror still being considered for award, deficiencies, significant weakness, and adverse past performance information to which the offeror has not yet had an opportunity to respond. The contracting officer also is encouraged to discuss other aspects of the offeror's proposal that could, in the opinion of the contracting officer, be altered or explained to enhance materially the proposal's potential for award. However, the contracting officer is not required to discuss every area where the proposal could be improved. The scope and extent of discussion are a matter of contracting office judgment."
9. Ibid.
10. *FC Construction Company, Inc.,* B-287059, 4/10/01.

CHAPTER 4

PRE-AWARD: WEIGHTING PAST PERFORMANCE INFORMATION

"Past performance is one indicator of an offeror's ability to perform the contact successfully." FAR[1]

This chapter provides guidance to the source selection authority in determining the usefulness of past performance information as an indicator of an offeror's ability to perform the prospective contract. Usefulness will depend on the answer to this question: "Is the past performance information from a contract that is similar to the solicitation requirement?" If it is, then the weight that will be assigned to it will depend on the following considerations.

FAR CONSIDERATIONS

The FAR[2] specifies four areas that must be considered in determining whether the past performance information is useful in the instant acquisition:

1. Currency and relevance of past performance information
2. Source of past performance information
3. Context of the data
4. General trends in contractor performance.

Currency and Relevance of the Past Performance Information

Currency refers to the state or quality of being current, i.e., recent. The more recent the contract, the greater assurance that the offeror still has the same managerial, technical, and human resource capacity. Older contracts may have employed different managers, technology, or personnel. Unless the solicitation sets a specific time limit, contracts completed within the last three years are generally considered current.

But currency is not necessarily time-related. For example, one offeror has an excellent performance record on contracts for developing systems for database management, but all the systems were based on technology that is now obsolete.

A second offeror also has excellent performance but has developed its systems for database management using innovative technology that is now considered the leading edge of current technology. The past performance information on the first offeror lacks currency because the technology used on the referenced contracts is no longer useful or acceptable. The information on the second offeror has currency because the technology it uses is still prevalent or still in use.

Relevance refers to the "same and similar effort." If the past performance information relates to work of a different nature from that of the instant acquisition, the contracting officer should disregard it because it does not show how well the offeror might perform under the instant acquisition. For example, under a solicitation for base housing maintenance and repair services, including plumbing, electrical, mechanical, and structural work, a review of one offeror's past performance revealed that it had done only painting and painting-related work in the past. It had not performed any of the other required work. This offeror's past performance information is not as relevant as that of an offeror that has performed the full array of services noted in the solicitation. Less weight is given to the past performance information of the offeror that has done only painting and painting-related work.

If a connection cannot be made between the past effort and the prospective acquisition, the past performance information is not relevant. The RFP, however, may be more precise and specify that the referenced contracts are those that are similar with respect to size, scope, and complexity. Or, the RFP may even specify the type of contract, e.g., fixed price. The more relevant the contract, the more weight is given to it.

Source of the Past Performance Information

Some past performance information sources are better than others. Contractor performance reports carried out in compliance with FAR 42.15 are the best source. They contain input from the agency's acquisition team and ratings for the key performance elements. The contractor was given the opportunity to review and comment on the ratings before they were finalized. Information close at hand (i.e., information personally known to the contracting officer or evaluators) is an important source. The most common sources of past performance information are the responses to questionnaires sent to the contacts referenced in the proposal.

Information that is at variance with other information received should be verified with the responding agency. If the information is negative, consideration should also be given to permitting the offeror to rebut such information. Information from commercial sources should be handled with care because although the federal government is required to maintain past performance information in its files, commercial sources might or might not routinely retain such information in a useable form. Adverse past performance information from commercial sources must be in writing.

Context of the Data

Context relates to the circumstances in which an event occurs. For example, one contractor has had very successful past performance constructing roads in urban settings but has had no contracts for constructing highways. Under a solicitation for road construction throughout the state, this offeror's past performance might not be as good an indicator of the offeror's ability to perform the contract as that of another offeror that has had similar successful past performance in both urban and rural settings.

Past performance information should be examined to ensure that the narrative description of an offeror's past performance and the assigned ratings mesh. Past performance information may be considered in context when the narrative substantiates the ratings. It is out of context when there is no narrative or the narrative inadequately supports the rating assigned. Adjectival ratings, numerical scores, color codes, or other rating indicators are of little value without a supporting narrative or description of the offeror's past performance.

General Trend of Past Performance

When reviewing past performance, evaluators often focus on a single problem contract rather than looking at the general trend of the offeror's past performance. An offeror's past performance should not necessarily be downgraded because of a single problem contract, particularly if the trend of the offeror's past performance (over time or a number of other contracts) does not show such problems. Evaluation of past performance information is not a mathematical or mechanical exercise. Problem contracts should be examined and then balanced with the general trend of the offeror's past.

An offeror's performance should be evaluated on the preponderance of its past efforts to determine whether past performance deficiencies are usual or unusual in terms of the offeror's performance record. If the preponderance of an offeror's past efforts are deficient, this fact should be treated as an unacceptable risk factor and evaluated as such.

OTHER CONSIDERATIONS

The areas identified in the FAR are not the only areas that should be considered in determining the usefulness of past performance information. The following should also be considered when evaluating an offeror's past performance information:

- Adverse past performance information
- Extent of government's responsibility
- New firms/firms with no past performance history
- Performance of predecessor companies, key personnel, or subcontractors.

Adverse Past Performance Information

When evaluating an offeror's past performance, assess the extent to which the offeror's past performance is likely to affect its performance on the prospective contract. A demonstrable relationship should exist between the offeror's past performance and the prospective performance, particularly if there is adverse past performance information. For example, if past problems have been corrected and are not likely to recur, these problems should not be used to downgrade the offeror's proposal. Or, if the past poor performance occurred in a corporate division that will not be involved in the prospective contract, the past problems should not be counted against the offeror unless it can be demonstrated that the problems originated at the corporate level and thus, unless corrected, would be likely to affect the prospective effort adversely. On the other hand, poor past performance on an effort similar to the prospective contract, if not explained satisfactorily, is a good indicator that the performance on the prospective contract will also be poor.

When considering the impact of an offeror's past performance on prospective performance, the nature and severity of past problems and the effectiveness of any corrective action taken by the offeror in terms of the prospective performance should be assessed. If the past problems have not been corrected, are they likely to recur and will they adversely affect the chance of successful performance? If the past problems have been successfully corrected or are unlikely to recur, they are not germane to the prospective contract. An offeror can still receive a high rating for past performance as long as problems identified during performance were handled to the satisfaction of the client.

Performance problems are not necessarily poor performance, as can be seen from the GAO decision in *The Communities Group,* B-283147, October 12, 1999, summarized in Example 4.1.

Example 4.1—Performance problems are not necessarily adverse past performance.

Issue: The Communities Group (TCG) protested the award of a contract to Management Solutions of America, Inc., contending that Housing and Urban Development (HUD) had failed to conduct meaningful discussions and properly evaluate proposals. Specifically, in rating Management Solutions' past performance, HUD had failed to consider the negative past performance of the firm's subcontractor on a current HUD contract for similar services.

Resolution: TCG was correct that the subcontractor had problems with the contract. However, HUD did not consider the problems negative performance because the subcontractor had taken prompt and appropriate remedial action. The Comptroller General found that HUD's evaluation of the offeror's subcontractor was reasonable and consistent with the evaluation criteria specified in the proposal and denied the protest.

For an abridged version of the GAO decision in *The Communities Group,* see Appendix B, Example 4.1.

Note that at the time Management Solutions' past performance was evaluated, the problem with its subcontractor had not been investigated and, because the facts of the matter were not known, the problem could not be considered in the evaluation. By the time of the protest, however, it was found that MTB had taken appropriate corrective action and the problem was not likely to recur. Thus, an adverse past performance finding would be inappropriate because the problem would have no effect on the prospective performance.

GAO reached a similar decision in *Dynacs Engineering Co., Inc.,* B-284234; B-284234.2; B-284234.3, March 17, 2000, which is summarized in Example 4.2.

Example 4.2—Clarifying adverse past performance information during discussion.

Issue: A NASA source evaluation board (SEB) learned that a contracting officer's representative (COR) administering another NASA contract intended to give Federal Data Corporation (FDC) a negative performance rating for its transition effort on that contract. This information was not used to downgrade FDC's past performance, and the other offeror protested that the past performance evaluation was unreasonable.

Resolution: The Comptroller General denied the protest, stating:

After learning of the COR's potential negative rating, NASA asked FDC to respond to this information. FDC did so, both explaining its position, and sending the SEB a copy of the response it had sent to the COR. According to FDC's response, the transition effort did not go well for reasons other than FDC's actions; FDC maintained that the follow-on contractor caused many of the problems. Since the COR had not actually assigned FDC a final negative rating, the SEB considered the issue unresolved and did not use it to downgrade FDC in the past performance evaluation... Since the COR had not provided a final rating by the time the SEB was completing its past performance evaluation, and FDC provided a response in which it denied that it was responsible for the difficult transition, it was reasonable not to automatically attribute the problems to FDC. We think the SEB therefore reasonably could conclude that the information available did not support a finding of deficient past performance, and thus did not warrant downgrading FDC.[3]

For an abridged version of the GAO decision in *Dynacs Engineering Co., Inc.,* see Appendix B, Example 4.2.

As with Example 4.1, if a matter dealing with adverse past performance information is not officially resolved at the time of the evaluation, the evaluators are not required to consider it. However, if the evaluators are aware of a problem, they should allow the offeror to comment on the adverse information, and the offeror's response must be credible. If FDC had not responded with reasonable arguments, the matter might have been resolved differently.

Examples 4.1 and 4.2 involved acquisitions in which discussions were to be conducted and there was time to consider these matters before award. But what happens when award will be made without discussions and time is of the essence? The FAR[4] states that where award will be made without discussions, the agency may (but is not required to) give the offeror an opportunity to clarify adverse past performance information to which the offeror has not previously had an opportunity to respond. Example 4.3, taken from the GAO decision in *A.G. Cullen Construction, Inc.,* B-284049.2, February 22, 2000, provides clarification on this point.

Example 4.3—Clarifying adverse past performance information where award will be made without discussions.

Issue: The solicitation provided for award, without discussion, to the offeror whose proposal represented the best value to the government based on price/performance tradeoff, with past performance significantly more important than price. The award went to DiCicco. Its price was five percent higher than Cullen's, but it had an excellent past performance rating compared to Cullen's very good rating. One of Cullen's references had provided negative past performance information. Because the award was made without discussion, Cullen had no opportunity to address the negative information. Cullen protested.

Resolution: The Comptroller General explained:

With regard specifically to clarifications concerning adverse past performance information to which the offeror has not previously had an opportunity to respond, we think that, for the exercise of discretion to be reasonable, the contracting officer must give the offeror an opportunity to respond where there clearly is a reason to question the validity of the past performance information, for example, where there are obvious inconsistencies between a reference's narrative comments and the actual ratings the reference gives the offeror. In the absence of such a clear basis to question the past performance information, we think that, short of acting in bad faith, the contracting officer reasonably may decide not to ask for clarifications.

Applying this standard here, we think that the contracting officer reasonably exercised his discretion in deciding not to communicate with Cullen regarding the adverse past performance information received from one of Cullen's references. There is nothing on the face of the reference that would create concerns about its validity. Given the permissive language of FAR 15.306(a)(2), the fact that Cullen may wish to respond to the reference does not give rise to a requirement that the contracting officer give Cullen an opportunity to do so.

For an abridged version of the GAO decision in *A.G. Cullen Construction, Inc.*, see Appendix B, Example 4.3.

Note that while the FAR is permissive about giving an offeror a chance to respond, the Comptroller General states that the offeror must be given an opportunity to respond if there is reason to question the validity of the adverse past performance information. The agency has the discretion to do so in all other cases.

Even if award is to be made without discussions, it is suggested that offerors be permitted to clarify adverse past performance information in all cases where the adverse information might be an important factor in the award decision (i.e., the offeror might otherwise be in line for award), regardless of any questions about the validity of the reference's information. Without the offeror's input, it would be difficult to assess the impact the problem might have on prospective performance. Although this might add a few days to the procurement process, a protest (even a losing one) will cause even greater disruption. It should be noted, however, that this suggestion applies only where the offeror's clarification will not result in any changes to the proposal. Proposal changes are not permitted when award will be made without discussions.

When discussions will be held, the FAR[5] states that communications must be held with offerors where adverse past performance information is a determining factor preventing them from being placed in the competitive range, and the offeror has not had a prior opportunity to respond to such information. Technically, this would not include adverse information about contracts the offeror has referenced because, theoretically, the offeror would know of any problems on these contracts and should comment on such problems in its proposal.

In reality, however, contractors are not always informed of government-perceived problems during contract performance, particularly on contracts that end satisfactorily. These problems, however, might be noted on responses to a query about past performance from another agency.

It would be good policy, therefore, to permit offerors to comment on any adverse past performance information before determining the competitive range or making an award without discussions if the adverse information might be a determining factor preventing the offeror from being included in the competitive range or considered for award. With offeror comments in hand, evaluators are better prepared to assess the impact of the problems on prospective performance. Permitting such comments might help avoid a protest.

If it is decided that an offeror is to be included in the competitive range despite some adverse past performance information, this information should be identified as a discussion question to be addressed during discussions.

In any event, if an offeror fails to provide information on past problems and the associated corrective action in its proposal, or fails to respond to questions about such problems, the government may determine that the problems have not been corrected and evaluate the offeror's past performance accordingly, as shown in Example 4.4 taken from the GAO decision in *Smith of Galeton Gloves, Inc.*, B-271686, July 24, 1996.

Example 4.4—If an offeror fails to respond to questions about past problems, you may assume that the problems have not been corrected.

Issue: Smith of Galeton Gloves, Inc., protested the award to Nationwide Glove Company, stating that the agency had improperly downgraded its proposal under the past performance evaluation factor. Smith had listed two past contracts, both of which did not meet the RFP's currency requirement. The agency researched its own files and found two previous contracts with Smith. Based on timeliness deficiencies on the two contracts, the agency gave a marginally acceptable past performance rating. The agency sent a discussion letter asking Smith to address the delinquency problems. Smith failed to do so.

Resolution: The Comptroller General denied the protest, stating:

Given the agency's discussion letter, which clearly placed Smith on notice that the firm needed to furnish additional evidence to improve its past performance rating, and Smith's failure to respond—in any fashion—to the agency's past performance concerns, we think the agency reasonably found Smith's proposal marginally acceptable under the past performance factor.

For an abridged version of the GAO decision in *Smith of Galeton Gloves, Inc.,* see Appendix B, Example 4.4.

While this case involved discussions after the competitive range was established, the ruling also would apply to an offeror that failed to respond adequately to a clarification request prior to an award without discussions or the establishment of the competitive range.

A contracting officer should be careful, however, about what is evaluated as poor past performance. A contractor's exercise of its rights during contract performance should not be evaluated as poor performance, as noted in Example 4.5, from the GAO decision in *AmClyde Engineered Products Co., Inc.,* B-282271; B-282271.2, June 21, 1999.

Example 4.5—Filing of contract claims is not poor performance.

Issue: AmClyde Engineered Products Company, Inc., protested the award to Samsung Heavy Industries Company, LTD, for the design and manufacture of portal cranes. AmClyde argued that the Navy should not have downgraded its proposal for making claims because this is a mechanism that a contractor is entitled to pursue whenever there is a dispute on the contract, and many of AmClyde's claims were meritorious.

Resolution: The Comptroller General denied the protest, reasoning that:

[W]e find no basis to conclude that AmClyde would have been entitled to a materially better or an outstanding rating, even if it had been able to eliminate claims history as an area of concern, since the other aforementioned past performance problems still remain.

Although the protest was denied, GAO agreed with AmClyde's position that filing claims should not downgrade a contractor's performance. A footnote to the AmClyde decision explained the GAO position as follows:

While the claims apparently had no impact here, we agree with the protester that, absent some evidence of abuse of the process, agencies should not lower a firm's past performance evaluation based solely on its having filed claims. Contract claims, like bid protests, constitute remedies established by statute and regulation, and firms should not be prejudiced in competing for other contracts because of their reasonable pursuit of such remedies in the past.

For an abridged version of the GAO decision in *AmClyde Engineered Products Company, Inc.,* see Appendix B, Example 4.5.

This decision encompasses more than the taking of formal contractual actions, such as claims, disputes, and appeals. Disagreements with the government about contract administration, such as contract interpretation, do not constitute poor past performance unless they are determined to be frivolous or deliberately misleading.

Extent of Government's Responsibility

One of the more difficult past performance evaluation areas is determining the extent to which government actions might have contributed to an offeror's deficient performance. Government actions, such as faulty specifications, late delivery of government-furnished property (GFP), delivery of faulty GFP, failure to provide timely testing or other approvals, and numerous contract changes, can contribute to cost overruns and late deliveries.

When faced with an allegation of deficient performance, the contractor often will blame the government, and the government usually will deny any responsibility. Resolving these issues is not easy; nevertheless, the extent of government involvement should be assessed before any decisions are made. It is not reasonable to penalize a contractor for problems resulting from, or significantly affected by, government actions.

For example, while discussing the background in a decision,[6] the Comptroller General noted that the contracting officer had asked an offeror about comments made by another agency indicating that the offeror's technical performance was considered inadequate. In response, the offeror produced a letter of commendation from the contracting agency's project manager on its performance under the contract in question, in which the project manager praised the offeror's performance as outstanding and tacitly admitted that the government was responsible for the alleged problems. Had the offeror been denied an opportunity to respond to the adverse comments, the record would have shown that the offeror had performed poorly on a contract when it actually had performed in an outstanding manner.

The validity of an offeror's contention that the fault lay with the government requires considering the arguments of both sides and deciding which side has the best argument. The evaluator should assess the government's allegations of poor performance against the offeror's other references. If the other references show high performance assessments, the matter should be investigated if a singular finding of poor performance would adversely affect the offeror's competitive position.

New Firms or Firms with No Past Performance History

The evaluation of past performance must provide for newly formed firms that lack a history of relevant past performance or firms for which there is no pertinent past performance information available (i.e., an established firm desiring to expand into new areas). The FAR[7] states that firms without a past performance record or for whom past performance information is not available may not be evaluated favorably or unfavorably on past performance. In effect, you are to give such a firm a neutral rating, which, in theory, does not affect its competitive position. The concept of "neutral" ratings is not new, as shown in Example 4.6 from the GAO decision in *Excalibur Systems, Inc.,* B-272017, July 12, 1996.

Example 4.6—Evaluating offerors with no past performance history (#1).

Issue: In the Excalibur Systems, Inc., decision, the Comptroller General discussed the use of neutral ratings where both offerors had received a green/low risk past performance rating, so award was made to the lowest-priced offeror. The protester argued that the awardee's past performance should have been given an insufficient data (neutral) rating because the awardee had never produced the item before, and the protester should have received award because its higher past performance rating and less-than-one-percent difference in price made it the best value.

Resolution: The Comptroller General denied the protest, stating:

Here, however, the Navy explains that its evaluation scheme does not call for rewarding a vendor with good past performance over a vendor with no relevant past performance. Rather, the Navy further explains, its evaluation scheme is intended to differentiate between those with good past performance and those with differing degrees of less than good performance. In other words, the Navy's position is that under the RFP an offeror with a green rating is superior to an offeror with a red or yellow rating but not to an offeror with a neutral insufficient data rating.

We have no basis to disagree with the Navy. In fact, we have previously recognized that this very evaluation scheme contemplates that "a green rating [is] to be given greater weight in the evaluation only when compared to a red or a yellow rating," and that an offeror's green rating is "not to be given greater weight in the evaluation when compared to an offeror['s] . . . insufficient data rating," so that in the circumstances here the agency is to compare the competing proposals "based on price."[8]

Accordingly, we conclude that even if Condor's green rating is changed to an insufficient data rating, the award decision would not change.

The Comptroller General denied this protest because the RFP clearly stated that offerors receiving insufficient data classifications "shall be evaluated solely on the basis of price [and that] [p]ast performance shall not be a consideration in their evaluation." This meant that a comparative assessment of past performance would be made only among those offerors with a past performance record, and then the offerors, including those with insufficient data ratings, would compete on the basis of price alone.

For an abridged version of the GAO decision in *Excalibur Systems, Inc.,* see Appendix B, Example 4.6.

The RFP's explanation of how the past performance of new firms or those with no past performance history will be evaluated must be worded carefully to express clearly the purpose of the evaluation. In Example 4.6, the Navy was clear as to how neutral past performance would be evaluated. What happens when the award turns on a tradeoff between price and past performance, and the two lowest-priced offerors have no past performance history? This can make things difficult, as shown in the GAO decision in *Phillips Industries, Inc.,* B-280645, September 17, 1998, which is summarized in Example 4.7.

Example 4.7—Evaluating offerors with no past performance history (#2).

Issue: The offerors were to be evaluated on the basis of price and past performance, and award was to be made on a best-value basis. Offerors with no past performance history with the agency were to be given a neutral past performance rating.

Two lowest-priced offerors had no performance history. The third lowest-priced offeror had an excellent past performance rating and a price that was within five percent of the two lower-priced offerors. The contracting officer found that the item was currently out of stock and that there were outstanding back orders. The contracting officer therefore concluded that the third lowest-priced offeror's price was worth the reduced risk of non-performance (as evidenced by its excellent past performance rating) in light of the high demand for items already in a back-ordered inventory position. The contracting officer awarded the contract to Amjay, the third lowest-priced offeror, as the best value.

Phillips Industries, the lowest-priced offeror, protested that it should have been awarded the contract under an evaluation scheme that provided for a neutral rating for an offeror with no performance history.

Resolution: The Comptroller General did not agree, noting:

The RFP listed certain factors, including delivery schedule/inventory status, which could affect the tradeoff determination. Here, the contracting officer decided, given the high demand and the backlog status for the item, that award to a slightly higher-priced firm which had an excellent performance history was justified to ensure timely delivery and represented the best value to the government. This was entirely consistent with the RFP evaluation scheme and the discretion afforded the contracting officer in making the tradeoff decision.[9]

The decision in this case turned on a bona fide need to ensure timely delivery because of the high demand and backlog status of the item being procured. This is what tradeoffs are all about—deciding, after the evaluations are completed and based on the circumstances of the instant procurement, which of the proposals offers the best value to the government.

For an abridged version of the GAO decision in *Phillips Industries, Inc.,* see Appendix B, Example 4.7.

Note that while a best-value determination may favor a higher-priced offeror with a favorable past performance rating over a lower-priced offeror with a neutral past performance rating, the evaluation scoring cannot penalize an offeror for its neutral rating.

OFPP guidance[10] suggests that when scoring an offeror with no past performance history, the offeror should be given the middle rating in whatever rating system is used (e.g., 50 on a 100-point scale, 3 on a 5-point scale, a satisfactory rating on an adjectival scale, or the middle color on a color-rating scale). Although the OFPP guidance indicates that this should happen rarely, proposals from new firms or firms with no pertinent past performance history are not that unusual. Giving a middle rating ensures that the offeror is not penalized for its neutral rating and is probably better than not scoring past performance at all (by avoiding possible confusion)—unless, of course, a situation like that in Example 4.7 applies. Careful attention should be paid to the wording of the evaluation scheme with respect to offerors with no performance history to ensure that the rating scheme itself does not work to downgrade new firms or offerors with no performance history.

Performance of Other Companies, Key Personnel, or Subcontractors

The FAR provides that the evaluation should take into account past performance information regarding predecessor companies, certain key personnel, or subcontractors that will perform major or critical aspects of the requirement.[11] The application of this FAR provision, however, can be problematic if the RFP does not explain how this will be done and what documentation or explanations the offeror should provide in its proposal.

Generally, the need to evaluate the past performance of other companies, key personnel, and subcontractors comes into play with newly formed firms or firms with little or no relevant past performance history. This does not, however, change the need to explain clearly how the past performance will be evaluated in such instances.

Performance of Other Companies—The evaluation team may consider the past performance of other companies when they are team members, affiliates, or significant subcontractors, as shown in the GAO decision in *Universal Building Maintenance, Inc.*, B-282456, July 15, 1999, which is summarized in Example 4.8.

Example 4.8—When should one company's past performance be attributed to another?

Issue: An agency improperly attributed the past performance of the parent company or its other subsidiaries to an awardee where the record did not establish that the parent company or subsidiaries would be involved in the performance of the protested contract.

Resolution: A protester argued that GSA had improperly evaluated the awardee's past performance by considering the contracts of the awardee's parent company. The record showed that the awardee, Service Star USA, Inc., had performed only one of its five referenced contracts. In fact, although not made clear by the awardee in its written proposal, four of the five contracts listed had been performed by two subsidiaries of Service Star's parent company, Service Star International, Inc.

The GSA responded that it had properly considered the parent company's and its other subsidiaries' contracts in its evaluation, citing FAR 15.305(a)(2)(iii) as the basis for its decision to consider these contracts. This FAR reference provides, in essence, that a past performance evaluation should consider information regarding predecessor companies, key personnel, or subcontractors that will perform major or critical aspects of the requirement when such information is relevant.

The Comptroller General did not agree with GSA's position.

We have stated that in determining whether one company's performance should be attributed to another, an agency must consider the nature and extent of the relationship between the two companies—in particular, whether the workforce, management, facilities, or other resources of one may affect contract performance of the other. In this regard, while it would be inappropriate to consider a company's performance record where that record does not bear on the likelihood of successful performance by the offeror, it would be appropriate to consider a company's performance record where it will be involved in the contract effort or where it shares management with the offeror. We conclude that the agency did not reasonably evaluate the relationship of the companies for purposes of attributing the past performance of the parent company or its other subsidiaries to Service Star USA, Inc., and therefore could not consider four of the five contracts referenced by Service Star USA, Inc. in evaluating its past performance.

Although a firm might not have a past performance history of its own, it still can have a performance history through other companies, as long as the other companies will be significantly involved in performing the prospective contract. In this case, however, GSA went beyond what was in the written proposal and either assumed performance by these other companies or simply ignored the fact that the proposal did not demonstrate the participation by these other companies. Therefore, the Comptroller General sustained the protest.

The point here is that while the performance of other companies may be used to demonstrate an offeror's past performance, this can be done only when the proposal clearly explains how these other companies will be significantly involved in the proposed contract. It might be beneficial to explain this in the RFP's description of how past performance will be evaluated. Otherwise, this information might not be provided in an offeror's proposal.

For an abridged version of the GAO decision in *Universal Building Maintenance, Inc.,* see Appendix B, Example 4.8.

Performance of Key Personnel—The FAR permits the evaluation of past performance to be broadened to include the experience of a firm's key personnel. This can be important to new firms or firms with no past performance history. Note, however, that the evaluation of the experience of key personnel involves how well they performed under the referenced contract, not simply that they had worked under the particular contract.

This concept assumes that if the referenced contract was performed successfully, the success is imputed to the named key person for purposes of the evaluation of past performance. This may present problems, however, if the contract was not performed successfully or if the reference's response was otherwise negative.

Downgrading an offeror under the past performance factor solely because some of its proposed key personnel were involved with a past problem contract might be difficult to justify without some evidence that the subject personnel were responsible for the problems. To presume that particular individuals are responsible for past problems requires definitive evidence. There are many reasons why a contract has problems that may be beyond the control of the responsible contractor personnel. Note, however, that the presence of such individuals, if they were deemed responsible for the problems on the referenced contract, could be determined to be a performance risk and evaluated as such.

Offerors should be advised to establish clearly a proposed key person's contribution to the success of the referenced contract when relying on that person's prior experience under the past performance evaluation factor. A failure to establish this relationship could result in a finding of insufficient information and a neutral past performance rating.

Evaluating the past performance of key personnel can become complicated, as shown in the GAO decision in *SWR Inc.,* B-286044.2; B-286044.3, November 1, 2000, which is summarized in Example 4.9.

Example 4.9—Evaluating the past performance of key personnel.

Issue: Past performance evaluation is unobjectionable where it was conducted in accordance with stated evaluation criteria and is supported by the record. The protester's proposal was reasonably rated neutral under the past performance factor where it showed no relevant prior performance by the offeror. The protester argued that the relevant experience of its proposed project manager should have been attributed to the protester. The agency declined to do so where the individual was not currently employed by the protester. Furthermore, the proposal did not contain a firm commitment by the individual to work for the protester.

Resolution: The protestor, SWR, submitted seven past performance references, all of which rated its performance as exceptional or very good under each past performance subfactor. The agency, however, found that the referenced contracts were not similar in nature and scope to the RFP requirements and therefore were not relevant. SWR's proposal thus was rated neutral overall for past performance.

SWR protested the award on the basis that its neutral past performance rating was not proper. SWR argued that the agency was required—under the terms of the RFP and the FAR—to consider the experience of its proposed project manager, a key employee who had worked in the same capacity for the incumbent contractor for three years. SWR concluded that had the agency considered the project manager's past performance, SWR would have received a higher rating and, based on its lower price, its proposal would have been determined to be the best value to the government.

The Comptroller General denied the protest, but not because the proposed project manager did not have the requisite experience, stating:

SWR's proposal indicated that the individual it was proposing as project manager was not a current SWR employee, but was employed as the project manager for the incumbent contractor. The possibility that, due to unforeseen circumstances, a proposed key individual may not be hired by the offeror, is an appropriate consideration for an agency in deciding whether the individual's experience should be imputed to the offeror for evaluation purposes.[11] *The letter included in SWR's proposal established no commitment on the part of the proposed individual to work for SWR and, indeed, did not even refer to SWR, and there was nothing else in the proposal indicating that SWR and the individual had even discussed specific employment terms. We think the agency reasonably could decline to impute the proposed individual's experience to SWR based on the absence of stronger evidence of an employment commitment, or other evidence that the individual would in fact be employed by SWR.*

For an abridged version of the GAO decision in *SWR Inc.,* see Appendix B, Example 4.9.

Example 4.9 contains lessons for both government and contractor personnel. For the government it shows that an RFP should always require firm letters of commitment from key personnel who are not currently employed by an offeror. The RFP also should explain that, at a minimum, the letter should be signed by the individual concerned and should show a firm commitment to be employed by the firm. Requiring valid letters of commitment can help avoid protests such as the one in Example 4.9.

Contractor personnel also should be aware of the need for a valid letter of commitment from proposed key personnel not currently employed by an offeror. Contractor personnel should recheck the validity of the letters of commitment when there is a significant period of time between the submission of the proposal and the time set for the submission of the final proposal revisions. It is the offeror's responsibility to ensure that the key personnel proposed will be available for contract performance.

Performance of Subcontractors—The past performance of proposed subcontractors may be evaluated if the subcontractors will perform major or critical aspects of the requirement and if the past performance is relevant to the current requirement. The GAO decision in *Battelle Memorial Institute,* B-278673, February 27, 1998, deals specifically with evaluating the past performance of subcontractors. It is summarized in Example 4.10.

Example 4.10—Evaluating the past performance of subcontractors.

Issue: Can subcontractors be listed as past performance references?

Resolution: Here is what the Comptroller General said:

With regard to its claims regarding Porton's work on two of the contracts, Battelle is essentially arguing that the only entity that may properly list a prior contract for purposes of past performance evaluation is the concern which actually performed the work relevant to that covered in the solicitation. We disagree. The general rule is that the prime contractor under a government contract is responsible for the performance of its subcontractors.[12] Further, subcontractors and joint venturers perform various portions of contracts and accordingly may obtain experience useful in predicting success in future contract performance. Where an offeror was involved as a subcontractor or joint venture in performing work under a prior contract similar to work to be included under the instant contract, such experience may properly be considered in assessing that offeror's past performance.[13]

For an abridged version of the GAO decision in *Battelle Memorial Institute,* see Appendix B, Example 4.10.

The key to evaluating a subcontractor's past performance is relevance. The government must look for it, and the offeror must clearly demonstrate it in the proposal. Keep in mind, however, that what is to be evaluated is how well the subcontractor performed the referenced contracts, not simply that it performed similar work.

NOTES

1. FAR 15.305(a)(2)(i).
2. FAR 15.305(a)(2)(i). "...The currency and relevance of the information, source of the information, context of the data, and general trends in contractor' performance shall be considered."
3. *The Communities Group,* B-283147, 10/12/99, 99-2 CPD ¶101 at 5,6.
4. FAR 15.306(a)(2). "If award will be made without conducting discussions, offerors may be given the opportunity to clarify certain aspects of proposals (e.g., the relevance of an offeror's past performance information and adverse past performance information to which the offeror has not previously had an opportunity to respond) or to resolve minor or clerical errors."
5. FAR 15.306(b)(1)(i). "[Communications] [s]hall be held with offerors whose past performance information is the determining factor preventing them from being placed within the competitive range. Such communications shall address adverse past performance information to which an offeror has not had a prior opportunity to respond; and (2) May only be held with those offerors (other than offerors under paragraph (b)(1)(i) of this section) whose exclusion from, or inclusion in, the competitive range is uncertain; ..."
6. *Columbia Research Corp.,* B-247073; B-247073.2, 4/23/92, GCR 106,570.
7. FAR 15.305(a)(2)(iv). "In the case of an offeror without a record of relevant past performance or for whom information on past performance is not available, the offeror may not be evaluated favorably or unfavorably on past performance."
8. *Espey Mfg. & Elecs. Corp.,* B-254738.3, 3/8/94, 94-1 CPD ¶180.
9. *Excalibur Systems, Inc.,* B-272017, 7/12/96, 96-2 CPD ¶13 at 3.
10. Office of Federal Procurement Policy, *Best Practices for Collecting and Using Current and Past Performance Information,* May 2000, p. 24.

11. FAR 15.305(a)(2)(iii). "The evaluation should take into account past performance information regarding predecessor companies, key personnel who have relevant experience, or subcontractors that will perform major or critical aspects of the requirement when such information is relevant to the instant acquisition."
12. *Neal R. Gross & Co., Inc.*, B-275066, 1/17/97, 97-1 CPD ¶30 at 4.
13. *Phillips National, Inc.*, B-253875, 11/1/93, 93-2 CPD ¶252 at 6.

CHAPTER 5

PRE-AWARD: EVALUATING PAST PERFORMANCE

"An agency shall evaluate competitive proposals and then assess their relative qualities solely on the factors and subfactors specified in the solicitation." FAR[1]

Evaluating past performance differs from evaluating the other non-cost evaluation factors. Past performance is based on information gathered from sources outside the proposal. The offeror is given the opportunity to identify past and current contracts for efforts similar to the government requirement. The burden is on the government to gather past performance information on the identified contracts.

For those contracts that have not been evaluated in compliance with FAR 42.15, the primary information-gathering activity is checking the references of the contracts identified by the offeror. For contracts with federal agencies that have been evaluated, it is a simple matter of accessing the respective report card from the Past Performance Information Retrieval System (PPIRS). For contracts with states, local governments, and private firms, reference checks are performed. Even with some federal contracts, reference checks will have to be done when the contracting agency is in the process of conducting an evaluation of the identified contract or simply did not perform the required evaluation.

When conducting the evaluation, a number of specific areas concerning past performance information warrant particular attention. These areas have been the subject of numerous protests, and both government and contractor personnel should be aware of potential pitfalls and how to avoid them. Attention should be given to:

- Checking references
- Using information close at hand
- Using personal knowledge
- Allowing offerors to respond to adverse past performance information
- Applying rating systems
- Documenting the evaluation findings.

CHECKING REFERENCES

Checking past performance references provided by offerors is time-consuming. It requires contacting the references, asking questions, receiving the answers, and sorting it all out. This process can be facilitated by limiting the number of references offerors must provide or simply by not contacting all the references.

Will the agency get in trouble if it fails to contact all the references? The Comptroller General has consistently ruled that there is no requirement that an agency contact all the references an offeror provides.

In *Universal Building Maintenance, Inc.*, B-282456, March 15, 1999, footnote 2, the Comptroller General stated:

> *The protester objects to the agency's inability to contact the two other references. The agency, however, is only required to make a reasonable effort to contact the references, and it is not objectionable to evaluate an offeror's past performance on less than the maximum possible number of references the agency could have received. See IGIT, Inc.*[2] *(although agencies are required to evaluate the past performance of all offerors on the same basis, there is no general requirement that an agency contact all of an offeror's references, or contact the same number of references for each offeror).*

Note that the Comptroller General indicated that an agency must make a reasonable effort to contact references but there is no requirement to contact all references. This should be taken to mean that: (1) if an agency makes a reasonable attempt to contact a reference but with no success, the agency is not required to make repeated attempts or to take unusual steps to contact the reference; and (2) an agency may check some, but not necessarily all, references provided by an offeror.

The key to an acceptable past performance evaluation is not how many references are checked but how well the evaluation is conducted; that is, the evaluation process must result in a well-informed and reasonable evaluation of an offeror's past performance. The Comptroller General's position on the requirement to check all references is probably best summed up by the following:[3]

> *There is no legal requirement that all past performance references listed in an offeror's proposal be checked or included in a valid review of past performance.*[4] *Rather, what is critical is whether the evaluation is conducted fairly, reasonably, and in accordance with the stated evaluation criteria, and whether it is based upon relevant information sufficient to make a reasonable determination of the offeror's overall past performance rating, including relevant information close at hand or known by the contracting personnel awarding the contract.*[5]

Example 5.1, from the GAO decision in *Advanced Data Concepts, Inc.*, B-277801.4, June 1, 1998, addresses what happens when the questionnaires are not returned.

Example 5.1—What Happens When Past Performance Questionnaires Are Not Returned?

Issue: The awardee referenced three prior Department of Energy (DOE) contracts, and all of the references returned the past performance questionnaires. The protester, ADC, referenced two current DOE contracts and one from another agency. When none of the protester's references returned the past performance questionnaires, the protester was awarded a neutral past performance rating.

Resolution: The Comptroller General ruled:

Despite ADC's arguments to the contrary, there is no legal requirement that all past performance references be included in a valid review of past performance.[6] *For our Office to sustain a protest challenging the failure to obtain or consider a reference's assessment of past performance, a protester must show unusual factual circumstances that convert the failure to a significant inequity for the protester.*[7] *... In short, without a showing that the DOE evaluators here should have been aware of the assessments that would have been received, and without some other showing that an agency's evaluation was unreasonable, we deny this protest ground.*

This case presents some issues that, while dismissed in this instance, warrant some thought: (1) should DOE have refused to permit offerors to comment on their performance of the referenced contracts and (2) should DOE have compelled the return of the questionnaires from at least the DOE components?

DOE prohibited offerors from commenting on their performance of the referenced contracts because it planned to obtain this information itself. DOE attempted to obtain the information from the protester's references, but none of them replied, thus giving the protester a neutral past performance rating as provided for in the RFP. The protester argued that the neutral rating was unreasonable because FAR Subpart 42.15 requires agencies to share past performance information and DOE should have taken action to compel return of the questionnaires.

It is suggested that offerors should be encouraged, not discouraged, to make such comments (except when it concerns contractor performance reports that the offeror has already had the opportunity to review). One of the best indications of a problem is when the offeror and the responding agency differ significantly in their assessment of the offeror's past performance. In these situations, the responding agency should be queried again to validate its initial response. Here, DOE deprived itself of this information. The result was a protest and, although the agency won, it still had to devote time and resources to respond to the protest.

For an abridged version of the GAO decision in *Advanced Data Concepts, Inc.*, see Appendix B, Example 5.1.

USING INFORMATION CLOSE AT HAND

The fact that the agency is not required to check all references is not an excuse for not checking other information "close at hand." This term refers to information that is, or should be, known personally by the contracting officer or the evaluators, as clarified in the GAO decision in *TRW, Inc.*, B-282162 and B-282162.2, June 9, 1999, which is summarized in Example 5.2.

Example 5.2—Clarifying "close at hand."

Issue: Information regarding the awardee's allegedly deficient prior performance on subcontracts was not so "close at hand" that it had to be considered by the agency.

Resolution: The Comptroller General denied the protest, stating:

While agencies generally need not evaluate all past performance references or those not reflected in the proposals, our Office has recognized that in certain limited circumstances an agency evaluating an offeror's past performance has an obligation (as opposed to the discretion) to consider "outside information" bearing on an offeror's past performance.[8] Where we have charged an agency with responsibility for considering such outside information, the record has demonstrated that the information in question was "simply too close at hand to require offerors to shoulder the inequities that spring from an agency's failure to obtain, and consider, the information."[9] ... However, the "close at hand" information in these cases generally concerned contracts for the same services with the same procuring activity, or at least information personally known to the evaluators.[10]

Here, the contracts on which Motorola's performance was allegedly unsatisfactory were between Motorola and TRW, with Motorola acting as a subcontractor and TRW as the prime contractor to the agency; they were not contracts between Motorola and the same procuring activity, such that the agency would necessarily have information concerning Motorola's prior performance close at hand. ... In sum, the record does not demonstrate that there was outside information so "close at hand" regarding Motorola's prior performance that the agency either improperly ignored or erroneously failed to obtain.

For an abridged version of the GAO decision in *TRW, Inc.*, see Appendix B, Example 5.2.

Example 5.3 illustrates the problems that arise when a contracting officer fails to consider past performance information close at hand simply because administrative procedures were not followed.

Example 5.3—Past performance information close at hand.

Issue: The protester alleged that the agency had failed to consider its past performance on a contract involving the same agency, the same services, and the same contracting officer because an individual in the agency did not complete and return the past performance evaluation materials.

Resolution: The Comptroller General agreed with the protester:

Where an RFP identifies past performance and price as the evaluation factors and indicates that an offeror with a better past performance record than that of another offeror can expect a higher past performance rating, proposals must be evaluated on that basis. The selection official, however, has the discretion to decide the appropriate tradeoff between past performance and price in determining which proposal represents the best value to the government.[11] *Such a tradeoff is not precluded under an evaluation scheme specifying a "neutral" rating for vendors with no past performance record.*[12]

Our disagreement with the agency springs from its overly mechanical application of its procedures for evaluating past performance. While the VA is correct in its view that there is no legal requirement that all past performance references be included in a valid review of past performance,[13] *some information is simply too close at hand to require offerors to shoulder the inequities that spring from an agency's failure to obtain, and consider, the information.*[14]

In this case, the Comptroller General found that had the agency considered the second referenced contract, which was rated as "exemplary" performance, the contracting officer might not have found the two offerors essentially equal with respect to past performance, and the tradeoff between price and past performance might have had a different result. The Comptroller General recommended that the agency redo the evaluation properly.

For an abridged version of the GAO decision in *International Business Systems, Inc.,* see Appendix B, Example 5.3.

Examples 5.2 and 5.3 illustrate that "close at hand" refers to information that the contracting officer knew about on a first-hand basis. A contracting officer is not expected to know about every contract the agency awarded. However, checking the records to see if an offeror had previous contracts with the agency and how well such contracts were performed is a sound practice.

USING PERSONAL KNOWLEDGE

May an evaluator use his or her own personal knowledge about an offeror when evaluating past performance? The answer is yes—under certain circumstances—as in the GAO decision in *Omega World Travel, Inc.*, B-271262.2, July 25, 1996, which is summarized in Example 5.4.

Example 5.4—An evaluator's personal knowledge may be used.

Issue: A protester maintained that its proposal had been improperly downgraded under past performance based on the undocumented personal knowledge of the evaluators. This allegation was based on narrative comments contained in the evaluation score sheets for two of the three evaluators, which stated, "info provided was responsive, but personal experience resulted in lower score."

Resolution: The Comptroller General did not agree with the protester, noting that:

An evaluator's personal knowledge of an offeror may properly be considered in a past performance evaluation.[15] *More specifically, where the solicitation provides for references to be used in the evaluation, as here, the agency may consider the unsatisfactory past performance of an offeror under a recent contract with the agency, thus, in effect, furnishing its own reference.*[16] *In an evaluation which takes into account the agency's own knowledge of offerors, the fundamental requirement that evaluation judgments be documented in sufficient detail to show that they are reasonable and not arbitrary still must be met.*

Based on these numerous documented complaints about Omega's past performance, which were the basis of the personal knowledge of two of the evaluators, and which are undisputed by the protester, we have no basis to question the downgrading of Omega's proposal under past performance.

Evaluators may use their personal knowledge when evaluating past performance, but this must be documented sufficiently to show the origin of the information and the basis for the findings. An evaluator may not, however, assume something based on third-party knowledge (i.e., other people said this firm performed poorly on some other contracts). Likewise, past performance evaluations may not be based solely on a firm's reputation (i.e., this is a successful company, so it must be a good performer). Personal knowledge may be used only when it is first-hand and can be documented.

For an abridged version of the GAO decision in *Omega World Travel, Inc.,* see Appendix B, Example 5.4.

An agency may base an evaluation of past performance on its reasonable perception of inadequate past performance, regardless of whether the offeror disputes the agency's interpretation of the facts. If this is the case, the evaluators may downgrade the offeror's proposal and eliminate the offeror from the competitive range, as determined by GAO in *Quality Fabricators, Inc.,* B-271431 and B-271431.3, June 25, 1996, which is summarized in Example 5.5.

Example 5.5—An agency's perception of poor past performance prevails when supported by sufficient evidence.

Issue: Quality Fabricators, Inc., (QFI) protested against downgrading of its performance based on evaluators' personal knowledge of complaints about its performance under an incumbent contract. The evaluators' judgments were documented in sufficient detail by an internal agency memorandum and surveys of agency travelers to show reasonableness of evaluation.

Resolution: The Comptroller General did not agree.

An agency's evaluation of past performance may be based upon the procuring agency's reasonable perception of inadequate prior performance, regardless of whether the contractor disputes the agency's interpretation of the facts.[17] *... We also conclude that QFI's proposal was reasonably excluded from the competitive range. Under the solicitation, past performance was considered significantly more important than price, and the agency was permitted to award to other than the lowest-priced offeror. Under this evaluation scheme, which placed paramount importance on past performance, it was a reasonable exercise of the agency's discretion to decide that a firm with an exceptional performance history (based on very favorable references and no deficiency reports) and a relatively low price would be the only firm with a reasonable chance for award when all other offerors had significantly higher prices and/or less attractive performance histories. This is particularly true since the agency's assessment of Tri-Way's past performance as exceptional is unchallenged. Since the agency reasonably concluded that QFI had no reasonable chance for award, the exclusion of its proposal from the competitive range is not legally objectionable.*[18]

The protester, citing our decisions holding that agencies have the discretion to eliminate from the competitive range proposals which do not include information required by the solicitation,[19] *suggests that agencies are required to eliminate such proposals from the competitive range. We disagree. The fact that an agency may eliminate a proposal from the competitive range for failure to include within the proposal information required by the solicitation does not mean the agency would be acting improperly if it included the proposal in the competitive range.*[20]

This case makes two points about an agency's discretion. First, the agency has the discretion to eliminate an offeror from the competitive range if it determines that the offeror's past performance is so poor that it should not be included in the competitive range even if the offeror disagrees. Second, the agency has the discretion to include an offeror in the competitive range if it determines that information deficiencies in the offeror's proposal are not so great as to warrant rejection. The agency must, however, have documented its determinations sufficiently to show that it has not abused its discretion.

For an abridged version of the GAO decision in *Quality Fabricators, Inc.,* see Appendix B, Example 5.5.

The evaluation of past performance is not a mechanical process—simply checking the boxes on a questionnaire or adding up scores. A "yes" or "no" answer without an explanation might be prejudicial.

Checking more than one or two references provides a broader picture of an offeror's ability to perform. There is, of course, a practical limit on the number of references that one can effectively check during the evaluation process. If there are multiple offerors with multiple references, the past performance evaluation will bog down and adversely affect the efficiency of the evaluation process. So, what to do?

As noted earlier, one solution is to establish a minimum number of references to be provided (typically, at least three references per offeror) and indicate that excess references may or may not be checked. In such instances a good-faith effort to check at least the minimum number of references should be made.

In the initial evaluation, negative past performance information generally draws more attention than positive information. However, the validity of the negative reports must be ensured before making any decisions.

ALLOWING OFFERORS TO RESPOND TO ADVERSE PAST PERFORMANCE INFORMATION

The opportunity to address adverse past performance information not known to the offeror depends on the stage of the pre-award process. With respect to an award that will be made without discussions, the FAR[21] states that offerors "may be given" the opportunity to clarify adverse past performance information to which the offeror has not previously had an opportunity to respond. With respect to competitive solicitations where discussions will be held, the FAR[22] states that communications "shall be held" with offerors whose past performance information is a determining factor preventing them from being placed in the competitive range when the offeror has not had a prior opportunity to comment on such information.

What the Government Should Do

Offerors are reluctant to accept an allegation of poor performance. Likewise, government officials may be reluctant to admit to another government agency that their actions contributed to an offeror's poor performance. A finding of poor past performance can easily degenerate into a dispute over facts and result in a protest that the offeror has not been treated fairly.

The likelihood of such protests might be minimized, however, if offerors are notified of adverse past performance information and allowed to respond to it when the adverse information might be an important factor in an award without discussions or a competitive range decision. Although this might add a few days to the procurement process, a protest (even when the agency wins) will cause even greater disruption.

Note that offerors' responses to adverse past performance information do not involve any changes to the proposal but merely provide explanatory information. The offeror is given one chance to reply in writing, and these comments must be considered in any decisions to be made. No discussions, proposal changes, or submission of new references is allowed.

Even a late delivery, which is a factual matter, can be interpreted as excusable under certain circumstances. To assume that poor past performance information is not subject to interpretation misses the point of the evaluation of past performance. The fact of a problem is important, but just as important is why it happened, whether it was corrected, and whether it is likely to affect the prospective performance. It is not a good practice to accept negative past performance information without looking at the circumstances, particularly when other sources have provided positive past performance information.

Generally, it is not a good idea to refuse an offeror the opportunity to respond to adverse past performance reports found during the initial evaluation when the adverse information might have a significant effect on the offeror's competitive position. FAR 15.306(b)(4) recognizes this in part in its statement that communications (before the establishment of the competitive range) shall address adverse past performance information on which the offeror has not previously had an opportunity to comment.

When offered the opportunity to respond to adverse past performance information, the offeror is responsible for providing an explanation of the poor performance. If the offeror fails to do this, the government is not required to pursue the matter further.

What the Offeror Should Do

When the government identifies negative past performance information, the offeror must respond with positive information, not generalizations, excuses, or promises. The offeror must specifically address each negative comment. There will be only one opportunity to explain past problems, so the explanation needs to be right the first time.

If the Adverse Information Is Correct

If the adverse information is correct, the offeror's response must show how the problems have been or will be corrected or, if applicable, how the reported problems will not affect the prospective performance. (This might apply, for example, if the problems involved a part of the company that will not be involved with the prospective contract.) If the problems have been corrected, the corrective action taken must be explained, along with how such action ensures that the problem will not recur.

If the offeror fails to show in its initial rebuttal that the problems were corrected (through either communications before the establishment of the competitive range or discussions after establishment of the competitive range), the government has no choice but to consider the problem unresolved and likely to recur. Contemporaneous documentation showing how the problem was, or will be, resolved (such as records kept during contract performance or letters from government personnel involved with the contract and written during contract performance) will bolster the rebuttal significantly.

If the Adverse Information Is Not Correct

If the offeror disagrees with the adverse past performance information or believes that the government was directly or indirectly responsible for the problems, the offeror must prove its case with facts, not generalized statements. In particular, one should not allege bias on the part of government personnel unless it can be proved with evidence sufficient to take to court. It is important that each allegation of poor past performance be addressed. Any point not addressed will be considered a tacit admission that the allegation is correct.

The offeror must show that the allegations were incorrect or that the problems were beyond its control (caused by third parties, the government, acts of God, etc.) and should not be considered adverse past performance information. Again, contemporaneous documentation that supports the offeror's position would be of significant help. If the offeror cannot provide contemporaneous documentation to prove its case, it is less likely to prevail. However, in the absence of contemporaneous documentation, a fact-based argument supported by written statements from personnel involved in the performance of the contract can help to make the case.

APPLYING RATING SYSTEMS

Past performance information includes the contracting officer's knowledge of and previous experience with the supply or service being acquired, customer surveys and past performance questionnaire replies, and contractor performance reports prepared in compliance with FAR 42.1502. The information must be reviewed, assessed, queried as necessary, and consolidated into a rating system.

One should not simply accept ratings without examining the accompanying narratives to ensure that they are consistent with the ratings. A single negative report on an offeror with an otherwise good record should be questioned to determine the degree to which the report should affect the overall assessment of the offeror's performance.

While past performance evaluations initially concentrate on negative findings, the need to identify positive aspects of an offeror's past performance should not be overlooked. Such information could be a deciding factor in a tradeoff determination when making the final source selection. Queries to third parties should always solicit comments on the positive aspects of an offeror's past performance.

Each evaluation criterion (i.e., past performance factor and significant subfactors) defined in Section M of the RFP must be rated. Any rating method, including adjectival or color-coded ratings, numerical weights, or ordinal ranking, may be used.[23] The recommended method is adjectival ratings, as described in Figure 5.1.

Figure 5.1 Adjectival Ratings

Exceptional. Performance <u>meets</u> contract requirements and <u>significantly exceeds</u> contract requirements to the Government's benefit. The contractual performance of the element or sub-element being assessed was accomplished with few minor problems for which corrective actions taken by the contractor were highly effective.

Very Good. Performance <u>meets</u> contractual requirements and <u>exceeds some</u> to the Government's benefit. The contractual performance of the element or sub-element being assessed was accomplished with some minor problems for which corrective actions taken by the contractor were effective.

Satisfactory. Performance <u>meets</u> contractual requirements. The contractual performance of the element or sub-element contains some minor problems for which proposed corrective actions taken by the contractor appear satisfactory, or completed corrective actions were satisfactory.

> Marginal. Performance does not meet some contractual requirements. The contractual performance of the element or sub-element being assessed reflects a serious problem for which the contractor has submitted minimal corrective actions, if any. The contractor's proposed actions appear only marginally effective or were not fully implemented.
>
> Unsatisfactory. Performance does not meet contractual requirements and recovery is not likely in a timely or cost-effective manner. The contractual performance of the element or sub-element contains serious problem(s) for which the contractor's corrective actions appear or were ineffective.

The essential element of this rating system is that the middle value is equivalent to meeting the requirement or norm. With five ratings, there are two levels above and two below, which allows for distinguishing between the better and best or the marginal and unsatisfactory.

Note that each rating has both an adjectival and a narrative description. Whether one uses adjectival, numerical, or color-coded ratings is immaterial as long as the description of the rating is the same as or similar to those used above.

Numerical Systems

Generally, numerical systems are established with a scoring range, an adjectival rating for that range, and a narrative description or standard to be met to get a score within that range. An example would be giving a score of 90 to 100 for Exceptional, 80 to 89 for Very Good, 70 to 79 for Satisfactory, 60 to 69 for Marginal, and 0 to 60 for Unsatisfactory.

Numerical scores convey a preciseness that might be misleading. For example, what is the real difference between a score of 88 and a score of 90? Numerical scores are only guides for the evaluators to point out differences between proposals and cannot be used as the basis for decisions. Decisions must be made based on the narrative explanations supporting the scores or rating assigned. It should be noted that documenting an evaluation using only the wording of the description of the rating is not a sufficient explanation for the scores assigned. The narrative explanation must show its relationship to specific past performance information (or lack thereof).

Color-Coding Systems

A color-coding system is similar to a numerical system in that it uses a color code (instead of a numerical range), an adjectival rating for that code, and a narrative description or standard to be met to receive each color code. For example, Dark Blue would be equivalent to Exceptional, Purple to Very Good, Green to Satisfactory, Yellow to Marginal, and Red to Unsatisfactory. Color coding provides a broad range, and the absence of numbers eliminates the implied precision of numerical scoring.

As with numerical scoring, evaluation narratives are required to support the color ratings assigned. The narratives must relate the problems (or strengths) found in the initial past performance evaluation to the rating assigned and its definition. An evaluation narrative using only the wording of the description provided earlier in Figure 5.1 for each rating is not an adequate explanation for the rating assigned.

Performance Risk Assessments

In addition to evaluating past performance information as an indicator of future performance, performance risk assessment is an effective evaluation technique. It relates to the evaluation of an offeror's current and past performance to assess the degree of confidence to be accorded to the offeror's ability to perform a prospective contract successfully. Performance risk is inherent in the evaluation of past performance and could be evaluated even if it was not listed as a specific evaluation factor. With respect to evaluating third-party evaluations, the broad range of the risk evaluation lends itself to the assessment of varying information sources. Figure 5.2 shows how performance risk might be evaluated.

Figure 5.2 Performance Risk

Very Low Performance Risk = Exceptional: Based on the offeror's performance record, <u>no doubt exists</u> that the offeror will successfully perform the required effort.

Low Performance Risk = Very Good: Based on the offeror's performance record, <u>little doubt exists</u> that the offeror will successfully perform the required effort.

Moderate Performance Risk = Satisfactory: Based on the offeror's performance record, <u>some doubt exists</u> that the offeror will successfully perform the required effort. Normal contractor emphasis should preclude any problems.

High Performance Risk = Marginal: Based on the offeror's performance record, <u>substantial doubt exists</u> that the offeror will successfully perform the required effort.

Very High Performance Risk = Unsatisfactory: Based on the offeror's performance record, <u>extreme doubt exists</u> that the offeror will successfully perform the required effort.

A risk analysis relates the strengths or weaknesses of the offeror's past performance to the likelihood of successful performance on the prospective contract. Performance risk analysis should consider the number and severity of problems, the effectiveness of corrective action taken, any demonstrated strengths, and the offeror's overall work record. The assessment of performance risk is not a simple arithmetic function of an offeror's performance on a list of contracts; instead, it should focus on the information deemed most relevant and significant to the offeror's likely performance on the prospective contract.

The advantage of a performance risk analysis is that it is not impeded by varying information sources. Each source can be evaluated based on the information provided without having to contend with differing scoring systems.

DOCUMENTING THE EVALUATION FINDINGS

The need to fully document all evaluation activity cannot be stressed enough. The initial evaluation findings by the individual evaluators and the evaluation team's consensus evaluation findings that provide the basis for the competitive range determination, the competitive range determination itself, and the final evaluations that support the evaluators' award recommendation must be documented and retained in the contract file. This documentation provides an audit trail to the factors that support the decisions made during the initial and final evaluation process and serves as the basis for the source selection official's tradeoff and final award decisions.

Proper documentation is particularly important with respect to the evaluation of past performance because much of the information used comes from sources outside the proposal itself. Past performance information provided by the offeror must be verified, agency contract records must be checked, contractor performance reports from other agencies must be examined, and, when appropriate, third parties must be queried about an offeror's past performance. All of this must be fully documented and retained in the contract files.

Documenting poor performance is important in determining the competitive range. Documenting strong points is important for tradeoff decisions and the source selection decision, where the strong points of an offeror's past performance may be a significant discriminator in determining the best value. Note that tradeoff decisions are made on the basis of the narrative supporting the assessment, not the adjectival ratings, numerical scores, or color codes—all the more reason to fully document the assessment, regardless of the scoring system used.

When evaluating best-value procurement, you are always subject to unintended consequences. The least important evaluation factor might become the deciding factor if all of the other factors are rated as essentially equal. The best way to deal with this potential problem is to ensure that the evaluation results are fully documented, particularly with respect to the evaluation of the differences between the proposals. The differences between proposals or lack thereof is often the basis for identifying the proposal offering the best value.

AVOIDING PROBLEMS

There is no sure way to avoid problems when evaluating an offeror's past performance. Offerors are not likely to simply accept a report of poor past performance if this is the primary factor in their exclusion from the competitive range or failure to receive the award. The following, however, might help minimize problems with offerors when evaluating past performance.

1. The RFP should warn offerors that they must address instances of performance problems in referenced contracts and explain how these problems were resolved. Indicate that a failure to explain past performance problems satisfactorily will have an adverse effect on the evaluation of past performance.
2. The RFP also should advise offerors to submit information on any awards or commendations received regarding their past performance because these could have a positive effect on the past performance evaluation.
3. Adverse past performance information identified during the initial evaluation—both that concerning referenced contracts and that identified by other sources—should be revealed to the offeror if the adverse information might affect the offeror's competitive standing. The offeror should be afforded the opportunity to rebut such information before an award without discussions or the establishment of the competitive range, even though this is not required by the FAR.
4. Past performance problems not resolved before establishment of the competitive range should be treated as significant weaknesses and addressed during discussions.
5. All past performance evaluations must be fully documented. Make note of any strong points found, as well as any adverse past performance information and the offeror's response to such information.
6. It is not necessary to open another round of discussions to address past performance problems first identified during discussions. Offerors should be advised to address such issues in their final proposal revisions.

7. If offerors do not satisfactorily explain how past performance problems were resolved in their final proposal revisions, the assumption is that the problems are unresolved and likely to recur.
8. The receipt of final proposal revisions marks the end of discussions. To avoid making an improper award, only in extreme circumstances are discussions reopened after receiving the final proposal revisions.

NOTES

1. FAR 15.305(a). "Proposal evaluation is an assessment of the proposal and the offeror's ability to perform the prospective contract successfully. An agency shall evaluate competitive proposals and then assess their relative qualities solely on the factors and subfactors specified in the solicitation. Evaluations may be conducted using any rating method or combination of methods, including color or adjectival ratings, numerical weights, and ordinal rankings. The relative strengths, deficiencies, significant weaknesses, and risks supporting proposal evaluation shall be documented in the contract file."
2. *IGIT Inc.,* B-275299.2, 6/23/97, 97-2 CPD ¶7 at 6.
3. *U.S. Technology Corp.,* B-278584, 2/17/98.
4. *Dragon Services, Inc.,* B-255354, 2/25/94, 94-1 CPD ¶151 at 8; *Questech, Inc.,* B-236028, 11/1/89, 89-2 CPD ¶407 at 3.
5. *International Business Systems, Inc.,* B-275554, 3/3/97, 97-1 CPD ¶114 at 5.
6. *Dragon Services, Inc.,* B-255354, 2/25/94, 94-1 CPD ¶151 at 8; *Questech, Inc.,* B-236028, 11/1/89, 89-2 CPD ¶407 at 3.
7. *International Business Systems, Inc.,* B-275554, 3/3/97, 97-1 CPD ¶114 at 5, GCR 109,877.
8. Ibid.
9. *International Business Systems, Inc.,* B-275554, 3/3/97, 97-1 CPD ¶114 at 5, GCR 109,877.
10. *Morrison Knudsen Corp.,* B-280261, 9/9/98, 98-2 CPD ¶63 at 5-5.
11. *Excalibur Systems, Inc.,* B-272017, 7/12/96, 96-2 CPD ¶13 at 3.
12. *Engineering and Computation Inc.,* B-275180.2, 1/29/97, 97-1 CPD ¶47 at 4-5; *Excalibur Systems Inc.,* supra.
13. *Dragon Services, Inc.,* B-255354, 2/25/94, 94-1 CPD ¶151 at 8; *Questech, Inc.,* B-236028, 11/1/89, 89-2 CPD ¶407 at 3.
14. *G. Marine Diesel,* 68 Comp. Gen. 577 (1989), 89-2 CPD ¶101 at 5-6; *New Hampshire-Vermont Health Serv.,* 57 Comp. Gen. 347 (1978), 78-1 CPD ¶202 at 12-13; *Continental Maritime of San Diego, Inc.,* B-249858.2; B-249858.3, 2/11/93, 93-1 CPD ¶230 at 6-8; *G. Marine Diesel; Phillyship,* B-232619; B-232619.2, 1/27/89, 89-1 CPD ¶90 at 4-5; *Inlingua Schools of Languages,* B-229784, 4/5/88, 88-1 CPD ¶340 at 5.
15. *TRESP Associates, Inc.; Advanced Data Concepts, Inc.,* B-258322.5; B-258322.6, 3/9/95, 96-1 CPD ¶8.
16. *G. Marine Diesel; Phillyship,* B-232619; B-232619.2, 1/27/89, 89-1 CPD¶90.

17. *Quality Fabricators, Inc.,* B-271431; B-271431.3, 6/25/96, GCR 109,553.
18. *Counter Technology Inc.,* B-260853, 7/20/95, 95-2 CPD ¶39; *Engineering & Computation Inc.,* B-258728, 1/31/95, 95-1 CPD ¶155.
19. *Panasonic Communications & Systems, Co.,* B-239917, 10/10/90, 90-2 CPD ¶279.
20. *Intermagnetics General Corp.*- Recon., 73 Comp. Gen. 333 (1994), 94-2 CPD ¶119.
21. FAR 15.306(a)(2). "If award will be made without conducting discussions, offerors may be given the opportunity to clarify certain aspects of proposals (e.g., the relevance of an offeror's past performance information and adverse past performance information to which the offeror has not previously had an opportunity to respond) or to resolve minor or clerical errors."
22. FAR 15.306(b)(1)(i). "[Communications] [s]hall be held with offerors whose past performance information is the determining factor preventing them from being placed within the competitive range. Such communications shall address adverse past performance information to which an offeror has not had a prior opportunity to respond; and …(4) Shall address adverse past performance information to which the offeror has not previously had an opportunity to comment."
23. FAR 15.305(a). "…Evaluations may be conducted using any rating method or combination of methods, including color or adjectival ratings, numerical weights, and ordinal rankings."

CHAPTER 6

PRE-AWARD: PAST PERFORMANCE AND SOURCE SELECTION

"The objective of source selection is to select the proposal that represents the best value." FAR[1]

The source selection authority (usually the contracting officer, but it may be another appointed official for major acquisitions) makes the final award decision based on the accumulated evaluation information developed during the course of the acquisition process. That information includes the initial evaluation report supported by the individual evaluators' comments, documentation of the competitive range determination, the final evaluation report with its supporting documentation, and the award recommendation.

SOURCE SELECTION DECISION

While the source selection authority may follow the results and advice of the evaluators, he or she is not required to do so. Evaluation results are considered advisory only, and the source selection authority, after examining the evaluation results, may come to a different conclusion and make award to an offeror other than that recommended by the evaluators.[2]

The source selection decision must represent the source selection official's independent judgment. This decision must be fully documented and include the rationale for any tradeoffs or business judgments made, including the benefits associated with additional costs. The rationale should address the relative differences between the competing proposals, including their relative strengths, deficiencies, significant weaknesses, and risks, and how these differences would have an impact (positive or negative) on performance of the prospective contract.

The rationale does not involve changing assigned ratings but is an assessment of the relative value of the proposals. The rationale must then show how the source selection official balanced these differences with the proposed cost or price in making the source selection decision. Note that tradeoffs are based on the evaluated pricing (proposed pricing plus or minus any adjustments made as a result of cost or price analysis and cost realism analysis) rather than the pricing proposed in the offeror's proposal.

Lowest-Priced Technically Acceptable Proposal

Some source selection decisions are fairly straightforward, such as when the RFP calls for award to be made to the offeror with the lowest-priced technically acceptable proposal. In this type of acquisition, the relative quality of the competing proposals is not considered. The proposals only have to meet the minimum technical requirements; quality above the minimum is not germane. Therefore, once the evaluators have identified the technically acceptable proposals, the final decision is based on the lowest evaluated price.

Although the source selection official has the authority to disagree with the selection of the technically acceptable proposals or with the determination of the lowest evaluated price, and to change these results, generally this does not happen. However, should such an occasion arise, the source selection official would be required to document fully the reasons for the changes.

BEST-VALUE AWARDS

When awarding on the basis of best value, the source selection decision is more complicated. Here, the relative quality of the competing proposals is a primary consideration, and award may be made to other than the lowest evaluated price. The source selection official must first examine the results of the evaluation to determine if the differences between the proposals actually represent differences in terms of contract performance. (It should again be noted that the scores or ratings assigned by the evaluators are only guides to point out the differences between proposals. Decisions are made on the basis of the evaluation narratives on which the assigned scores or ratings are based.) The source selection official then examines the evaluated cost or price and, if appropriate, makes a tradeoff to determine which proposal offers the best value.

In best-value procurement, the RFP should indicate that the government reserves the right to award to other than the lowest-priced proposal. This gives the government the flexibility to balance the value of the technical aspects and the cost or price of the competing proposals and make a tradeoff to determine which proposal offers the best value to the government.

Highest Technically Rated, Lowest-Cost Proposal

If the highest technically rated proposal also has the lowest cost or price, and the source selection official agrees with the evaluation findings, the source selection decision is relatively easy. The source selection official merely has to show why he or she agrees with the evaluation findings. This requires more than a simple "I agree," however—every source selection decision must be a stand-alone document with the award rationale fully addressed.

Highest Technically Rated, Not-Lowest-Cost Proposal

If the highest technically rated proposal does not offer the lowest cost or price, the source selection decision is more difficult. To justify an award to the highest technically rated proposal, the source selection decision must show how such an award is worth the price premium to be paid. Conversely, to justify an award to a proposal that is not rated the highest technically but offers the lowest price, the source selection decision must show how award to the highest technically rated proposal is not worth the price premium to be paid. In short, all source selection decisions must show how the source selection official balanced the technical and pricing aspects of the competing proposals and why a particular proposal was selected for award.

Multiple Non-Cost Evaluation Factors

There are times, however, when using multiple non-cost evaluation factors can produce unintended results. For example, an RFP called for the evaluation of technical excellence, management capability, and past performance, with past performance having the least weight in the evaluation. The evaluation found the technical excellence and management capability factors of the competing proposals roughly equal (they do not have to be determined to be exactly equal, only close enough that one could not reasonably be considered better than the other). In such an instance, past performance would become the primary discriminating factor, and the award would have to be made on the basis of past performance and price regardless of the original intent of the evaluation. The source selection decision would have to show how the technical excellence and management capability factors were determined to be roughly equal and how the tradeoff between past performance and price was made.

PAST PERFORMANCE TRADEOFFS AND SOURCE SELECTION DECISIONS

Because the competitive range consists of only the most highly rated proposals, most offerors with serious past performance problems will be eliminated before discussions begin. This does not mean, however, that past performance is no longer an issue. In acquisitions where past performance is an evaluation factor, it can play a significant role in the source selection decision.

Some of the more common problem areas in making a source selection decision when past performance is a significant, or the only, non-cost evaluation factor are:

- Determining which proposal offers the best value when all are equally rated
- Making tradeoffs between past performance and price
- Properly documenting the source selection decision.

Determining Best Value When Proposals Are Equally Rated

Only the most highly rated proposals remain after discussions and the final evaluation are completed. What happens when those proposals are equally rated? The simple answer is that evaluation factors other than past performance will prevail.

Offerors, however, consider their performance better than others even when given a rating of excellent or outstanding and will find some grounds on which to protest the award. Example 6.1, taken from the GAO decision in *Airwork Limited-Vinell Corp. (a Joint Venture),* B-285247 and B-285247.2, August 8, 2008, illustrates the importance of documenting the rationale for the ratings.

Example 6.1—Determining the best of the best.

Issue: AWV, the incumbent, protested the agency's past performance evaluation, in which both protester and awardee were rated excellent/high confidence. AWV asserted that its additional, relevant past performance would contribute to better satisfying the agency's stated needs so as to warrant a significantly higher rating under the past performance factor.

Resolution: The Comptroller General found that both offerors had received a valid past performance rating and denied the protest, noting:

We recognize that, as asserted by AWV, that company possesses extensive, relevant experience. For example, AWV is not only the incumbent Air Force WRM contractor in Southwest Asia; it has also provided base operations and maintenance services for Air Force bases in Turkey; training, logistics and related support to the Saudi Arabian National Guard; and personnel support services for

United States personnel in Egypt. However, AWV received the highest possible rating under this factor, reflecting the high quality and relevance of its past performance, and the agency was not obligated to reduce the rating reasonably assigned to DynCorp even if, as AWV contends, AWV's past performance was even better. Agencies are not required to give evaluation credit for proposal features it determines will not contribute in a meaningful manner to better satisfying the agency's needs.[3] *Here, given DynCorp's highly-rated relevant past performance, it is unclear how AWV's additional relevant past performance would contribute to better satisfying the agency's stated needs so as to warrant a significantly higher rating under the past performance factor. In any event, ...there is no basis for concluding that a marginally higher rating for AWV under the past performance factor would affect the outcome here.*

For an abridged version of the GAO decision in *Airwork Limited-Vinell Corp.*, see Appendix B, Example 6.1.

In Example 6.1, the protester argued that its proposal should not have received the same past performance rating as the awardee's because the protester had better past performance. The protestor stated that the awardee's past performance rating should be lowered and the protester should receive the award. However, where two offerors are given the highest past performance rating possible, the fact that one might have an even better past performance record than the other is not material unless it can be shown that there is a clear benefit to be gained by awarding to the offeror with the better past performance record.

In this case there was no clear benefit, and based on the past performance evaluation, both proposals represented the same low risk. Past performance ratings and the other non-cost evaluation ratings are assigned independently of other proposals and generally are not changed as a result of a comparative assessment. Although the assigned ratings are not changed, however, the relative value of a particular evaluation factor in one proposal when compared to another proposal can be a discriminator during a tradeoff determination to decide the best value. In this case, however, the value of past performance was not a discriminating factor; the award decision turned on the fact that the awardee's technical proposal was rated higher than the protester's proposal and was lower priced.

Even if past performance had been the only non-cost evaluation factor, the protester's argument would have been invalid. Because the past performance of both offerors was evaluated as exceptional/high confidence, the award would have been based on price alone and the award decision would have remained the same.

Past performance can be a point of contention right up to the source selection decision, even when all proposals are highly rated for past performance. It should be noted here that the decision reached in Example 6.1 was based on a fully documented record that showed how the past performance ratings were established. Good decisions require good documentation.

Making Past Performance/Price Tradeoffs

Even if not originally intended, past performance may become the determinative factor if all other technical evaluation factors are evaluated as roughly equal. If the offeror with the best past performance rating is not also the lowest-priced offeror, the source selection official must make a past performance/price tradeoff to determine which proposal offers the best value. Any award to other than the lowest-priced offeror must be supported by a tradeoff rationale showing that the benefits of the higher-priced award are worth the price premium to be paid. Past performance/price tradeoffs are often required when the only evaluation factors are past performance and price, as in the GAO decision in *H.F. Henderson Industries,* B-275017, January 17, 1997, which is summarized in Example 6.2.

Example 6.2—Past performance/price tradeoffs.

Issue: In a solicitation that cited price and past performance as the only and equally weighted evaluation factors, the agency selected the offeror with the low performance risk rating instead of the lower-priced offeror with a reasonably based moderate performance risk rating. The lower-priced offeror's moderate risk rating was based on prior contract delinquencies, while the higher-priced offeror received a low performance risk rating because of its early or timely performance under its contracts. The lower-priced offeror protested that its risk rating should have been better and that it should have received the award.

Resolution: The Comptroller General did not agree and denied the protest.

In a best value procurement, price is not necessarily controlling in determining the offer that represents the best value to the government. Rather, that determination is made on the basis of whatever evaluation factors are set forth in the RFP, with the source selection official often required to make a cost/technical tradeoff to determine if one proposal's technical superiority is worth the higher cost that may be associated with that proposal. In this regard, price/past performance tradeoffs are permitted when such tradeoffs are consistent with the RFP evaluation scheme.[4]

In making the performance/price trade-off, the Air Force found that the price premium associated with making award to Datacom, instead of Henderson, was justified, given Datacom's low performance risk, based on its consistent timely and early contract deliveries, as compared to Henderson's moderate performance risk, which evidenced a greater potential for untimely deliveries under this contract. The Air Force explained that it was imperative that the kits be delivered on schedule, and that award to a higher-priced offeror with a low performance risk was warranted in these circumstances because of the potential for additional costs to the government due to slips in delivery of these kits and the detrimental impact that delays would have on the mission-essential fleet upgrade.

Proposals must be evaluated with respect to the criteria set forth in the solicitation. And as stated earlier, in a best-value procurement, award may be made to other than the lowest-priced offeror, but only if a tradeoff determination clearly demonstrates the benefits to the government of such an award. Note that the reverse also is true. If award is to be made to the lowest-priced offeror, where the technical factors (including past performance) were cited as being equal to or more important than price, a tradeoff determination must be made to demonstrate that the higher technical/higher-priced proposal is not worth the price premium to be paid.

For an abridged version of the GAO decision in *H.F. Henderson Industries,* see Appendix B, Example 6.2.

One of the more difficult tradeoff areas is a past performance/price tradeoff between a firm with a neutral past performance rating and an established firm with an excellent past performance rating. Such tradeoff determinations usually involve more than just a simple comparison of offerors' past performance, as in the GAO decision in *National Aerospace Group Inc.,* B-281958, May 10, 1999, which is summarized in Example 6.3.

Example 6.3—Using past performance to evaluate new firms or firms with no performance history—making price/past performance tradeoffs.

Issue: Award was made to a higher-priced proposal with a good performance record over a lower-priced proposal with no performance history. The unsuccessful offeror protested that the contracting officer had not made a proper price/past performance tradeoff.

Resolution: The Comptroller General sustained the protest.

In a recent case involving DLA's use of ABVM scoring, we concluded that the use of a neutral rating approach to avoid penalizing a vendor without prior experience does not preclude a determination to award to a higher-priced firm with a good past performance record over a lower priced vendor with a neutral past performance rating. Indeed, such a determination is inherent in the concept of best value. In Phillips,[5] the contracting officer's determination to select a higher priced vendor with an excellent ABVM score, rather than a new supplier with a neutral rating, was reasonable where the record in that case showed that the agency had backorders for the item and timely delivery was critical. Nonetheless, we expressed concern that the vendor without a performance history not be disqualified for award merely because it lacked a performance history; we pointed out that such an approach would be inconsistent with the FAR and the DLA ABVM clause. As DLA recognized in that case, FAR 15.305(a)(2) provides that in the case of an offeror without a record of relevant past performance or for whom information on past performance is not available, the offeror may not be evaluated favorably or unfavorably on past performance.[6] *The ABVM clause states that lack of performance history is not grounds for disqualification for award.*

Unlike in Phillips, there is no indication that the item was in backlog or high demand status or that timely delivery was critical and worth the price premium to avoid the risk of using a vendor with no performance history. We conclude that the contracting officer failed to make a meaningful best value determination consistent with the SPA to justify paying a price premium to Tara. As a result, DLA's decision was tantamount to rejecting National's quotation based on its lack of performance history, which is inconsistent with 41 U.S.C. sect. 405(j)(2), FAR 15.305(a)(2), and the clauses which implement the ABVM program, as discussed in the Phillips decision.

We therefore sustain National's protest of the order to Tara under RFQ-A426.

Note that in the *Phillips* case (see Example 4.7), the decision was exactly the opposite. An award to the higher-priced offeror with an excellent performance history over a lower-priced offeror with no performance history was justified because of the need for timely delivery. The difference between these two cases is that in *Phillips* the tradeoff determination provided a justification for the price premium to be paid (out-of-stock, backlogged orders and a need to ensure timely delivery), whereas in *National* there was not only no tradeoff determination but also no pressing need to ensure timely delivery, and thus there was no justification for paying a price premium.

For an abridged version of the GAO decision in *National Aerospace Group Inc.*, see Appendix B, Example 6.3.

A neutral rating is assigned to new firms or firms with no performance history (e.g., when an established firm is trying to enter a new market or in circumstances where it was not possible to verify an offeror's past performance with any of the references provided) to avoid penalizing an offeror with no past performance history, thus enhancing the competition. This applies only to the rating approach, however, to avoid an otherwise arbitrary rejection of an offeror's proposal. A tradeoff determination that results in an award to a higher-priced offeror with a good past performance record over a lower-priced offeror with a neutral past performance rating, because the higher-priced offeror represents the best value to the government, demonstrates the basic concept of best value.

The decision to award to the higher-priced offeror, however, must be documented to show that such an award is worth the price premium to be paid—for example, by showing that timely and effective contract performance must be assured to meet the government's needs and that this assurance, based on past performance history, is found in an award to the higher-priced offeror.

Documenting Tradeoff Determinations and Source Selection Decisions

As noted earlier, the source selection decision, supported by any tradeoffs made, must be documented to show the rationale and basis for the decisions made, including the benefits associated with additional costs.[7] When tradeoffs are performed, this documentation must include an assessment of each offeror's ability to meet the technical requirements and a summary, matrix, or qualitative ranking with an appropriate supporting narrative related to each of the RFP's evaluation factors.

A failure to meet this requirement could result in a successful protest and a requirement to redo all or part of the competition or, in extreme cases, a directed award. While development of the appropriate documentation can be a chore, particularly when there is no disagreement between the source selection official and the evaluators, it is better and less time-consuming to do the job correctly in the first place than to risk a successful protest and a requirement to do it all over again.

When making a source selection decision involving past performance (or any other non-cost evaluation factor), the source selection authority's assessment of the competing proposals often must go beyond just the assigned ranking and supporting narrative. It must be based on an assessment of the differences between the competing proposals and the source selection authority's judgment concerning the significance of the differences in light of the RFP's evaluation scheme. With respect to past performance, this assessment includes a comparative assessment of the relative complexity of offerors' past efforts when determining which proposal offers the best value to the government. This judgment must be fully documented and show that it was reasonable and adequately justified. This is particularly important when award will be made to other than the lowest-priced offeror. When the source selection official fails to do this, the Comptroller General is likely to sustain a protest of the award, as in the GAO decision in *PMT Services, Inc.,* B-270538.2, April 1, 1996, which is summarized in Example 6.4.

Example 6.4—When evaluating past performance, the comparative assessment of complexity cannot be superficial.

Issue: PMT Services, Inc., protested the award of a contract to Moheat Environmental Services, Inc. PMT challenged that the selection of a substantially higher-priced proposal for award was unreasonable where the agency did not meaningfully consider the complexity of PMT's prior contracts vis-à-vis the complexity of the contract to be awarded.

Resolution: The Comptroller General sustained the protest, stating that:

While contract size may be relevant to contract complexity,[8] evaluating "complexity" of contract requirements based on size alone, without considering such other indicators of complexity, may not yield a meaningful conclusion about an offeror's probability of future success. An increase in the amount of waste to be disposed of under a contract, for example, or the number of pick-up locations are factors to be considered, but it does not follow that the complexity of the requirement has increased merely because of increases under these factors. … On the other hand, the contractor may have to do considerably more, such as develop new procedures for handling hazardous waste with which it has no experience, provide more trucks and drivers, and coordinate the additional resources committed to the effort. The point to be made on the record is that one cannot simply say that because the size of the contract has increased, its complexity has also increased.

There has been absolutely no showing on this record that what is primarily a two-location requirement is more complex than the one-location requirement PMT previously serviced. In this regard the agency's evaluation did not identify any types of waste, handling procedures, staffing requirements, or quantity and management resources which could make this RFP work meaningfully more complex than that performed under the Tooele contract. In sum, on this record, we cannot say that an agency's reliance on the size and number of waste generation locations reflects a reasonable analysis of PMT's prior contracts and, in the absence of a meaningful distinction in the complexity of this work as compared to PMT's previous work, that the agency's evaluation of PMT's past performance as "marginal" is reasonably based.

Although the SSA [source selection authority] discounted the number of waste generation locations in increasing Moheat's past performance rating, the record shows that the SSA did not similarly consider the immateriality of those locations to PMT's rating. To the contrary, PMT's lack of experience with multiple locations under a single contract was a specific concern stated by the SSA in his selection decision.

The SSA selected Moheat for award after determining that the evaluated difference in the firms' past performance justified a more than one million dollar (49 percent) price premium. This tradeoff decision, however, is based upon an inadequate evaluation of PMT's past performance. Until there is a proper assessment of PMT's past performance, the SSA cannot reasonably determine whether Moheat's past performance is worth the 49 percent price premium.

For an abridged version of the GAO decision in *PMT Services, Inc.*, see Appendix B, Example 6.4.

In this case, the SSA simply accepted the evaluation results without a careful review of the basis for the evaluation results. The SSA then compounded the problem by treating the offerors differently with respect to the number of waste generation locations. The fact that the basic evaluation was superficial and not well thought out escaped everyone's attention. The concept that the contract was bigger, and therefore more complex, was accepted without sufficient analysis. Had the SSA attempted to document the source selection decision properly, the documentation process might have revealed the problems with the award decision. The Comptroller General pointed out what should have been considered and why an award could not be made on the stated basis.

Example 6.5, taken from the GAO decision in *Si-Nor, Inc.,* B-282064 and B-282064.2, May 25, 1999, provides another example of how a lack of proper documentation can derail an acquisition.

Example 6.5—Past performance/price tradeoffs must be fully documented.

Issue: In a solicitation for a fixed-price requirements contract for refuse collection and disposal services, offers were to be evaluated on the basis of two evaluation factors, past performance/experience and price/cost, which were to be approximately equal in weight. Past performance and experience also were approximately equal in weight. Award was to be made on a best-value basis.

Resolution: The two primary contenders were Si-Nor and Eagle. Both proposals were rated low risk for experience; however, Si-Nor's proposal was rated only satisfactory for past performance, whereas Eagle's was rated outstanding. Eagle's evaluated proposal price was $858,656.80 higher than Si-Nor's evaluated price. Despite the price difference, the source selection official determined that Eagle's proposal represented the best value, primarily because of its outstanding past performance rating as compared to Si-Nor's satisfactory rating.

Si-Nor protested on the grounds that the agency had failed to document why any advantage reflected in Eagle's higher past performance rating warranted payment of an $858,636.80 premium. Si-Nor argued that its lower evaluated price warranted a determination that its proposal represented the best value to the government.

The Comptroller General agreed and sustained the protest.

Based on our review of the record, we conclude that the determination to award to Eagle was not adequately justified. The tradeoff rationale set forth in the new selection official's revised source selection decision stated as follows:

"I have determined [Eagle]'s proposal to be of better value than [Si-Nor]'s proposal. Both offerors received a low risk rating for experience. However,

[Eagle] received an outstanding past performance rating based on their past performance record, meeting all contract requirements and exceeding some of the contract requirements, compared to the satisfactory rating given [Si-Nor]. . . . I believe that [Eagle]'s outstanding past performance outweighs the lower price offered by [Si-Nor], a difference of $858,636.80 for the total cost."

This determination—as well as the record as a whole—includes no explanation for the agency's conclusion as required by FAR 15.308. While the record clearly sets forth the agency's conclusion that Eagle's past performance rating was worth an $858,636.80 price premium, it includes no documentation, evidence or explanation of the benefits that the agency associated with Eagle's superior past performance rating which would outweigh the additional price. This lack of documentation is significant in light of the fact that price was essentially twice as important as past performance under the stated evaluation scheme.

This is a good example of the need to consider and document tradeoff decisions carefully. Note that this decision did not turn on the price difference itself but on the failure of the selection official to document specifically the reasons why Eagle's superior past performance was worth the price premium to be paid.

For an abridged version of the GAO decision in *Si-Nor, Inc.*, see Appendix B, Example 6.5.

Proper documentation, whether of evaluation findings, tradeoffs, or source selection decisions, is critical to a successful acquisition. In the event of a protest, the quality of decision-making is immaterial if the record is not fully documented. The need for full documentation starts with the initial evaluation and continues throughout the acquisition process.

EVALUATING PAST PERFORMANCE IS NOT EASY

Evaluating past performance in a competitive environment is not easy. The informational requirements encompass both negative and positive information, and both must be well documented. Positive information (proposal strong points) is usually easier to obtain and is as important as negative information, particularly when making tradeoffs between past performance and other factors. Negative information is harder to deal with because it must be documented in greater detail. A comparative assessment requires sufficient information to enable evaluators to compare one proposal to another to determine the most highly rated proposals for inclusion in the competitive range and later for the source selection official to determine which proposal offers the best value to the government.

Past Performance as a Risk Factor

One way to simplify the process is by evaluating past performance as a risk factor. Evaluating past performance is essentially assessing an offeror's past performance to determine its ability to perform the proposed effort successfully. Chapter 3 suggests seven questions. For a risk assessment, however, the number of questions could be reduced to three:

1. If the offeror did not perform well, what were the problems, and how poor was its performance?
2. If there were problems, were they satisfactorily corrected?
3. If the offeror performed well, were there any particular strong points?

In the initial evaluation of past performance, the emphasis should be on identifying the offerors with poor past performance histories so they can be eliminated from the competition. The first two questions address poor past performance. Because only the most highly rated proposals are included in the competitive range, the final evaluation of past performance would involve a comparative assessment of offerors' strong points, which is addressed by the third question. While this suggestion might be an oversimplification, the emphasis should be on simplifying the evaluation process by seeking only that information needed to make a reasoned decision and eliminating the gathering of unnecessary details.

Contractor Performance Reports

Evaluating past performance information in source selection requires that the RFP clearly define how past performance will be evaluated (Chapter 2); that past performance information be not only accessible but also current and relevant (Chapter 3); that offerors have the opportunity to respond to adverse past performance (Chapter 4); and that evaluators provide documentation supporting their ratings (Chapter 5) so that the source selection authority can discriminate among the offerors and make best-value tradeoff decisions (Chapter 6).

Contractor performance reports are a key source of past performance information and an important consideration in awarding new contracts. Although using contractor performance reports does not eliminate the need to verify information provided by the offeror (e.g., reference checks on non-federal government and commercial contracts), the availability of these reports will greatly simplify the evaluation process.

Chapters 7 through 12 address the post-award evaluation of a contractor's performance and the preparation of contractor performance reports.

NOTES

1. FAR 15.302. "Source selection objective. The objective of source selection is to select the proposal that represents the best value."
2. FAR 15.308. "Source selection decision. The source selection authority's (SSA) decision shall be based on a comparative assessment of proposals against all source selection criteria in the solicitation. While the SSA may use reports and analyses prepared by others, the source selection decision shall represent the SSA's independent judgment. The source selection decision shall be documented, and the documentation shall include the rationale for any business judgments and tradeoffs made or relied on by the SSA, including benefits associated with additional costs. Although the rationale for the selection decision must be documented, that documentation need not quantify the tradeoffs that led to the decision."
3. *Consolidated Engineering Services, Inc.,* B-279565.5, 3/19/99, 99-1 CPD ¶76 at 3-4: see Tecom Inc., B-275518.2, 5/21/97, 97-1 CPD ¶221 at 7 (agency reasonably concluded that offeror was not entitled to higher rating where requirements were not exceeded in a manner that would increase benefit to the agency); Computer Systems Development Corp., B-275356, 2/11/97, 97-1 CPD ¶91 at 7-8.
4. *Excalibur Systems Inc.,* B-272017, 7/12/96, 96-2 CPD ¶13; *Dragon Services Inc.,* B-255354, 2/25/94, 94-1 CPD ¶151.
5. *Phillips Industries, Inc.,* B-280645, 9/17/98, 98-2 CPD ¶74 at 5.
6. 41 U.S.C. section 405(j)(2) (1994).
7. FAR 15.308. "...The source selection decision shall be documented, and the documentation shall include the rationale for any business judgments and tradeoffs made or relied on by the SSA, including benefits associated with additional costs. Although the rationale for the selection decision must be documented, that documentation need not quantify the tradeoffs that led to the decision."
8. *Chem-Services of Indiana, Inc.,* B-253905, 10/28/93, 93-2 CPD ¶262.

CHAPTER 7

POST-AWARD: CONTRACTOR PERFORMANCE EVALUATIONS

"Past performance information is relevant information, for future source selection purposes, regarding a contractor's actions under previously awarded contracts." FAR[1]

The effective use of past performance as an evaluation factor in source selection depends on the availability of contractor performance information on contracts with requirements similar to the requirements of the solicitation. The best source of past performance information is performance evaluations conducted during and upon completion of contract activities. Thus, the FAR, in requiring that past performance be used as an evaluation factor in source selection,[2] also requires that contracts and orders be evaluated annually and on completion of activities.[3]

LOW COMPLIANCE

Implementing the requirement to evaluate contractor performance is more challenging than implementing the requirement to use past performance in source selection. Past performance, which once was an optional source selection factor, has become mandatory for most acquisitions. Evaluating a contractor's performance and making the results available to other agencies are new responsibilities for agencies, requiring fundamental changes in the way that agencies administer contracts.

Those changes include creating a system for evaluating contracts and for maintaining evaluation results and making them available when needed in source selection. All agencies have now developed a system or adapted another agency's system to meet their particular needs. In addition, an agency-wide depository that receives evaluation reports and makes them available to all agencies is now functioning. In spite of these developments, compliance with the FAR requirement remains low. As a result, past performance has not yet met its potential as an effective evaluation factor in source selection.

The reasons for the low compliance are many. Contracting personnel complain that they do not have the time to conduct the evaluations; therefore, many evaluations are never initiated. Of the evaluations that are initiated, many are not completed because the technical offices are reluctant to participate. Some are reluctant to participate because they see no purpose in evaluating the contractor after the contract is completed. Of the performance evaluations that are completed, the assessments are often vague because some government officials are disinclined to say anything negative about a contractor with whom they have had close personal contact and would like to maintain good relations.

The result is that many contracts are not being evaluated, and of those that are, the usefulness of many of the evaluations is questionable. This would not be so, however, if contractor performance evaluations were understood correctly. Contractor performance evaluations can be done expeditiously and are actually easy to conduct. They require little more than documenting the key interactions of the agency's acquisition team with the contractor for a time span not exceeding one year.

Because contracting officers have the authority to conduct contract performance evaluations, the guidance in this chapter is primarily directed at them. The information is useful, however, to all who participate in the process, particularly the government technical and program personnel who monitor contractor performance. It is also useful to contractors whose performance is evaluated and who are given the opportunity to review the evaluation before final assessment is made.

PURPOSE OF THE EVALUATIONS

Contractor performance evaluations are conducted on contracts or orders upon completion of activities. Contracts or orders with a period of performance exceeding one year should be evaluated on an interim basis. The purpose of contractor performance evaluations is to provide information that can be used in future source selection. It is important to keep the purpose in mind because it affects how the evaluations are conducted and how the results are maintained.

Contractor performance evaluations are not meant to correct current performance; that is achieved primarily through monitoring actions by the government acquisition team member responsible for a particular aspect of the contract (e.g., technical, financial, legal). Nor are contractor performance evaluations contractually required. They are requirements for the agency but not for the contractor. Unlike evaluations that are contractually required (e.g., evaluations used in determining incentive or award fees), the results of contractor performance evaluations do not affect payments to contractors. Contractor performance evaluations simply record how well contractors performed.

Although these evaluations do not affect the contract directly, they can affect future contracts if the award of those contracts is based on past performance.

Contractor knowledge of this fact motivates contractors to optimum performance. In this sense, contractor performance evaluations are effective tools of contract administration. This does not imply that contractor performance evaluations should be used during execution of the contract to evaluate performance. The purpose of contractor performance evaluations is to obtain performance information, and the only time that a contractor performance evaluation is conducted, other than upon completion of activities, is when there is a need to provide current information for source selection purposes on a contract where the period of performance exceeds one year.[4] This means that only one contractor performance evaluation need be conducted in a year on any single contract or order.

CONTRACTOR PERFORMANCE EVALUATIONS

FAR Subpart 42.15 requires contractor performance evaluations for contracts and orders that exceed the simplified acquisition level.[5] The only exception are contracts awarded under FAR Subpart 8.7 with nonprofit agencies employing people who are blind or severely disabled.[6] Construction and architect-engineer services contracts, however, are not subject to the simplified acquisition threshold. Construction contracts of $550,000 or more and any that are terminated for default must be evaluated. Architect-engineer services of $30,000 or more and any terminated for default must be evaluated. Orders placed against a Federal Supply Schedule contract or under a task order contract or a delivery order contract awarded by another agency also must be evaluated. For single-agency task order and delivery order contracts, the contracting officer may require performance evaluations.[7]

Although annually evaluating contracts is another contract administration responsibility, it does not necessarily mean increased work for contracting officers. It does, however, require modifying some contract administration procedures.

Evaluating Contractor Performance Is Not a Complex Procedure

To begin, evaluating contractor performance is not a complex procedure. The evaluations focus on performance issues, such as quality of product or service, timeliness, cost control, and business relations. The targets to be met (i.e., the requirements) have been stipulated in the contract. The assessment is based on the performance standards that have been established for each requirement.

Performance Evaluations Are Based on Current Information

Performance evaluations document, at a point in time, actions that have been taken by members of the government's acquisition teams who have been monitoring performance as part of their responsibility or involvement in contract administration. The actions are with respect to the contractor's performance in meeting the requirements either stipulated or referenced in the contract. They include determinations regarding the contractor's conformance to specifications or performance standards, adherence to schedules, forecasting and control of costs, and compliance with the administrative aspects of the contract.[8] The evaluations do not ask open-ended questions, nor do they require essay-type answers. The questions are limited to the requirements of the contract, and the answers assess how well the contractor performed in meeting the particular requirements. The result of the evaluation is a contractor performance report.

Report Cards for Contractors

Performance reports are for contractors what reports cards are for students. Teachers monitor students' performance against the curriculum goals. They observe classroom participation, note completion of assignments, and give periodic and final exams. At the end of the term, they give a report card based on performance during that period. Contracting officers monitor contractors' performance against the contract. The contracting officer determines whether the contractor has met the requirements stipulated in the contract. When the contract is completed, the contracting officer prepares an evaluation, rating the contractor's performance.

Evaluating versus Accepting/Rejecting Performance

Evaluating contractor performance is a new, but not necessarily an additional, contract administration responsibility for contracting officers. It is a different way of fulfilling the responsibility to see that the contractor complies with the requirements of the contract. Evaluating goes beyond accepting or rejecting the contractor's performance. It requires an assessment or appraisal of the contractor's performance in delivering the product or service. It does not change contract administration procedures during the course of contract execution. The contracting officer continues to make accept/reject decisions based on contractors' performance in meeting contract requirements. It is only upon completion of activities or, in the case of an interim evaluation, completion of a year, that the contracting officer is required to assess and record how well the contractor met the contract requirements.

Evaluating rather than merely accepting or rejecting performance is similar to a teacher's giving a grade to students rather than making a pass/fail determination. Contracting officers are now required to grade the contractor's performance on delivery of the product or service, rather than simply accepting or rejecting the product or service. A pass/fail determination suffices to recognize that the student has met the class requirements. An accept/reject determination suffices to authorize payment to a contractor. Grades, however, provide a basis for comparing the qualifications of students applying for higher education. Rating a contractor's performance provides a basis for comparing the qualifications of offerors submitting proposals.

The only additional work for a contracting officer is rating the contractor and recording those ratings annually. The effort expended, however, can be more than compensated for by the benefits derived. Contract administration is improved, and future source selection decisions, which make use of past performance information obtained from performance evaluations, are more efficient and effective.

Shared Responsibility

Although the contracting officer is responsible for evaluating contractors' performance, he or she relies on the acquisition team to provide information about that performance. The acquisition team consists of the procurement personnel and the customers who receive the product or service.[9] Each member of the acquisition team has specific responsibilities and periodically updates the contracting officer regarding contractor performance. Based on this information, the contracting officer or the authorized representative of the contracting officer (contracting officer's representative [COR] or contracting officer's technical representative [COTR]) makes decisions and judgments during the period of performance. Upon completion of activities, the contracting officer accepts or rejects the contractor's performance.

The contracting officer now must evaluate the contractor's performance. He or she uses the same information to evaluate the contractor's performance that was used to accept or reject it. If the contracting officer needs to verify or supplement a specific aspect of a contractor's performance, he or she can turn to the member of the acquisition team who has been monitoring that aspect of the contract. Before making a final determination, the contracting officer allows the contractor to review the preliminary findings. The contractor's comments, additional information provided, or rebutting statements are considered before making the final performance rating.

TIMING/FREQUENCY

The FAR requires that the evaluations be conducted upon completion of activities. It is important to do this before the contract acquisition team takes on new duties—the sooner the better, because memory of details fades with time. Interim evaluations should not be done on contracts with a period of performance exceeding one year until enough time has elapsed to allow the contractor to demonstrate its performance potential. Thus, interim evaluations are not usually performed more frequently than once a year.

Many consider annual or more frequent evaluations of multiyear contracts to be good contract administration practice. Contractor performance evaluations are designed to assess performance, not to correct it. If evaluations are critical for effective contract administration, they should be tailored to the particular needs of the contract. The same can be said for using contractor performance evaluations to make a decision whether to exercise an option year on a contract. A more focused evaluation can be a more effective and efficient way of making this decision. Contractor performance evaluations have a specific purpose—collecting past performance information—and should not be used for purposes other than the purpose for which they have been designed.

Contractor performance evaluations are not substitutes for other types of evaluations required for a particular contract. On the other hand, the evaluations required as part of a contract's post-award administration can help to satisfy the requirement to prepare contractor performance reports. For example, evaluations to determine incentive or award fee payments provide some, if not all, of the contractor performance information that is collected in a contractor performance evaluation. In conducting a contractor performance evaluation of an incentive or award fee contract, the contracting officers should begin with a review of the information available from completed incentive or award fee evaluations. This not only facilitates the process[10] but also ensures consistency between evaluations.[11] The same can be said for evaluations that are part of quality assurance surveillance plans for performance-based contracts. If the agency is using earned value management systems to monitor contract performance, the systems reports should serve as a basis for the contractor performance evaluations.[12]

CONTENT

Because the purpose of the evaluation is to obtain performance information for use in source selection, the content of the evaluations is limited to information on a contractor's performance,[13] that is, information that is an indicator of an offeror's ability to perform the contract.[14] That information falls under the following categories:

- **Quality of Product or Service**—Information on conformance to contract technical requirements or to standards of good workmanship. It is an indicator of an offeror's technical ability.
- **Timeliness**—Information on adherence to contract schedules, such as milestones, delivery dates for interim or final products, or reporting requirements. It is an indicator of an offeror's reliability.
- **Cost Control**—Information on forecasting and controlling costs; submitting reasonably priced change proposals; and providing current, accurate, and complete billings. It is an indicator of the offeror's financial management capability.
- **Business Relations**—Information on the working relationship between the contractor and the government's acquisition team. It is an indicator of an offeror's management philosophy and practice.

DISTINGUISHING FEATURES OF CONTRACTOR PERFORMANCE EVALUATIONS

The timeliness, the rating system, and the contractor's participation in the evaluation distinguish contractor performance evaluations from other types of performance evaluations. Conducting an evaluation immediately on termination of activities can improve its accuracy. Rating the performance improves the quality of the information obtained. Finally, contractor participation in the evaluation adds to its fairness. The result is that contractor performance evaluations can be an objective source of past performance information.

- **Timing**—Conducting the evaluation during contract performance or upon completion ensures that those who have been intimately involved with the contract, including the contracting officer, the members at the acquisition team, and the end users, are available to provide input regarding the contractor's performance. Past performance information obtained through a timely evaluation is superior to past performance information obtained through reference checks after the fact. For example, interviews or questionnaires sent to the contacts listed by the offerors to collect performance information have limitations with respect to the informants and are not timely. They may reach only one or two individuals who were involved with the contract, and they are done months or even years after the contract is completed.

- **Rating performance**—Rating performance as opposed to accepting or rejecting it provides information that can be used to compare and discriminate among offerors in source selection. Past performance information that accepts or rejects the contractor's performance—confirming that the contractor was successful or unsuccessful—serves only to distinguish the good performers from the bad.
- **Contractor review**—Having the contractor review and respond to an initial assessment of performance adds legitimacy to the evaluation. It ensures that the final assessment reflects not just the government's perspective, but the contractor's as well.

MINOR CHANGES, MAJOR BENEFITS

Compliance with the requirement to evaluate contractors' performance can be accomplished with minimal changes in contract administration procedures. The evaluation is made on only the contractor's performance in complying with requirements contained in the contract. The contracting officer bases his or her assessment of the performance on information provided by the members of the acquisition team who have responsibility for monitoring the contractor's compliance with contract requirements. Rather than simply accepting or rejecting the contractor's performance, the contracting officer now rates it.

A contracting officer does not have to conduct evaluations more often than annually. The added work amounts to sharing the preliminary assessment with the contractor and preparing an evaluation report. The report has value to the government in that it is an indicator of a contractor's ability to perform a contract and can be used in making future source selection decisions regarding similar contracts. The process improves communication among the acquisition team members and results in better contractor performance.

NOTES

1. FAR 42.1501. "General. Past performance information is relevant information, for future source selection purposes, regarding a contractor's actions under previously awarded contracts. It includes, for example, the contractor's record of conforming to contract requirements and to standards of good workmanship; the contractor's record of forecasting and controlling costs; the contractor's adherence to contract schedules, including the administrative aspects of performance; the contractor's history of reasonable and cooperative behavior and commitment to customer satisfaction; the contractor's record of integrity and business ethics, and generally, the contractor's business-like concern for the interest of the customer."

2. FAR 15.304(c)(3)(i). "Except as set forth in paragraph (c)(3)(i) of this section, past performance shall be evaluated in all source selections for negotiated competitive acquisitions expected to exceed the simplified acquisition threshold."
3. FAR 42.1502. "Policy."

   "(a) Past performance evaluations shall be prepared as specified in paragraphs (b) through (g) of this section at the time the work under the contract or order is completed. In addition, interim evaluations shall be prepared as specified by the agencies to provide current information for source selection purposes, for contracts or orders with a period of performance, including options, exceeding one year. The evaluations are generally for the entity, division, or unit that performed the contract or order. The content of the evaluation should be tailored to the size, content, and complexity of the contractual requirements.

   "(b) Except as provided in paragraphs (e), (f), (h) of the section, agencies shall prepare an evaluation of contractor performance for each contract that exceeds the simplified acquisition threshold.

   "(c) Agencies shall prepare an evaluation of contractor performance for each order that exceeds the simplified acquisition threshold placed against a Federal Supply Schedule contract, or under a task order contract or a delivery order contract awarded by another agency (i.e. Governmentwide acquisition contract or multi-agency contract). This evaluation shall not consider the requirements under paragraph (g) of this section.

   "(d) For single-agency task order and delivery order contracts, the contracting officer may require performance evaluations for each order in excess of the simplified acquisition threshold when such evaluations would produce more useful past performance information for source selection officials than that contained in the overall contract evaluation (e.g., when the scope of the basic contract is very broad and the nature of individual orders could be significantly different). This evaluation need not consider the requirements under paragraph (g) of this section unless the contracting officer deems it appropriate.

   "(e) Past performance evaluations shall be prepared for each construction contracts of $550,000 or more, and for each construction contract terminated for default regardless of contract value. Past performance evaluations may also be prepared for construction contracts below $550,000.

   "(f) Past performance evaluations shall be prepared for each architect-engineer services contract of $30,000 or more, and for each architect-engineer services contract that is terminated for default regardless of contract value. Past performance evaluations may also be prepared for architect-engineer services contracts below $30,000.

   "(g) Past performance evaluations shall include an assessment of contractor performance against, and efforts to achieve the goals identified in the small business subcontracting plan when the contract includes the clause at 52.219-9 Small Business Subcontracting Plan.

   "(h) Agencies shall not evaluate performance for contracts awarded under Subpart 8.7."
4. FAR 42.1502(a). "...In addition, interim evaluations should be prepared as specified by the agencies to provide current information for source selection purposes, for contracts or orders with a period of performance, including options, exceeding one year..."
5. FAR 2.101. "'Simplified acquisition threshold' means $100,000, except for acquisitions of supplies or services that, as determined by the head of the agency, are to be used to

support a contingency operation or to facilitate defense against or recovery from nuclear, biological, chemical, or radiological attack, means (1) $250,000 for any contract to be awarded and performed or purchase to be made, inside the United States; and (2) $1 million for any contract to be awarded and performed, or purchase to be made, outside the United States."

6. The Javits-Wagner-O'Day Act requires the government to purchase supplies or services from nonprofit agencies serving people who are blind or severely disabled. FAR 8.7 details the rules and regulations governing these acquisitions.
7. FAR 42.1502(d). "For single-agency task order and delivery order contracts, the contracting officer may require performance evaluations for each order in excess of the simplified acquisition threshold when such evaluations would produce more useful past performance information for source selection officials than that contained in the overall contract evaluation."
8. For examples of relevant past performance information, see FAR 42.1501.
9. FAR 1.102(c). "The acquisition team consists of all participants in government acquisition, including not only representatives of the technical, supply, and procurement communities but also the customers they serve and the contractors who provide the products and services."
10. FAR 42.1503(b). "…Evaluations used in determining award or incentive fee payments also may be used to satisfy the requirement of this subpart."
11. Although evaluations for determining fees under award or incentive fee contracts and contractor's performance evaluations are different, "the fee amount paid to contractors should be reflective of the contractor's performance, and the past performance evaluation should closely parallel the fee determinations." See FAR 42.1500.
12. Office of Federal Procurement Policy, *Best Practices for Collecting and Using Current and Past Performance Information*, May 2000, p. 9.
13. FAR 42.1501. "General. Past performance information is relevant information, for future source selection purposes, regarding a contractor's actions under previously awarded contracts."
14. FAR 15.305(a)(2). "*Past performance evaluation.* (i) Past performance information is one indicator of an offeror's ability to perform the contract successfully…."

CHAPTER 8

POST-AWARD: DESIGNING A CONTRACTOR PERFORMANCE EVALUATION SYSTEM

"Differing number and type of rating factors and rating scales agencies use to document contractor performance limit the usefulness of the information." GAO[1]

Although the content of performance evaluations should be tailored to the size, content, and complexity of the contractual requirement, there needs to be some commonality in all contractor performance evaluation systems used throughout the federal government. Otherwise, it will be difficult, if not impossible, to compare past performance information collected by one agency with that collected by other agencies. Every agency's contractor performance evaluation system should collect information on the same basic assessment areas,[2] use comparable rating systems, and structure evaluations to ensure that prescribed procedures are followed.[3]

This chapter is directed primarily at agency procurement analysts who can affect policy. It offers guidance in designing a contractor performance evaluation system that meets specific agency needs and, at the same time, is compatible with other agencies' systems.

CONTENT

For the past performance information obtained by the evaluations of one agency's system to be useful in source selection for other agencies, every contract performance evaluation should collect past performance information in four basic assessment areas—quality of product or service, timeliness, cost control, and business relations.[4] Agencies may add to this list or subdivide the assessment areas according to their particular needs. In addition, all agencies should use systems for rating the assessment areas that have the same number of values with comparable weights.

Basic Assessment Areas

The assessment areas that were originally considered indicators of an offeror's ability to perform a contract successfully were quality of product or service, timeliness of performance, cost control, business practices, customer (end user) satisfaction, and key personnel past performance.[5] These six areas have been reduced to four[6] and are described as follows:

- **Quality of Product or Service**—An assessment of the contractor's performance in making sure that the product or service conforms to contractual requirements, performance standards, or both.
- **Timeliness**—An assessment of a contractor's adherence to contract schedules, such as milestones, delivery dates for interim or final products, or reporting requirements.
- **Cost Control**—An assessment of a contractor's performance with respect to forecasting costs; controlling costs; submitting reasonably priced change proposals; and providing current, accurate, and complete billings. (Applicable only to cost reimbursement, time and materials, and labor-hour contracts.)
- **Business Relations**—An assessment of the contractor's business management philosophy and practice that includes both the external relations of the contractor with the government's acquisition team (including end users) and internal relations with its own staff and subcontractors.

Additional Assessment Areas

Other assessment areas may be added at the discretion of the agency. Adding assessment areas might create more work for the evaluators and should be balanced against the improved quality of the past performance information obtained.

When a contract has a Small Business Subcontracting Plan, the contactor's performance in achieving the goals must be assessed.[7] This may be done as a separate assessment area or under the business relations assessment area.

Another assessment area that some agencies have added is management of key personnel.[8] Assessing a contractor's performance regarding the management of key personnel should be limited to assessing compliance with the key personnel requirements stated in the contract. For example, did the contractor replace key personnel in a timely manner with equally qualified professionals? Management of key personnel may be assessed under business relations. Evaluating it that way is usually preferable to creating a separate assessment area.

Tailoring Content to Contractual Requirements

The content of the evaluation can be tailored to an agency's specific needs by subdividing the four basic assessment areas. An example of this is the Department of Defense's (DoD's) performance assessment elements for large systems acquisitions. DoD has four major assessment areas, which are referred to differently but are essentially the same as the four basic assessment areas mentioned above: technical (quality of product), schedule, cost control, and management. The technical sub-elements are product performance, systems engineering, software engineering, logistic support/sustainment, product assurance, and other technical performance. The management sub-elements are management responsiveness, subcontractor management, program management, and other management.[9]

Areas Not Assessed

Some areas should not be evaluated separately. Contractor performance evaluations should not be used to evaluate end user satisfaction, the performance of key personnel, or the performance of subcontractors.

- **End Users**—Input from end users of the product or service should be obtained, if appropriate, in evaluating contractor performance. This does not mean that an assessment of end user satisfaction should be made separately from the other assessment areas. Input from end users of the product or service might be an appropriate source of information regarding the contractor's performance in meeting the quality, timeliness, cost, or business relations requirements of the contract. End user satisfaction is a concern when the end user is the primary customer.

  End user satisfaction is not usually relevant when the end users are different from the primary customer—for example, the participants of a training course contracted at the request of the agency's personnel office. Here the primary customer is the personnel office, and the ultimate users are the trainees. If the contractor met the requirements of the primary end user (the personnel office) and the ultimate users (the trainees) were not satisfied, the contracting entity (the personnel office) is responsible, not the contractor.

  On the other hand, a contract may require a level of end user satisfaction. In most cases, it would be subsumed under or assessed as a subcategory of the quality assessment element.
- **Key Personnel**—The evaluation should not be used to evaluate key personnel. The contractor is responsible for the key personnel's performance. If key personnel were responsible for missing a schedule event, this fact will be reflected in the assessment of timeliness. If key personnel made a significant

contribution to the quality of a product or service, this will be reflected in the assessment of quality. If the contractor failed to replace key personnel in a timely manner, this will be reflected in the evaluation of the contractor's management practice element of business relations.

Experience has shown that when key personnel are evaluated, the assessment has little value. Obtaining information on key personnel is usually difficult because of the infrequency of contact with the key personnel. When there is a close working relationship between a member of the government's acquisition team and his or her contract counterpart, there is a propensity to be positive and a reluctance to be negative. The result is that the evaluation of key personnel is often subjective or ambiguous.

- **Subcontractor Performance**—The evaluation should not be used to evaluate subcontractor performance. As with key personnel, the prime contractor is responsible for the subcontractor's performance. The successes and failures of the subcontractor are the successes and failures of the prime contractor. The evaluation is limited to the prime contractor's performance in managing the subcontract.

Rating Principles

Because past performance information will be used by other agencies, it is essential that the rating system be comparable to other rating systems throughout the government. The basic element of a rating system is to have the middle value equivalent to meeting the contractual requirements or standard.[10] The range should be five values.[11] Numerical, adjectival, or color-coded denominations can be used to express the scale values.

The advantage of the five-point scale is that it provides more options than a three-point scale. Having two values above the satisfactory level allows for discriminating between the better and best performers, and having two values below the satisfactory level allows for discriminating between the marginal and unsatisfactory performers. With a three-point scale, all good performers are above and all poor performers below.

With a five-point scale, each value must be described in a way that clearly distinguishes it from the next higher or lower value. This is important so that those making the rating (the evaluators) and those receiving the rating (the contractors) interpret the rating in the same way.

For shorthand purposes, the value can have a numerical, color-coded, or adjectival denomination. For consistency, the highest rating should correspond with the highest number. Suggested denominations for the five-point scale are (5) or dark blue = exceptional; (4) or purple = very good; (3) or green = satisfactory; (2) or yellow = marginal; and (1) or red = unsatisfactory.

Description of Ratings

The description of the value distinguishes each value from the next higher or lower value. With respect to quality of product or service, timeliness, or cost control, the evaluation criteria are the contractual requirements. With respect to business relations, the evaluation criteria are generally accepted professional business standards. Note that an important element distinguishing one value from another is how well the contractor handled problems. The five values are described as follows:

- **Exceptional**—Performance meets contract requirements and significantly exceeds contract requirements to the government's benefit. The contractual performance of the assessment area or element thereof being assessed was accomplished with a few minor problems for which corrective actions taken by the contractor were highly effective.
- **Very Good**—Performance meets contractual requirements and exceeds some to the government's benefit. The contractual performance of the assessment area or element thereof being assessed was accomplished with some minor problems for which corrective actions taken by the contractor were effective.
- **Satisfactory**—Performance meets contractual requirements. The contractual performance assessment area or element thereof contains some problems for which proposed corrective actions taken by the contractor appear satisfactory, or completed corrective actions were satisfactory.
- **Marginal**—Performance does not meet some contractual requirements. The contractual performance assessment area or element thereof being assessed reflects problems for which the contractor has submitted inadequate corrective actions, if any. The contractor's proposed actions appear only minimally effective or were not fully implemented.
- **Unsatisfactory**—Performance does not meet contractual requirements and recovery is not likely in a timely or cost-effective manner. The contractual performance of the assessment area or element thereof had problems for which the contractor's corrective actions appear or were ineffective.

Narrative Supporting Ratings

A narrative summary provides the rationale for the rating. The narrative must justify a rating higher than three and explain a rating lower than three. If the score is three, the narrative should not merely state that the contractor met the requirements for the assessment area or element thereof but should be used to motivate a contractor to optimal performance or to explain why a higher score was not given.

FORMAT

The FAR requires several procedures that agencies must take into consideration when establishing a format for the performance evaluations. For example:

- The evaluations shall provide for input from the technical office, contracting office, and, if appropriate, end users of the product or service.[12]
- The contractor shall be provided the opportunity to review the evaluation.[13]
- Agencies shall provide for review at a level above the contracting officer to consider disagreements between the parties regarding the evaluation.[14]
- Agencies shall submit past performance reports electronically to the Past Performance Information Retrieval System (PPIRS) at www.ppirs.gov.[15]

A basic evaluation format that would ensure the incorporation of all the above-cited FAR requirements would be:

- **Background Information**—Includes the contractor's name and address; the contractor's representative and his or her email address; the contract/order number; the value, including options; the award date and anticipated completion date; and the type of contract. Note that most of the information has already been entered into the Federal Procurement Data System - Next Generation (FPDS-NG) and can be pre-populated if auto-registration is used.
- **Description of Requirement**—Provides a description of the work being done under the contract and identifies the key performance indicators.
- **Initial Evaluation**—Rates and supports the ratings of the contractor's performance in each of the assessment areas prepared by the contracting officer or his or her delegate after consultation with the acquisition team.
- **Contractor Review**—Contains comments, additional information, or rebuttals received from the contractor.
- **Upper-level Review**—Reports on a review at a level above the contracting officer when there are disagreements between the contractor and the contracting officer.
- **Final Evaluation**—Contains the final ratings with supporting narratives, incorporating the response of the contractor and the resolution of disagreements between the contracting officer and the contractor.
- **Evaluation Report**—Documents the final ratings and supporting narratives for each of the assessment areas. Using a report card facilitates the maintenance of the past performance information in an automated system,

which is indispensable if it is to be accessible to source selection authorities in other agencies.

USING A FORM

A form is an essential element of performance evaluation systems. It summarizes the results of the evaluation and facilitates maintaining and accessing the past performance information when it is needed in source selection.

Design of a Form

The form should be designed to document past performance information that is useful for source selection officials. There should be space for background information, a description of the requirement, and the rating and rating narrative for each assessment area. A description of the requirement is critical because source selection officials use it to determine whether the evaluation report is relevant to the solicitation being considered. The central part of the form is the narrative supporting each rating, which should clearly show that the contractor had the opportunity to review the ratings and that any disagreements were resolved at a level above the contracting officer.

Proposed Sample Report Form

The simpler the evaluation form, the better. It should be easy for the contracting officer to fill out, providing only relevant past performance information. The basic form should cover the following fields:

- Name and address of the contractor
- Contract number
- Contract date
- Description of the requirement
- Rating and narrative supporting the rating for the four assessment areas
- Verification that the contractor was given the opportunity to review the assessment
- Verification that the agency reviewed disagreements between the contractor and the contracting officer
- Signature of the contracting officer
- Date the evaluation was submitted to the PPIRS and a copy given to the contractor.

The form should not contain information on subcontractors, teaming, or joint venture partners. This just adds to the reporting burden of the contracting officer. If this information is needed during source selection, it can be obtained by contacting the agency. The same can be said regarding the listing of key personnel. The occasional need to verify that a particular firm was a subcontractor or that a person was a key employee on a contract does not justify including this information on the report form.

There is no need to include on the form the question of whether the rating officer would select the firm again. This is the kind of question that is asked when conducting a reference check. It elicits a "yes" or "no" answer and not an assessment of how well the contractor performed. It only distinguishes good from bad performers and does not provide information that is helpful in discriminating among good performers.

Asking a question regarding the contractor's commitment to customer satisfaction is redundant because it is already covered under business relations. Addressing customer satisfaction again with a "yes/no" answer and without a supporting statement adds nothing to the evaluation. Without a rating and supporting narrative, the information is of little value in source selection.

The report form should contain information that helps the source selection committee make a judgment regarding the similarity of the requirement of the evaluated contract and that of the solicitation. Similarity is usually defined in terms of content, but it also includes size and complexity. Space, then, should be provided on the report form for a description of the requirement, the value of the contract, and the award date and completion dates. The type of contract should be noted because it affects the evaluation methodology. Including other fiscal data or significant dates would be at the agency's discretion. The guidance here is to limit the reporting burden for the contracting officer to the information needed by the source selection officials.

AUTOMATION

Automation is essential for maintaining past performance information and making it available, but it is not necessary for collecting past performance information. In some cases, an automated system for collecting past performance information can be a constraint. Automation should be used for preparing the evaluations only to the extent that it facilitates the process.

For an automated system to work efficiently, all the participants in the process must have compatible hardware and know how to use the software. The participants involved in evaluating contractor performance include, at a minimum, the contracting officer, at least one representative of the technical office, and the contractor. In some cases, the participation of the end users is appropriate, and, if there is a review to resolve differences between the contractor and the contracting officer, the participation of someone at a higher level than the contracting officer is required. If one participant does not have the hardware or does not know how to use the software, the evaluation becomes stalled and might never be completed.

Using an automated system for collecting performance information can become mechanical, resulting in the mere filling in of blanks rather than conducting a thoughtful evaluation. This can happen unintentionally when input is required from a member of the acquisition team who is unfamiliar with the software. The team member's concern about entering the information distracts from the content of the information.

With input required from so many participants, it is suggested that the person charged with preparing the evaluation collect the information using the communication technology that the respondent is familiar with and has access to. Once the information has been obtained from the acquisition team and has been reviewed by the contractor, and the final assessment has been made, the information is entered into an automated system. Thus, the preparer can use phone, fax, and email to collect information from the acquisition team, to obtain the contractor's review, and to resolve disagreements. The preparer controls entry of the information into the automated system.

Phone, fax, and email are used in the private sector when information is required from many respondents. For example, a physician doing a diagnostic examination of a patient bases his or her findings on information obtained from other specialties (e.g., laboratory work, x-rays). This information is communicated to the physician by fax, phone, email, or regular mail. The physician makes his or her diagnoses based on the information received.

Technology that allows for full automation of the system is available. Experience has shown, however, that full automation can be a constraint to completing the evaluations. The objective should be to get the evaluations completed in a timely manner using communication technology with which the respondents are most comfortable. Email might be the preferred way of communicating within the agency, but contractors might prefer to use regular mail, even when they have access to the Internet. Faxing the form with the initial assessment of performance might be acceptable to some contractors and objectionable to others. As a general rule, use the same means of communicating with the acquisition team for preparing the evaluation that you have used for communicating with the team on other contract administration matters.

SIGNATURES

The contracting officer should sign the evaluation only after the contractor has had an opportunity to review it and all differences have been resolved. In signing the evaluation form, the contracting officer attests that all agency policies and procedures have been followed. The name of any person who provided information regarding the contractor's performance should not appear on the evaluation report.

NOTES

1. Government Accountability Office, *FEDERAL CONTRACTORS - Better Performance Information Needed to Support Agency Contract Award Decision,* April 2009, p. 17.
2. Office of Federal Procurement Policy, *Best Practices for Collecting and Using Current and Past Performance Information,* May 2000, p. 9.
3. FAR 42.1503. Procedures.
4. FAR 42.1501. "General. Past performance information is relevant information, for future source selection purposes, regarding a contractor's actions under previously awarded contracts. It includes, for example the contractor's record of conforming to contract requirements and to standards of good workmanship; the contractor's record of forecasting and controlling costs; the contractor's adherence to contract schedules, including the administrative aspects of performance; the contractor's history of reasonable and cooperative behavior and commitment to customer satisfaction; the contractor's record of integrity and business ethics, and generally, the contractor's business-like concern for the interest of the customer."
5. Office of Federal Procurement Policy, supra, p. 13.
6. Ibid., p. 10.
7. FAR 42.1503(g). "Past performance evaluation shall include an assessment of contractor performance against, and efforts to achieve, the goals identified in the small business subcontracting plan when the contract includes the clause at 52.219-9, Small Business Subcontracting Plan."
8. Department of Defense, *A Guide to Collection and Use of Past Performance Information,* May 2003, Appendix D.
9. Ibid.
10. Office of Federal Procurement Policy, supra, p. 2, 12–13, and Appendix III.
11. Department of Defense, supra, p. 8 and Appendix F.
12. FAR 42.1503(a). "Agency procedures for the past performance evaluation system shall generally provide for input to the evaluations from the technical office, contracting office and, where appropriate, end users of the product or service. Agency procedures shall identify those responsible for preparing interim and final evaluations. Those individuals identified may obtain information for the evaluation of performance from the program office, administrative contracting office, end users of the product or service, and any

other technical or business advisor, as appropriate. Interim evaluations shall be prepared as required."

13. FAR 42.1503(b). "Agency evaluations of contractor performance prepared under this subpart shall be provided to the contractor as soon as practicable after completion of the evaluation. Contractors shall be given a minimum of 30 days to submit comments, rebutting statements, or additional information. Agencies shall provide for review at a level above the contracting officer to consider disagreements between the parties regarding the evaluation. The ultimate conclusion on the performance evaluation is a decision of the contracting agency. Copies of the evaluation, contractor response, and review comments, if any, shall be retained as part of the evaluation. These evaluations may be used to support future award decisions, and should therefore be marked 'Source Selection Information.' Evaluation of Federal Prison Industries (FPI) performance may be used to support a waiver request (see 8.604) when FPI is a mandatory source in accordance with Subpart 8.6. The completed evaluation shall not be released to other than Government personnel and the contractor whose performance is being evaluated during the period the information may be used to provide source selection information. Disclosure of such information could cause harm both to the commercial interest of the Government and to the competitive position of the contractor being evaluated as well as impede the efficiency of Government operations. Evaluations used in determining award or incentive fee payments may also be used to satisfy the requirements of this subpart. A copy of the annual or final past performance evaluation shall be provided to the contractor as soon as it is finalized."
14. Ibid.
15. FAR 42.1503(c). "Agencies shall submit reports electronically to the Past Performance Information Retrieval System (PPIRS) at www.ppirs.gov. The process for submitting such reports to PPIRS shall be in accordance with agency procedures."

CHAPTER 9

POST-AWARD: EVALUATING CONTRACTOR PERFORMANCE

"Agency procedures for the past performance evaluation system shall generally provide for input to the evaluations from the technical office, contracting office and, where appropriate, end users of the product or service." FAR[1]

CONTRACTING OFFICE'S RESPONSIBILITY

Agencies must identify the individuals responsible for preparing the interim and final evaluations.[2] "Those individuals identified may obtain information for the evaluation of performance from the program office, administrative contracting office, end users of the product or service, and any other technical or business advisor, as appropriate."[3] Since contracting officers are responsible for ensuring performance of all necessary actions for effective contracting,[4] the assumption is that those individuals would be contracting officers or contracting administrative officers specifically authorized by the contracting office.[5]

TAILORING THE EVALUATION TO THE CONTRACT

The contracting officer identified by agency procedures to conduct the evaluation depends on other members of the acquisition team[6] to provide information not just in evaluating the contractor's performance but also in designing the evaluation. The design should tailor the content of the evaluation to the size, content, and complexity of the contract.[7]

Evaluation questions need to be prepared to ascertain how well the contractor performed in meeting the specific contractual requirements and in managing the contract. Each of these questions should fall under one of the four assessment areas or a sub-element of it. The answers to the questions provide the assessment of the contractor's performance.

For small contracts, the contracting officer may be able to conduct the evaluation with the help of a representative of the technical or program office. As contracts become larger and more complex, the contracting officer will have to contact more members of the acquisition team to obtain a complete and accurate evaluation of performance. The time needed to conduct the evaluation, however, should not necessarily increase proportionally to the increase in the contract size or complexity if the members of the acquisition team understand their respective roles and responsibilities. This chapter is directed at not only the contracting officers but also the entire acquisition team. Understanding one's role and responsibilities is the key to conducting the contractor performance evaluations efficiently.

FORMAT, NOT FORM

Some agencies use a form for conducting the evaluations. The contracting officer initiates the process by sending the form to the technical person who has been monitoring contractor performance. This person is requested to make an initial assessment of the contractor's performance regarding four assessment areas. The assessment evaluation includes scoring each assessment area and providing a supporting narrative for the score given. The form is then returned to the contracting officer, who reviews the assessment, edits as he or she sees fit, and sends the form with the initial assessment to the contractor for review.

Using the form in this way might be an efficient way to collect past performance information, but it does not necessarily produce a fair and accurate assessment of a contractor's performance. First, a form might not provide enough space to address issues thoroughly, particularly for large or complex contracts or when problems have arisen. A form limits input to one respondent, usually the technical officer, to the exclusion of other members of the acquisition team. Contracting officers who forward the form to the contractor for review in a perfunctory manner further weaken the process.

A form can serve as an outline of the evaluation to ensure that all the required assessment areas are covered and the required procedures followed. It should not be used to collect the information from the acquisition team. The contracting officer should get responses to the evaluation questions from the appropriate member or members of the acquisition team, analyze the responses by assessment area, and then enter the rating and supporting narrative for each assessment area on the form. The ratings and supporting narratives are then shared with the contractor for review. After the response from the contractor is received and any disagreements are resolved, the rating and supporting narrative are finalized.

USE A FORM TO RECORD INFORMATION, NOT TO COLLECT IT

A form is essential for recording the findings of the evaluation. It provides a convenient way to maintain past performance information and to make that information available when required for source selection purposes. A one- or two-page form that summarizes past performance information in a systematic way is easy for the source selection authority to use. It facilitates the source selection evaluation team's work not only in reviewing past performance information but also in comparing the findings among many offerors.

THE INITIAL PERFORMANCE ASSESSMENT

The initial performance assessment consists of collecting information on the contractor's performance, analyzing the data, and assigning a rating with a supporting rationale. This requires contacting the members of the acquisition team who are knowledgeable about the contractor's performance with respect to quality, timeliness, cost control, and business relations. The number of those contacts will vary depending on the size and complexity of the contract. Small contracts might mean contacting only one person, the technical officer who has been responsible for monitoring the contract for the customer. Larger and more complex contracts will involve contacting more members of the acquisition team, such as program managers, item managers, field contract administrators, or auditors. Those contracts might require contacting a different member for each of the assessment areas or several members for one assessment area or another. Contacting end users of the products or service might even be required.

The contracting officer should use the same method of contacting the members of the acquisition team that he or she has used for other contract administration activities. The contracting officer can communicate directly or indirectly through the authorized representative (COR, COTR). Which members the contracting officer or the authorized representative should contact is determined in accordance with agency procedures regarding contract administration.

For large or complex contracts, if an interim evaluation is anticipated, the scope of the contractor performance evaluation or evaluations should be incorporated into the contract administration plan. When it is necessary to initiate an evaluation of the contractor's performance, the contracting officer will know which members of the acquisition team to contact, and the members of the acquisition team will know what information they are to provide and, if not directly to the contracting officer, through whom.

The contracting officer already knows much of the information needed to assess performance. In the course of administering the contract, the contracting officer has been making decisions or has been informed of decisions being made by the acquisition team. Thus, the contracting officer is usually knowledgeable regarding the contractor's performance, particularly with respect to quality, timeliness, and cost control. The contracting officer has direct knowledge of the contractor's performance regarding business relations based on their interaction in the execution of the contract. When the time comes to prepare the evaluation, the contracting officer will need to complement his or her knowledge of the contractor's performance by contacting specific members of the acquisition team.

The initial assessment requires analysis, rating, and a narrative summary for each of the assessment areas. It should not entail a review by team members, redrafting of sections, or clearance by different offices. The rating and the rationale for that rating are left to the judgment of the contracting officer. The contracting officer has fulfilled his or her responsibility by obtaining input from the "program office, administrative contracting office, end users of the product or service, and any other technical or business advisor, as appropriate."[8] Once the contracting officer has made the initial assessment, he or she sends it to the contractor for review.[9]

BASIS FOR APPRAISING THE ASSESSMENT AREAS

The assessment areas are appraised by comparing the actual performance of the contractor against the contractual requirements, which are found in various sections of the contract. Sections B[10] and C[11] of the contract schedule contain requirements regarding supplies or services. Section D[12] contains requirements for packaging, packing, preservation, and marking. Inspection, acceptance, quality assurance, and reliability requirements are in Section E.[13] Requirements for time, place, and method of delivery or performance are in Section F.[14] Sections G,[15] H,[16] and I[17] contain other requirements regarding administration of the contract.

The first thing that the contracting officer must do is identify the performance questions by assessment area—quality, timeliness, cost control, and business relations. There can be more than one performance question for an assessment area, or there may be none. For example, there would be no assessment of cost control on fixed-price contracts.

Contractual requirements have performance standards. The contracting officer formulates questions to elicit information regarding how well the contractor met the standard for the specific requirement. If the requirement has an explicit performance standard, the question is easy. For example, if the contract stipulates that the contractor is to deliver the product by the first of May, the question is:

Did the contractor deliver the product by the first of May? If not, what were the problems, who was responsible for the problems, what action did the contractor take to resolve the problems, and how effective was the contractor's response?

For each of the key contractual requirements, the contracting officer asks the member or members of the acquisition team who have had responsibility for that aspect of the contract for information on well the contractor met the performance standard for that requirement. The contracting officer then analyzes the information collected by assessment area and gives an initial rating and a rationale for the rating.

Rating Performance

The basis of the rating system for evaluating a contractor's performance is that the middle value is equivalent to meeting the explicit or implicit standard for the specific requirement. For most requirements, the middle value, or satisfactory performance, is the expected rating. This is what the government requires, i.e., delivery of the product on time, according to specifications, and within cost.

On a five-point scale, if the contractor did not meet the requirements, an unsatisfactory rating is given. If the contractor did not fully meet the requirements, a marginal rating is given. If the contractor complied with the performance requirements for an assessment area, a satisfactory rating is given. A very good rating is given when the contractor's performance exceeded the performance requirements. An exceptional rating is given if the contractor is outstanding.

Obtaining a rating above satisfactory is not always possible. Rating a contractor above satisfactory recognizes performance that was above and beyond what was expected in the contract and resulted in a benefit to the government. Not every contract provides such opportunities. One circumstance that could warrant a higher rating would be when the contractor's initiative improved contract execution or the quality of the product or service. Another circumstance would be when the contractor's actions successfully resolved unintended or unanticipated problems. The more complex the contract, the more likely that problems will occur; the simpler the contract, the less likely problems will occur.

On the other hand, obtaining a rating below satisfactory is always possible. If the contractor's performance fell below the standard, the rating would be marginal. If the contractor failed, the rating would be unsatisfactory.

Satisfactory Is a Good Rating

A satisfactory rating on a contractor performance evaluation is a good rating. A satisfactory rating on an evaluation of an offeror's past performance in source selection might not be good enough. These are two different kinds of evaluations. The evaluation of a contractor's performance relates to the performance standards for the requirements. The contractor is rated but not ranked. The evaluation of an offeror's past performance in source selection is in relation to the past performance of other offerors. In evaluating the offerors' past performance in source selection, the offerors are both rated and ranked.

Objectivity

If used correctly, the five-point scale, with the middle value being equivalent to meeting the requirement, contributes to the objectivity of the evaluation. The middle value serves as the benchmark—a point of reference from which other measurements can be made. By anchoring the ratings on the middle value, the five-point scale allows for two ratings above and below. Any rating higher or lower is in relation to meeting the standard (i.e., performing to the satisfaction of the customer).

The ratings reflect how well the contractor performed according to the standards for the requirements of an assessment area. The ratings are based on factual evidence. Giving a rating above satisfactory says not only that the contractor met the standards but also that, in meeting the standards, the contractor's action demonstrated very good or exceptional performance. One way to distinguish satisfactory performance from very good or exceptional performance is to consider the contractor's performance in dealing with problems and the solutions or remedial action taken. Another way would be to look at added benefits to the government that resulted because of the contractor's action. Not every contract has problems or provides opportunities to add benefits, so a satisfactory rating is all that is expected of a contractor.

Incomplete Information

In those cases in which there are some but not sufficient grounds to give a contractor a higher rating, it is suggested that the score be biased downward when preparing the initial rating (i.e., before the contractor's review) and biased upward when making the final rating (i.e., after the contractor has responded). That is, if the contractor's performance appears to be between satisfactory and very good or between marginal and satisfactory, give the lower rating. Challenge the contractor to make the case for the higher rating. If there is still doubt after the response from the contractor, favor the contractor and give the higher rating.

After making a reasonable effort to obtain the information from other members of the team regarding the contractor's performance, if there is insufficient information to determine that the contractor met the requirement, presume that the contractor did indeed meet the requirement and give a satisfactory rating. If there is no information, indicate that the information was not available. The important consideration here is to expedite the process. This is the initial assessment, and the final assessment will not be made until the contractor has had the opportunity to respond.

Comments

Comments on the initial assessment are the government's perspective of the contractor's performance and are not final until the contractor has had a chance to review them and to respond. Comments are supporting narrative rationales for the ratings. They should describe the action taken by the contractor that contributed to the contractor's success or failure in meeting the requirement.

Initial comments may be written so as to elicit a response from the contractor. Contractors are members of the acquisition team, and it is important to obtain their perspective. Every effort should be made to avoid a rebuttal by the contractor. If there are ongoing problems, try to resolve them before sending the evaluation to the contractor for review. The contractor has a right to rebut the initial assessment, but that rebuttal should be based on factual discrepancies and not merely differences of opinion or interpretation.

If a satisfactory rating is given, comments are optional. The rating speaks for itself: The contractor met the requirement. Comments are required to support a rating above satisfactory or to explain a rating below satisfactory. Comments should address the requirement or standard as articulated in the contract and should be supported by facts and not personal opinions. This is particularly important when giving a rating below satisfactory. Deficiencies should be brought to the contractor's attention before the evaluation takes place. If they have been, the comment should reflect the responsiveness of the contractor in correcting the deficiencies.

Although comments are optional when a satisfactory rating is given, there are occasions when comments should be given. Comments for a satisfactory rating on an interim evaluation can motivate a contractor to optimum performance. Comments might be necessary for large or complex contracts to explain why a higher rating was not given. Comments for a satisfactory rating on a final evaluation are expected if the contractor has unsuccessfully rebutted the rating. (See Chapter 10.)

GUIDANCE FOR RATING THE FOUR ASSESSMENT AREAS

Ratings higher than satisfactory are not given for merely exceeding the performance standard. A very good rating for going over the standard or an exceptional rating for significantly exceeding the standard would be given only if exceeding the standard meant added value to the government. Ratings higher than meeting the performance standards are given in most instances to recognize superior performance in responding to problems that arise during the execution of the contract. Those are not problems that are caused by the contractor but problems that are unexpected. They require a solution, and consequently they are a challenge to the contractor's technical or managerial ability.

Quality of Product or Service

Quality of the product or service is an indicator of the technical ability of the contractor. The assessment is made by comparing the product or service delivered by the contractor to the specifications for the product or the performance standards for the service indicated in the contract. If the contractor met the specifications or performance standards, the rating would be satisfactory.

A rating higher than satisfactory could be given if this were a performance-based acquisition contract in which the performance standards were expressed in terms of an acceptable range. If the contractor met the low end of the range, the rating would be satisfactory. The rating would be very good if the contractor consistently met the high end of the range. An exceptional rating could be given if the contractor surpassed or always met the high end of the range.

A contractor's response to a problem can result in receiving a rating higher than satisfactory. The corrective action would need to have made a positive impact on the quality of the product or service. For example, without the contractor's technical expertise, specifications or performance standards would not have been met. Another example would be surpassing the performance standards to the benefit of the government because of the contractor's technical expertise. In the latter case, the rating could be very good or exceptional, depending on the resulting added value to the government.

A marginal rating would be given if some of the requirements were not met but the failure to meet them was not serious enough to deny payment. An unsatisfactory rating would be given only if the contractor did not deliver the product or service, or if the delivered product or service was of no value to the government.

Timeliness

Timeliness assesses the contractor's reliability. The assessment is made by comparing the contractor's adherence to the requirements for time of delivery of a product or service as specified in Section F of the contract schedule. It is an objective assessment because it measures something factual. The two most common ratings would be satisfactory and unsatisfactory because the contractor would either have met or missed the scheduled dates.

A contractor could meet the delivery dates and receive a marginal rating. An example would be if the contractor failed to adhere to other timeliness requirements, such as submitting reports on their due dates. Whether to give a marginal rating would depend on the adverse effect that the failure to adhere to other timeliness requirements had on the contract's ultimate objective. Giving a rating above satisfactory for timeliness is unlikely. However, it would be appropriate to do so where, but for decisive actions by the contractor, the schedule would not have been met.

Cost Control

Cost control assesses a contractor's financial management ability, which encompasses forecasting costs, controlling costs, submitting reasonably priced change proposals, and providing current, accurate, and complete billings. The evaluation involves the contractor's record of how accurately it estimated costs and how well it controlled the costs expended. This is the easiest assessment area to rate. If the contractor is doing better than projected, the rating is very good; if the contractor is not meeting projections, the rating is marginal. If the contractor is on target, the rating is satisfactory. An exceptional rating would be given when the contractor's actions have resulted in a significant cost savings for the government.

Business Relations

Business relations address the contractor's business management philosophy and practice, which includes the working relationship between the contractor and the government's acquisition team. The basis of the assessment is the administrative requirements implied or explicit in the contract. These could include the following elements:

- Reasonable and cooperative behavior
- Commitment to customer satisfaction
- Business-like concern for the interest of the customer
- Problem identification and quality of corrective action
- Timely award and management of subcontracts
- Efforts to achieve the goals identified in a small business subcontracting plan[18]
- Record of integrity and business ethics.

A marginal rating would be given to a contractor for failing in any one of these elements that was considered critical to the success of the effort. If the contractor substantially met the critical elements, the rating would be satisfactory. A very good rating could be given if the contractor met the standard in all the critical elements. An exceptional rating is usually not given for business relations.

TIME NEEDED TO PERFORM THE EVALUATION

The time needed to prepare the evaluation will depend on the size and complexity of the contract. Larger and more complex contracts will have more members on the acquisition team. The additional burden on the contracting officer, however, will be minimal if you follow the guidance provided. Performance evaluations require an appraisal of a contractor's performance in four assessment areas. The ratings are based on actions already taken by the acquisition team. The additional work for the contracting officer is rating, writing a supporting narrative for the rating, and preparing the evaluation report. This is done once for a contract or order on completion of activities or annually for contracts or orders with a period of performance exceeding one year.

NOTES

1. FAR 42.1503(a).
2. FAR 42.1503(a). "...Agency procedures shall identify those responsible for preparing interim and final evaluations."
3. FAR 42.1503(a). "...Those individuals identified may obtain information for the evaluation of performance from the program office, administrative contracting office, end users of the product or service, and any other technical or business advisor, as appropriate."
4. FAR 1.602-2. "Responsibilities. Contracting officers are responsible for ensuring performance of all necessary actions for effective contracting, ensuring compliance with the terms of the contract, and safeguarding the interests of the United States in its contrac-

tual relationships. In order to perform these responsibilities, contracting officers should be allowed wide latitude to exercise business judgment. Contracting officers shall— (a) Ensure that the requirements of 1.602-1(b) have been met, and that sufficient funds are available for obligation: (b) Ensure that contractors receive impartial, fair, and equitable treatment; and (c) Request and consider the advice of specialists in audit, law, engineering, information security, transportation, and other field, as appropriate."

5. FAR 42.302(b)(11). "Prepare evaluations of contractor performance in accordance with Subpart 42.15."
6. FAR 1.102(c). "The Acquisition Team consists of all participants in Government acquisition including not only representatives of the technical, supply, and procurement communities but also the customers they serve, and the contractors who provide the products and services."
7. FAR 42.1502(a). "...The content of the evaluations should be tailored to the size, content, and complexity of the contractual requirements."
8. FAR 42.1503(b). "... Agency procedures shall identify those responsible for preparing interim and final evaluation. Those individuals identified may obtain information for the evaluation of performance from the program office, administrative contracting office, end users of the product or service, and any other technical or business advisor, as appropriate."
9. FAR 42.1403(b). "Agency evaluations of contractor performance prepared under this subpart shall be provided to the contractor as soon as practicable after completion of the evaluation. Contractors shall be given a minimum of 30 days to submit comments, rebutting statements, or additional information..."
10. FAR 15.204-2(b). "*Section B, Supplies or services and price/costs.* Include a brief description of the supplies or services; e.g., item number, national stock number/part number if applicable, nouns, nomenclature, and quantities. (This includes incidental deliverables such as manuals and reports.)"
11. FAR 15.204-2(c). "*Section C, Description/specification/statement of work.* Include any description or specifications needed in addition to Section B (see Part 11, Describing Agency Needs)."
12. FAR 15.204-2(d). "*Section D, Packaging and marking.* Provide packaging, packing, preservation, and marking requirement, if any."
13. FAR 15.204-2(e). "*Section E, Inspection and acceptance.* Include inspection, acceptance, quality assurance, and reliability requirements (see Part 46, Quality Assurance)."
14. FAR 15.204-2(f). "*Section F, Deliveries or performance.* Specify the requirements for time, place, and method of delivery or performance (see Subpart 11.4, Delivery or Performance Schedules, and 47.301-1)."
15. FAR 15.204-2(g). "*Section G, Contract administration data.* Include any required accounting and appropriation data and any required contract administration information or instructions other than those on the solicitation form. Include a statement that the offeror should include the payment address in the proposal, if it is different from that shown for the offeror."

16. FAR 15.204-2(h). "*Section H, Special contract requirements.* Include a clear statement of any special contract requirements that are not included in Section I, Contract clauses, or in other sections of the uniform contract format."
17. FAR 15.204-3. "Part II-Contract Clauses. *Section I, Contract clauses.* The contracting officer shall include in this section the clauses required by law or by this regulation and any additional clauses expected to be included in any resulting contract, if these clauses are not required in any other section of the uniform contract format. An index may be inserted if this section's format is particularly complex."
18. FAR 42.1502(g). "Past performance evaluations shall include an assessment of contractor performance against, and efforts to achieve, the goals identified in the small business subcontracting plan when the contract includes the clause at 52.219-9, Small Business Subcontracting Plan."

CHAPTER 10

POST-AWARD: CONTRACTOR REVIEW AND RESPONSE

"Agency evaluations of contractor performance...shall be provided to the contractor as soon as practicable after completion of the evaluation. Contractors shall be given a minimum of 30 days to submit comments, rebutting statements, or additional information." FAR[1]

The unique feature of contractor performance evaluations is that the contractor participates in the process. This participation is reactive: The government prepares the initial assessment, and the contractor is given an opportunity to review and respond to it before the final assessment is made.

CONTRACTOR'S INPUT

The contractor participates as a member of the acquisition team.[2] The contractor's input and that of the government are equally important. The contractor may provide a different perspective, add new information, or even rebut the government's initial assessment of performance. The final assessment is not made until the contractor has had an opportunity to respond and all disagreements between the contractor and the government have been resolved. All the procedures related to contractor's review, response, and resolution of differences are aimed at achieving a fair and accurate evaluation of the contractor's performance.

Alerting the Contractor

The evaluation should not be a surprise to the contractor. Although not required, it is recommended that the contract schedule include a statement regarding the contractor performance evaluation, or evaluations, if the period of performance exceeds one year. The statement should alert the contractor that the evaluation will be conducted for the purpose of obtaining past performance information that may be used in future source selections. The statement may be included in Section H of the contract schedule.[3] At a minimum, the statement should contain the following:

> On completion of contract activities, the Government shall prepare an evaluation of contractor performance in accordance with FAR 42.15. (In addition,

interim evaluations shall be conducted annually.) The contractor will have 30 days to review and respond to the evaluation(s) before final assessment is made. The evaluation(s) may be used for future source selection purposes.

Experience has shown that the knowledge that the evaluations will take place and that the information obtained might be used in future source selection decisions is an incentive for the contractor to perform at optimal levels.

Contractor Should Understand the Process

In addition to being alerted about the evaluation, the contractor should understand the process. The more informed the contractor is about the evaluation process, the more efficacious the response and the fewer chances for problems. The contractor should understand the basis on which the initial assessment was made, including the scoring procedures; the purpose of the contractor's review and the response options; how disagreements will be resolved; and how the evaluation will be used.

Guidance for Contractors

It is recommended that every agency prepare a guide for use by contractors in reviewing the initial assessment. The agency guide need not be lengthy—just one or two pages—and should include the following:

- **Basis on which the evaluation is made**—Emphasizes that the evaluation assesses contractors' performance against the performance standards for the requirements stipulated in the contract with respect to the quality of the product or service, timeliness, cost control, and business relations.
- **The rating procedures**—Explains that there are five ratings—exceptional, very good, satisfactory, marginal, and unsatisfactory—and that a satisfactory rating is equivalent to meeting the performance standard for a requirement. Show that a rating above or below satisfactory is in relation to satisfactory performance. Describe what must be demonstrated to achieve a rating higher than satisfactory.
- **Contractor review and resolution of disagreements**—Explains that the contractor is given 30 days to review the initial evaluation and provide comments, rebutting statements, or additional information. Describe the process for resolving disagreements. Make sure that it is understood that if the contractor does not respond, the initial evaluation stands and the contractor will not have a chance to comment later if the evaluation is used in future source selections.

- **Final ratings and evaluation reports**—Makes clear that the final ratings are made only after the contractor has had an opportunity to provide its input to the evaluation. Reassure the contractor that a copy of the final report will be provided to the contractor as soon as it is finalized. Explain that the report will be maintained in the Past Performance Information Retrieval System (PPIRS) and made available to other agencies for source selection purposes. Let the contractor know that the report will not be retained in PPIRS for more than three years (six years for construction contracts).

Alerting the contractor that the evaluation will be conducted and providing guidance to the contractor on reviewing and responding to the initial evaluation are good business practices. Taking these steps ensures fair treatment of all contractors, helps facilitate the process, and avoids unnecessary conflict.

Contacting the Contractor

The contracting official who prepares the evaluation should be the one who forwards the evaluation to the contractor for review. The evaluation should be sent in the name of the person who signed the contract for the contractor. If the agency has been dealing with a person other than the person who signed the contract, notifying that official might expedite the response. A cover letter to the contractor might contain the following:

> The Agency has prepared an initial assessment of performance for the subject contract. Your comments, rebutting statements, or additional information will be considered before making the final assessment. Please review the enclosed evaluation. If we do not hear from you in 30 days, the Agency's assessment will be considered final. These evaluations may be used to support future award decisions. You will receive a copy of the evaluation once it is finalized.
>
> Information regarding the evaluation procedures is available at the Agency's website at www.agency.gov/contractor/evaluation/guide.

CONTRACTOR'S REVIEW

The purpose of the review is to complete the evaluation. The technical and contracting offices and, where appropriate, the end users, have provided input. An initial rating and supporting statement have been made for each assessment area. The contractor is now asked to review the initial assessment for accuracy, completeness, and fairness.

Review Process

The contractor's review of the evaluation should focus on the rating and the summary supporting narrative for the rating of each assessment area evaluated. This is the contractor's opportunity to improve the ratings if it can show that the government has reached its conclusion based on inaccurate, incomplete, or erroneous information. The contractor should review each rating by asking the following questions:

1. Did the agency assess the contractor's performance on all major requirements? If not, what was left out?
2. Did the agency interpret requirements in the same way as the contractor? If not, what are the differences?
3. Are the narrative statements supporting the ratings factually correct? If not, what should be corrected?
4. Do the narratives support the ratings, i.e., justify a rating higher than satisfactory or explain a rating lower than satisfactory?
5. Does the contractor agree with the ratings? If not, what evidence would support a higher rating?

How to Respond to the Agency

Based on the review, the contractor makes a decision as to whether a response to the agency is necessary. A response by the contractor can add to the integrity of the evaluation. That the contractor has provided comments, rebutting statements, or additional information makes for a better evaluation. There are three situations in which a response is needed:

- **Correcting Factual Errors**—A factual error must be corrected by the contracting officer. The contractor would be expected to provide evidence to support its claim.
- **Providing Additional Information**—Additional information must be considered by the contracting officer but does not have to be incorporated into the evaluation. The exception would be when the additional information could affect the rating or the rationale for the rating.
- **Rebutting the Government's Assessment**—If the contractor disagrees with the rating, it must convince the contracting officer that the agency's rating is incorrect. This may be done by providing information that was not taken into consideration in making the initial rating or showing that the initial rating was based on inaccurate or false information or on a misinterpretation of what transpired. If, after receiving the contractor's rebuttal, the contracting

officer disagrees with the contractor, the disagreement must be resolved at a level above the contracting officer. (See Chapter 11.)

Contractors should feel free to informally discuss less-than-satisfactory ratings with agency personnel for clarification before responding in writing. The discussion would usually be with the contracting officer but could be with other members of the acquisition team with whom the contractor has been working.

Common Misconceptions of the Ratings

When the contractor does not understand the review process, the three most common reactions are: (1) the contractor responds by rebutting the satisfactory ratings, (2) the contractor does not respond because the ratings were all above satisfactory, and (3) the contractor does not respond to low ratings because it does not believe anything can be changed. Each of these reactions is misguided.

Satisfactory Ratings—If a contractor does not understand that a satisfactory rating is equivalent to meeting the standard and interprets it as average performance, it is normal for the contractor to be concerned. The fact that the contractor competed for and won the contract indicates that it was the most qualified of the offerors and definitely not an average performer. This mistaken understanding of a satisfactory rating usually ends in a lengthy rebuttal that adds nothing to the evaluation. Contractors must understand that a satisfactory rating on a performance evaluation is a good rating. It means that the contractor complied with contractual requirements for the assessment area. It does not mean that performance was average.

Inflated Ratings—The opposite reaction comes from the contractor that is given exceptional or very good ratings on all the assessment areas. The contractor is pleased and therefore does not respond. This is a mistake because such ratings could be inflated or the narrative might not support the higher ratings. Exceptional means out of the ordinary, or one of a kind. When an exceptional rating is given, the narrative must support the rating. If the narrative does not support an exceptional rating or a very good rating, these ratings will not be credited as such when used in source selection. The source selection authority makes its judgment on the basis of the supporting narrative, not solely on an adjectival, numerical, or color-coded rating. The contractor should at least respond by proposing language or providing examples to support the higher ratings.

Low Ratings—Some contractors accept low ratings and do not respond because they believe nothing can be done to improve the rating. If a rating is negative but deserved, the best response is to accept responsibility for the failure and propose corrective action that will be taken to avoid failure in the future. This is especially critical if this is an interim evaluation, which will give the contractor the opportunity to prove itself on the subsequent evaluation. Trying to rebut negative ratings by offering excuses serves no purpose.

Final Note

There must be consistency between the contractor performance evaluation and other evaluations of contractor performance. For example, there should be consistency between the fee amount paid to contractors under award and incentive fee contracts and the contractor performance evaluation.

When comparing the same performance areas, the general rule would be: (1) the higher fee amounts are equivalent to a very good rating, (2) the lower fee amounts are equivalent to a satisfactory rating, and (3) no fee payment above the minimum fee amount is equivalent to a satisfactory rating or could be equivalent to a marginal rating, depending on the circumstances. Paying the highest fee amount does not automatically translate into an exceptional rating on a performance evaluation. It would be inconsistent, however, to give a negative rating if some fee payment were made. Contractors should rebut performance report ratings that do not closely parallel the fee determinations.[3]

NOTES

1. FAR 42.1503(b).
2. FAR 1.102(c). "The Acquisition Team consists of all participants in Government acquisition including not only representatives of the technical, supply, and procurement communities but also the customers they serve, and the contractors who provide the products and services."
3. FAR 42.1500. "...the fee amount paid to contractors should be reflective of the contractor's performance and the past performance evaluation should closely parallel the fee determinations."

CHAPTER 11

POST-AWARD: RESOLVING DISAGREEMENTS

"Agencies shall provide for review at a level above the contracting officer to consider disagreements between the parties regarding the evaluation." FAR[1]

The FAR requires that the contractor be given an opportunity not only to rebut the contracting officer's assessment of performance (Chapter 10) but also to provide for a review when the contracting officer denies the contractor's rebuttal. This chapter provides guidance to agencies to ensure that such reviews are carried out in an equitable and expeditious manner.

We begin with a definition of terms. What constitutes a "level above the contracting officer"? How are "disagreements" defined? Who are the "parties" involved? The following should be considered in preparing agency procedures regarding reviews at a level above the contracting officer.

DEFINITIONS

Level above the Contracting Officer—The level differs depending on the contracting authority's organizational structure. "Level above the contracting officer" is used in various sections of the FAR. It can be the supervisor of the contracting officer or an official outside the contracting officer's supervisory chain. The question that must be asked is whether that official is capable of making an independent review.[2] The official designated to review a protest should not have had previous personal involvement in the procurement.[3] Using the protest procedure as a precedent, the person designated could be in or outside the supervisory chain of the contracting officer. The contracting officer should not designate the official; this should be determined according to an established agency procedure.

Disagreements—For a disagreement to be reviewed at a higher level, the contractor must submit a rebutting statement, and the contracting officer must reject the contractor's rebuttal. By submitting a rebutting statement, the contractor demonstrates that it disagrees with the agency's initial assessment and argues for a change in the rating or ratings. By rejecting the contractor's rebuttal and not changing the rating or ratings, the contracting officer disagrees with the contractor. The higher-level review considers the opposing positions.

Not all disagreements are reviewed at a higher level; only those regarding the ratings are reviewed. Disagreements regarding interpretation of facts that do not affect the ratings are not subject to higher review. A disagreement exists when the contractor refutes the agency's initial rating or ratings by presenting opposing arguments and the contracting officer does not accept the contractor's arguments. Merely disagreeing with a rating without offering evidence or arguments to support a change in the rating is not sufficient to require a review.

Parties—The parties are the government and the contractor. The contracting officer, however, speaks for the government once the contractor responds to the initial assessment. The contracting officer is empowered to make the final assessment and does not have to obtain the concurrence of the acquisition team when he or she disagrees with the contractor's rebuttal. Going back to a member of the acquisition team where the disagreement involves the competency of that member (e.g., technical, audit, financial), however, is recommended to reinforce the contracting officer's decision to deny the rebuttal.[4]

HOW TO AVOID AGENCY REVIEWS

When sending the initial assessment to the contractor, it is recommended that the contractor have access to agency guidance on responding to the initial assessment of performance. It is particularly important if this is the first time that the contractor has had the opportunity to be evaluated by the agency. (The contractor might be familiar with the performance evaluations of other agencies that have different procedures.) The easiest way to do is to advise the contractor of the availability of guidance when forwarding the evaluation. It is not necessary to include the guide; indicating how to access the guide is sufficient.

If any of the ratings are negative, it is critical that there is backup documentation in the contract folder to support the agency's assessment. The evaluation should not be used to advise the contractor for the first time that its performance is unsatisfactory. Even when there is documentation, it might be useful to discuss this with the contractor before sending out the initial assessment. Personally contacting the contractor should prepare the contractor to accept the rating and could result in avoiding an unnecessary rebuttal. It is a good business practice and should be followed to the extent practicable.

If the contractor rebuts a rating and the contracting officer does not agree with the contractor, an agency review is in order. Contacting the contractor at this point is not recommended. The contractor is given one opportunity to rebut the ratings. Further dialogue might be instructive to both parties but will not change the past performance of the contractor.

REQUESTING A REVIEW

The evaluation with the contractor response need not be sent to the agency official for review. The review is limited to the areas of disagreement—that is, those ratings where the contractor has responded with a rebuttal statement. All that needs to be forwarded to the official making the review is the supporting statement for the ratings and the rebuttal from the contractor.

This material should be submitted in a way that facilitates the review process. The suggested approach is to use a four-part action memorandum.

The first part would be a request for a review to resolve the disagreement between the contracting officer and the contractor. The second part would be the agency's supporting statement of the rating or ratings in contention. Using cut and paste, the supporting statement can easily be copied from the evaluation to part two of the memorandum. The third part would be the contractor's rebuttal, which would be attached to the memorandum and only referenced in this part of the memorandum. The fourth part would be a place for the reviewing official to indicate whether he or she concurs with the contracting officer. Concurrence or non-concurrence would be needed for each rating in contention. Space should be provided to allow for comments by the reviewing official.

The following is an example of the suggested action memorandum.

To: Reviewing Official

From: Contracting Officer

Subj.: Review of Disagreement between (Contractor's Name) and the Agency

Ref: Contract No.

Problem: The contractor has submitted a statement rebutting the Agency's initial evaluation of performance. The contracting officer does not agree with the contractor's rebuttal. In accordance with FAR 42.1503(b), "Agencies shall provide for review at a level above the contracting officer to consider disagreements between the parties regarding the evaluation." You are hereby requested to review this matter and render a decision. The Agency's rating and supporting statement are provided below, followed by the contractor's rebuttal.

Agency's Rating: The following is a true and correct copy of the supporting statement(s) for the contested rating area or areas to which the contractor has responded. [Cut and paste statement from evaluation.]

Assessment Area: Timeliness *Rating: Satisfactory*

(Timeliness: The contractor met the deadline for delivery of the product. The contractor did encounter some problems that caused delay in meeting production milestones. Timely identification of these problems and appropriate corrective actions minimized any adverse effects the delays would have had on timely delivery. The contract met the timeliness requirements and therefore is rated Satisfactory.)

[Add other assessment areas and ratings, as necessary, and cut and paste appropriate supporting statements.]

Contractor's Rebuttal: The pertinent parts of the contractor's response in which the contractor did not agree with the Agency's evaluation are attached to this memorandum.

Reviewer's Decision: Please indicate your decision by initialing and dating in the appropriate area below. If you sustain the contracting officer, the rating and supporting statement stand. If you agree with the contractor, the rating and supporting statement will be changed accordingly.

I agree with the **contractor** with regard to the following assessment areas:

Assessment area(s): ______________________________

Comment: ______________________________

I agree with the **contracting officer** with regard to the following assessment areas:

Assessment area(s): ______________________________

Comment: ______________________________

Initials: ____________________ Date: ____________________

RESPONSIBILITY OF THE REVIEWER

The responsibility of the reviewing official is to consider the facts and decide whether he or she agrees with the contractor or the contracting officer. This decision should be in writing and should be issued within 15 days from receipt of a rebuttal statement.[5] Following the procedure explained above (i.e., using a four-part action memorandum) simplifies and expedites the process. In most cases, there is no need for additional comments; a simple concurrence suffices.

DECISION IS FINAL

Based on the decision of the agency review, the contracting officer finalizes the report.[6] Consulting with the acquisition team and further discussion with the contractor are not needed. There is no appeals process.

ADVISING CONTRACTOR OF DECISION

It is not necessary to advise the contractor that a higher-level review will take place. Once a decision is made, the contracting officer finalizes the evaluation by incorporating the decision of the reviewing official, as appropriate. The evaluation report should indicate that the agency review took place before the final assessment was made. The agency review document is filed with the contractor's rebuttal in the contract folder. No copy of the agency's review is given to the contractor. If copies are needed in the future, they can be obtained from the contract file.

Once finalized, a copy of the evaluation report is sent to the contractor. At the same time, an electronic copy of the report is submitted to the Past Performance Information Retrieval System (PPIRS).

NOTES

1. FAR 42.1503(b). "... Agencies shall provide for review at a level above the contracting officer to consider disagreements between the parties regarding the evaluation. The ultimate conclusion on the performance evaluation is a decision of the contracting agency."
2. This is not a technical review as was the case with reviewing officials for evaluations of construction contracts or for architect/engineer contracts. Construction and architect-engineer services contract evaluations were reviewed for technical and professional accuracy. FAC 2005-34 no longer requires technical reviews. The review that is required here is to determine the merits of the opposing positions regarding the evaluation of the contractor's performance. The reviewing official acts as a judge and not as an expert in the matter.
3. The FAR does not provide procedures for establishing a review at a level above the contracting officer when required by FAR 42.1503(b). However, the procedures in FAR 33.103(d)(4) for filing a protest with an agency regarding a contracting officer's decision are applicable with respect to review at a level above the contracting officer. FAR 33.103(d)(4): ". . . Agencies shall designate the official(s) who are to conduct this independent review, but the official(s) need not be within the contracting officer's supervisory chain. When practicable, officials designated to conduct the independent review should not have had previous personal involvement in the procurement."
4. The contracting officer should defer to the customer, particularly with regard to the ratings of quality and timeliness.
5. Office of Federal Procurement Policy, *A Guide to Best Practices for Past Performance,* May 1995, p. 42.
6. FAR 42.1503(b). "...The ultimate conclusion on the performance evaluation is a decision of the contracting agency."

CHAPTER 12

POST-AWARD: MAINTAINING PAST PERFORMANCE INFORMATION AND MAKING IT ACCESSIBLE

"Agencies shall submit past performance reports electronically to the Past Performance Information Retrieval System (PPIRS) at www.ppirs.gov." FAR[1]

The purpose of conducting contractor performance evaluations is to provide information for use in source selection. The effort expended in conducting contractor performance evaluations will be in vain if the information obtained is not available in making award decisions. Past performance information must be maintained in such a way that it is accessible to source selection officials when reviewing the qualifications of offerors.

MAINTAINING PAST PERFORMANCE INFORMATION

The evaluation is retained in the contract file, which includes the evaluation report, the contractor's response, and the agency review, if a review was required to resolve disagreements between the contractor and the contracting officer.[2] It does not include the working papers associated with conducting the evaluation, such as input from individual members of the acquisition team, the substance of which would have been incorporated into the evaluation. That material may be discarded once the evaluation is completed.

Treat as Source Selection Information

Because the evaluation may be used to support future award decisions, it should be identified as source selection information.[3] This is accomplished by marking "Source Selection Material" on a cover sheet for the evaluation documents or on the folder in which the documents are filed. It is not necessary to mark each page of the evaluation at this time, but only when the evaluation is released to source selection officials.[4]

Past Performance Information System

The final evaluation report or report card does not include the contractor's response or the agency's review comments. Although part of the evaluation, the contractor's response and the agency's review comments are not needed by source selection officials. The evaluation report contains pertinent information—the agency's rating and the rationale for the rating for each of the assessment areas. The source selection official does not reevaluate the agency ratings but accepts the agency's determination as final. The evaluation report must indicate that the contractor was given the opportunity to review the evaluation and, if there were disagreements between the contracting officer and the contractor regarding the ratings, whether a review was made at a level above the contracting officer.

On completion of the evaluation, the contracting officer sends a copy of the evaluation report to the contractor.[5] At the same time, the contracting officer submits an electronic copy of the evaluation report to the Past Performance Information Retrieval System (PPIRS) at www.ppirs.gov.

PPIRS: A SINGLE SOURCE FOR PAST PERFORMANCE REPORTS

PPIRS is a web-enabled enterprise application that stores past performance reports and makes them available to government acquisition officials for use in making source selection decisions. PPIRS assists acquisition officials from all agencies by serving as the single source for contractor performance evaluations conducted in compliance with FAR 42.15.

Problems with Multiple Past Performance Information Systems Resolved

With the proliferation of past performance information systems—each agency establishing its own system—retrieving data from many systems can be a laborious process. The fewer the past performance information systems, the more efficient the process will be. That is because of the need to have a user identification and password to gain access to each system. The user ID and password are required not just for the agency using the system but also for source selection officials from other agencies who want to retrieve data from the system. This is not a problem when the contracts listed by the offeror are from one agency, but it becomes more difficult to retrieve the data when the contracts listed by the offerors are from many agencies. A user ID and password are required for each system where past performance information is maintained.

An example of the inefficiencies created by multiple systems would be a solicitation in which there were five proposals, each listing seven contracts that were similar to the requirements of the solicitation. This would require accessing 35 evaluation reports, which could come from one or as many as 35 different past performance information systems. Even if it required accessing only five or six systems, it would mean obtaining a user ID and a password for that many systems for at least one source selection official. Every new solicitation would require obtaining a user ID and a password for different source selection officials.

PPIRS has resolved the problem by providing a government-wide depository of contractor performance reports and by making those reports accessible to source selection officials from all agencies.

Collecting Past Performance Information

PPIRS receives performance reports from past performance information systems including the following:

- Construction Contractor Appraisal Support System (CCASS)
- Architect-Engineer Contract Administration Support System (ACASS)
- Contractor Performance System (CPS)
- Past Performance Data Base (PPDB)
- Past Performance Information Management System (PPIMS)
- Contractor Performance Assessment Report System (CPARS).

Each of the above-mentioned past performance information systems no longer needs to make its evaluation reports available to source selection officials. They can now concentrate on their primary objective, which is to collect past performance information. A description of each past performance information system follows.

PAST PERFORMANCE INFORMATION SYSTEMS

The U.S. Army Corps of Engineers (USACE) has managed two past performance information systems for over two decades. These systems, known as the Construction Contractor Appraisal Support System (CCASS) and the Architect-Engineer Contract Administration Support System (ACASS), maintain performance evaluation reports on construction and architect-engineer contracts, respectively. Although the systems were originally established by USACE for its own use, all federal departments and agencies may now use the systems as appropriate.

Construction Contractor Appraisal Support System

CCASS is an automated database of performance evaluations on construction contractors. Its primary use is to make the responsibility determination in awarding sealed-bid contracts. Contractor performance evaluations are also used when past performance is an evaluation factor in the second phase of a two-phase design-build selection.[6] To retrieve the evaluation reports, the authorized user responds to a series of questions, and the results are transmitted to the requestor's computer. The cost of using CCASS is based on a fee for service to cover operating and maintenance costs. No profit is made from the system. The performance reports are automatically purged from the system after six years from the date of the reviewing official's signature.

The evaluations were conducted in accordance with FAR 36.201, which required the preparation of a report using a standard form (SF 1420). The evaluations are now conducted in accordance with FAR 42.1502(e)[7] using the Contractor Performance Assessment Reporting System (CPARS) module Construction. The resulting evaluation reports are automatically sent to PPIRS.

Architect-Engineer Contract Administration Support System

ACASS is a database of selected information on architect-engineer firms. In addition to performance evaluations, ACASS tracks the amount of work an architect-engineer firm was awarded by the Department of Defense and maintains qualifications and performance data on architect-engineer firms.[8] The reports are electronically transmitted to ACASS. Permission to access ACASS is granted to persons within any federal agency with the authority to contract with architect-engineer firms. Like CCASS, the cost of using ACASS is based on a fee for service to cover operations and maintenance. No profit is made on the system, and the evaluation reports are automatically purged from the system after six years.

ACASS performance evaluations were conducted in accordance with FAR 36.604, which required the preparation of a report using a standard form (SF 1421). The evaluations are now conducted in accordance with FAR 42.1502(f)[9] using the Contractor Performance Assessment Reporting System (CPARS) module Architect-Engineer. The completed evaluation reports are automatically submitted to PPIRS.

Contractor Performance System

The National Institutes of Health (NIH) has taken a leadership role in establishing a past performance evaluation system for civilian agencies. The NIH Contractor Performance System (CPS) is a multiple-agency, shared file system. Subscribers pay an annual fee based on the number of contracts that will be maintained for the department or agency. Authorized users have access to the completed evaluations of all subscribing agencies.[10] Each completed contractor performance report (CPR) is electronically submitted to PPIRS.

The CPR collects data for seven assessment areas—Quality of Product or Services, Cost Control, Timeliness of Performance, Business Relations, Comments on Subcontracts/Socioeconomic Goals, Comments on Key Personnel, and Customer Satisfaction. The rating scale gives a value of 5 or Outstanding, 4 or Excellent, 3 or Good, 2 or Fair, 1 or Poor, and 0 or Unsatisfactory.

Past Performance Data Base

The system used by the National Aeronautics and Space Administration (NASA) is known as the Contractor Performance Information and Past Performance Data Base (PPDB). Its purpose is to assist NASA's procurement officials in collecting, storing, and retrieving contractor performance reports. NASA uses its own form, which has four assessment areas (Quality, Timeliness, Pricc/Cost, and Other) and five ratings (Excellent, Very Good, Good, Satisfactory, and Poor/Unsatisfactory). The evaluation reports are electronically submitted to PPIRS for use, government-wide, in source selection.

Past Performance Information Management System

The Army and the Defense Information Systems Agency (DISA) used the Past Performance Information Management System (PPIMS) to support the contractor evaluation process using the performance assessment report (PAR). Completed PARs were electronically submitted to PPIRS. PPIMS is no longer in use. (See below.)

Contractor Performance Assessment Reporting System

CPARS is a web-enabled application that was developed by the Navy. In 2005 DoD chose CPARS to replace its Past Performance Automated Information System (PPAIS). In 2007 PPIMS migrated to CPARS, and the contractor performance assessment report (CPAR) replaced the PAR for the collection of past performance information. CPARS connects to PPIRS so that every completed contractor performance assessment report can be shared government-wide by source selection officials.

The CPAR collects information on five assessment areas—Quality of Product or Service, Schedule, Cost Control, Business Relations (which includes small business subcontracting goal accomplishment), and Management of Key Personnel. Color-coded and adjectival ratings are used: Dark Blue is equivalent to Exceptional; Purple, to Very Good; Green, to Satisfactory; Yellow, to Marginal; and Red, to Unsatisfactory. In rating performance, particular emphasis is given to the contractor's effectiveness in dealing with problems.

FEDERAL REPOSITORY OF PAST PERFORMANCE INFORMATION

One of the obstacles inhibiting the use of past performance as an evaluation factor in source selection was the accessibility of past performance information. PPIRS has resolved this problem with respect to past performance evaluations conducted in compliance with FAR 42.15.

NOTES

1. FAR 42.1503(3). "Agencies shall submit past performance reports electronically to the Past Performance Information Retrieval System (PPIRS) at www.ppirs.gov. The process for submitting such reports to PPIRS shall be in accordance with agency procedures."
2. FAR 42.1503(b). "... Copies of the evaluation, contractor response, and review comments, if any, shall be retained as part of the evaluation."
3. FAR 42.1503(b). "... These evaluations may be used to support future award decisions, and should therefore be marked "Source Selection Information."
4. FAR 3.104-4. "*Disclosure, protection, and marking of contractor bid or proposal information or source selection information.* (a) Except as specifically provided for in this subsection, no person or other entity may disclose contractor bid or proposal information or source selection information to any person other than a person authorized, in accordance with applicable agency regulations or procedures, by the agency head or the contracting officer to receive such information."
5. FAR 42.1503(b). "... Agency evaluations of contractor performance prepared under this subpart shall be provided to the contractor as soon as practicable after completion of the evaluation."
6. FAR 36.303-2 "Phase Two.

   "(a) Phase Two of the solicitation(s) shall be prepared in accordance with Part 15, and include phase-two evaluation factors, developed in accordance with 15.304. Examples of potential phase-two technical evaluation factors include design concepts, management approach, key personnel, and proposed technical solutions.

"(b) Phase Two of the solicitation(s) shall require submission of technical and price proposals, which shall be evaluated separately, in accordance with Part 15."

7. FAR 42.1502(e). "Past performance evaluations shall be prepared for each construction contract of $550,000 or more, and for each construction contract terminated for default regardless of contract value. Past performance evaluations may also be prepared for construction contracts below $550,000."
8. See FAR 36.603, *Collecting data on and appraising firms' qualifications statements.*
9. FAR 42.1502(f). "Past performance evaluations shall be prepared for each architect-engineer services contract of $30,000 or more, and for each architect-engineer services contract that is terminated for default regardless of contract value. Past performance evaluations may also be prepared for architect-engineer services contracts below $30,000."
10. Subscribers to the system include the Departments of Agriculture, Commerce, Energy, Health and Human Services, Interior, Justice, Labor, State, Transportation, and Veterans Affairs; the Environmental Protection Agency and Federal Emergency Management Agency; General Services Administration; U.S. Agency for International Development; Social Security Administration; Export-Import Bank; Architect of the Capital; Federal Trade Commission; National Labor Relations Board; and U.S. Government Printing Office. See National Institutes of Health, *Contractor Performance System,* About CPS, updated 9/29/2009.

CHAPTER 13

LEGAL ISSUES IN PAST PERFORMANCE

"Our Office will examine an agency's past performance evaluation only to ensure that it was reasonable and consistent with the stated evaluation criteria and applicable statutes and regulations..." GAO[1]

Although most of the legal challenges related to an agency's use of past performance information involve the agency's evaluation of past performance information in the source selection process, there are actions contractors can take during contract performance to enhance their competitive advantage in future procurements. The first part of this chapter addresses steps a contractor can take to avoid problems that might later damage its competitive position in the federal marketplace. The second part provides guidance to contractors with respect to their legal rights concerning alleged improper agency evaluations of past performance information based on GAO protest decisions.

HOW CONTRACTORS CAN USE PAST PERFORMANCE INFORMATION TO THEIR COMPETITIVE ADVANTAGE

Poor performance ratings can be nearly impossible to overcome and might seriously reduce business opportunities within the federal marketplace. Perhaps the most obvious way for contractors to avoid poor performance ratings is to perform well on their contracts. However, exemplary performance is not always possible or, for a host of reasons, not always recognized or acknowledged by agency evaluators. Thus, contractors should be vigilant and do everything possible to ensure an accurate evaluation of their contract performance.

Contractors can shape or influence the performance evaluation process and should take full advantage of every opportunity to do so to increase the likelihood that past performance information is accurate and is presented in the light most beneficial to the contractor.

As discussed below, contractors have four opportunities to provide input:

1. During and at the close of contract performance by submitting comments on performance evaluations

2. During and at the close of contract performance by requesting review by officials a level above the contracting officer when the contractor disagrees with the initial performance evaluation
3. During proposal preparation by preparing proposals that address known problems head-on and by presenting performance records in the best possible light
4. During proposal evaluation by participating actively in oral or written exchanges with the agency to ascertain and address each issue of potential concern to evaluators.

Submit Comments on Performance Evaluations

FAR 42.1503(b)[2] requires agencies to allow contractors to review their performance evaluations and to give contractors at least 30 days to submit comments and rebuttals. This is the contractor's opportunity to change the ratings or wording of the supporting narratives in the evaluation report.

Because the evaluation report may be used for future source selections, contractors should treat it as critical to their future success in winning contracts and devote as much time and resources toward ensuring its accuracy as is necessary. Contractors should understand that the 30-day period will be their only chance to comment on performance evaluations and thus should make the most of the opportunity. Any aspect of an evaluation report that could be perceived as negative or marginal should be addressed in as much detail as possible, within any space constraints imposed by the agency. In addition, if possible, documentation should be provided to bolster the credibility of the contractor's position.

Performance evaluations cover such areas as quality of product or service, timeliness, cost control, and business relations. Detailed explanations should address such factors as:

- The government's role in contributing to any perceived performance problems
- The excusable nature of the problem—how the problem was beyond the contractor's control
- Efforts the contractor undertook at the time to address the issue
- Corrective actions taken to prevent future occurrences of the problems
- The uncharacteristic nature of the problem in light of the contractor's overall performance record.

Obtain Review at a Level Above the Contracting Officer

In instances where the parties cannot come to terms and the contractor disagrees with how potentially damaging information is characterized, the contractor should be sure to take advantage of the provisions in FAR 42.1503(b)[3] requiring review of the evaluation at a level above the contracting officer. The contractor should prepare its case as thoroughly as possible and explain either why the performance problems were beyond its control or how the problems have been corrected and will not be repeated. Again, documentary support might be crucial for supporting the contractor's position and should be provided if available or reasonably attainable.

Prepare Proposals to Present Past Performance in the Best Light Possible

In addition to the performance evaluations available to procuring agencies, agencies will rely to varying extents on offerors' proposals as a primary source of past performance information. It follows that contractors should carefully consider the contracts and references they choose to identify in their proposals as "relevant." It should be assumed that procuring agencies will contact all such references and use them as a primary source of information. Contractors should also assume that relevant past performance information will come to light, even if it is not discussed in their proposals.

If a contractor has a poor performance record on a particular contract effort, it should closely examine all aspects of that contract to determine how best to distinguish it from the effort being solicited. In this way, inclusion of the problematic effort in the proposal as a relevant contract might be avoided. Factors such as (1) technical similarities, (2) dollar amount, (3) age, (4) contract type (fixed price or cost-type), (5) performance period, and (6) nature of customer may each be used as a distinguishing factor. If the contract cannot in good faith be distinguished and must be included in the proposal as a relevant contract, the circumstances surrounding any performance problems should be thoroughly explained.[4]

The issues addressed above—the government's role in contributing to the problems, the excusable nature of the problems, and the contractor's corrective action to prevent future occurrences—should be emphasized. Bad experiences should be cast as "lessons learned," and assurances should be given to the evaluator that, because of changes implemented, no similar problems will occur in the future.

Use Discussions to Enhance Your Position

FAR 15.306(b)(1)[5] requires agencies to allow offerors to address adverse past performance information to which they have not had an opportunity to respond (1) if the past performance information is the determining factor preventing them from being placed in the competitive range or (2) if their inclusion or exclusion from the competitive range is uncertain. Such past performance information, of course, normally will not include evaluation reports prepared under FAR 42.15 and past performance information the offeror has presented in its proposal. The provision is generally meant to address past performance information the agency has obtained from third-party sources that might be unknown to the offeror. Once such past performance information is raised with the offeror, the offeror should marshal its resources to research the circumstances that gave rise to the adverse past performance information and to provide strong responses, if possible, that address the issues summarized above.

Although disagreements on a personal level might, and often do, lead to poor references on a contract performance level, contractors should bear in mind that, under FAR 15.306(e)(4),[6] government personnel involved in the procurement are forbidden to disclose the names of the individuals providing reference information about an offeror's past performance. Thus, the substance of the information is the only material to which contractors are entitled during discussions. This fact might hinder a contractor's understanding of, and explanation for, why it received a poor past performance reference from what was otherwise presumed to be a friendly reference.

CHALLENGING AGENCY PAST PERFORMANCE EVALUATIONS

Protests of an alleged improper agency evaluation of past performance information in source selection are extremely commonplace, despite the fact that protesters face an uphill battle in trying to convince GAO that impropriety exists. GAO's general rule is that it "will examine an agency's past performance evaluation only to ensure that it was reasonable and consistent with the stated evaluation criteria and applicable statutes and regulations, since determining the relative merit of an offeror's past performance is primarily a matter within the contracting agency's discretion."[7]

Scope of the Past Performance Information Review—Relevancy and Currency

A significant body of GAO case law addresses the issue of what past performance an agency may, must, or should not consider in its evaluation. GAO has summarized its rulings on this issue as follows:

> *[A]n agency has discretion to determine the scope of the vendors' performance history to be considered, provided that it evaluates all submissions on the same basis and consistent with the solicitation. An agency properly may base its evaluation on contracts it believes are most relevant to the solicitation; it has discretion to consider information other than that provided by the vendors, and need not consider all references a vendor submits.*[8]

An agency may ignore an entire class of references when evaluating past performance.[9] For example, a protester complained that the agency had failed to contact any of its commercial references. GAO found that the agency had reasonably regarded the protester's government contracts to be more relevant to the instant procurement than its commercial contracts and thus had acted properly. Interestingly, the agency had made telephone calls to the protester's largest commercial customer, but its calls were not returned. GAO found that the agency had properly proceeded with its evaluations without that customer's reference because an agency is required only "to make a reasonable effort to contact a reference."

GAO has even accepted an agency evaluation in which the agency purposefully excluded the past performance of all key personnel as irrelevant.[10] GAO found reasonable the agency's contention that, because it was contracting with the corporate entity and not the individuals, the corporate entity's past performance information was more indicative of future performance.

In addition to considering whether a referenced project is relevant to the instant procurement based on the similarity of the subject matter of the two projects, agencies may also consider whether the size or scope of the projects makes them comparable for past performance purposes.[11] Indeed, an agency may even downgrade an offeror's past performance evaluation where its references provided high marks if the size or scope of the highly regarded performance nonetheless is incomparable to the instant procurement's size or scope.[12]

In another case, the protester was the incumbent on a contract considered so similar to the instant solicitation that it was used as the basis for the government's cost estimate. Additionally, the contracting officer's representative for the protester's contract was a member of the technical evaluation board for the instant solicitation. The agency defended its failure to consider the contract in its past performance evaluation by contending that the protester's failure to complete a contractor past performance data sheet for the contract had prevented the agency from sending out a past performance survey. Under the circumstances, however, GAO found that "the agency could not reasonably ignore personally known information" about the protester's prior experience "merely because the firm did not submit a Contractor Past Performance Data Sheet for that contract."[13]

The currency of past performance information may also affect an agency's scope of review during an evaluation of past performance. The FAR limits the "use of past performance information in PPIRS that is within three years (six for construction and architect-engineer contracts) of the completion of performance of the evaluated contract or order."[14] This limitation, however, pertains only to past performance information that has been in PPIRS.

It does not affect an agency's authority to include past performance information older than three years (six years for construction and architect-engineer contracts and orders) in its source selection determinations. Indeed, FAR Part 15, which governs the procedures for negotiated source selections, contains no such restriction on the age of past performance information. The FAR does specify that the currency of past performance information "shall be considered."[15] As a result, agencies may request past performance information from contracts completed more than or even less than three years prior to the instant solicitation.

It is important to bear in mind, however, that agencies will often adjust the value of past performance information according to the age of the prior contract to which it relates. GAO has approved of such weighting of past performance information, stating, not surprisingly, that agencies may give more weight to past performance information relating to recent contracts than they give to that relating to older contracts.[16]

Challenging the Accuracy of Past Performance Information

Agencies are generally required to consider past performance information of an exculpatory nature if it tends to counter negative past performance ratings; however, there is no requirement that agencies seek out such information. Rather, offerors are obligated to provide the agency with their most current past performance information, even if the agency could otherwise gain access to the past performance information. In one case, for example, the protester argued that the agency's past performance evaluation was flawed because the agency had failed to update its files to reflect a recent Armed Services Board of Contract Appeals decision that cast doubt upon the accuracy of an earlier negative past performance evaluation. The protester had not brought the decision to the attention of the agency prior to the past performance information evaluation. GAO dismissed the protest, holding that there is no legal obligation on the part of agencies to search for past performance information not already on hand.[17]

Time and again, GAO decisions show that protesters bear a heavy evidentiary burden when challenging past performance evaluations. For example, a protester[18] lost an Army contract for hospital nutritional care services because of a higher risk assessment derived from its past performance history. The Army's assessment was based in part on disputed information from another Army facility. The protester offered excuses, interpretations, and documentation that GAO admitted tended to place the past performance problems in a light more favorable to the protester. However, GAO still found that the protester had failed to meet its burden of showing that the disputed past performance information was inaccurate. It then reiterated its general rule that "an agency's evaluation of past performance may be based upon the procuring agency's reasonable perception of inadequate prior performance, even where the contractor disputes the agency's interpretation of the facts." In other words, as in other areas of bid protests, a contractor's mere disagreement with the agency on an evaluation issue will usually get the contractor nowhere; hard evidence showing that the agency's position is unreasonable must be provided.

There are limits to an agency's discretion to rely on or interpret the past performance information before it. In another case,[19] the agency had found the protester's past performance "marginal" during proposal evaluations, largely based on purported comments from a customer's technical specialist on a previous contract. At a hearing held by GAO, however, the technical specialist testified that he did not recall making certain statements the agency had attributed to him, that the agency had misinterpreted other statements, and that other statements in the agency's evaluation record were inaccurate or mischaracterized. GAO sustained the protest.

Exchanges Regarding Past Performance

After submission of proposals, exchanges between offerors and agencies regarding past performance vary depending on the stage of the source selection. As noted previously, exchanges may come in the form of "clarifications," "communications," or "discussions," each of which is treated distinctly by the FAR and GAO.

If the agency intends to make award without discussions, GAO has held that the contracting officer has "broad discretion" to decide whether to address an offeror's past performance history by seeking a "clarification."[20] If the clarification would involve adverse past performance information upon which the offeror has not had a chance to comment, the offeror must be given "an opportunity to respond where there clearly is a reason to question the validity of the past performance information, for example, where there are obvious inconsistencies between a reference's narrative comments and the actual ratings the reference gives the offeror."[21] Conversely, if the contracting officer has no reason to question the validity of past performance information, "he or she can reasonably rely on the information furnished without seeking to verify it or permitting the protester an opportunity to rebut it."[22]

Agencies must have "communications" with certain offerors if a competitive range is to be established.[23] With respect to past performance, communications must be held with offerors whose past performance information is the determining factor preventing them from being in the competitive range. In one of the few cases addressing this issue, GAO conducted a review of the agency's report, found nothing in that record showing that the protester's past performance information was the reason it had failed to make the competitive range, and thus denied the protest.[24]

If a competitive range is established, the contracting officer must discuss with each offeror any "significant weaknesses, deficiencies, and other aspects of its proposal," including past performance, that could be altered or explained so as to materially enhance the proposal's potential for award. Problems of past performance that fall under one or more of these descriptions must be discussed.

In determining whether an agency considered particular items of past performance information "significant weaknesses" or "deficiencies," GAO usually just refers to the agency evaluation report as in *Digital Systems Group.*[25] In that case, GAO denied a protest after it noted that, although the report had identified the disputed past performance information problems as "weaknesses," the evaluators considered them neither "significant weaknesses" nor "deficiencies." Conversely, in a similar case,[26] GAO sustained a protest where the agency's report did not even discuss, much less downplay, the significance of past performance information problems. GAO stated, "While these negative evaluations were not specifically relied upon in the [source selection board's] tradeoff, we cannot conclude that they did not have an impact on [the protester's] overall rating."

Agencies may not expend any effort to conduct discussions on past performance problems if they believe such discussions are unlikely to alter the evaluation result as in the Maytag Aircraft Corp. case.[27] In that case, the protester contended that the agency had failed during discussions to raise past performance issues that the agency considered to be weaknesses. The contracting officer explained that because the problems had been well documented by the protester and the agency, and because two of the pertinent references were also evaluators on the source selection committee, she had determined that additional discussions of the problems would not have changed the facts known to the evaluators. GAO agreed.

As with other protest grounds, it is not enough just to show that the agency did not hold proper discussions. The protester must also show that it was prejudiced by the agency's failure—that "but for the agency's actions, it would have had a substantial chance of receiving the award."[28] GAO has stated the threshold for prejudice as follows: "[A] reasonable possibility of prejudice is a sufficient basis for sustaining the protest .... In other words, we will deny a protest only where it is clear from the record that the protester was not prejudiced."[29]

Even when the agency errs in evaluating past performance, GAO has found that protesters are not prejudiced by erroneous negative comments if the record indicates that other significant negative comments were made about the protester's past performance.[30] In another case, GAO held that the protester was not prejudiced by a disputed past performance evaluation because it "would not have been able to improve its past performance rating of neutral, which was based on its lack of experience in manufacturing the same or similar items, through discussions (presumably if the protester had such experience, it would have mentioned it in its initial proposal) ...."[31]

Contractors should also keep in mind that to win over the agency during discussions, they might need to show not only that they adequately addressed past performance problems in a past contract, but also that they have taken action to minimize occurrence of the same problems in future contracts. A protester[32] argued that the agency had not conducted meaningful discussions on the protester's past performance problems. GAO noted that the protester had responded to the adverse past performance information at the time it was being compiled and had opportunity during discussions to respond to negative information received by the agency through customer feedback. GAO then stated that "[w]hile [the protester] provided responses that indicated that appropriate corrective action was taken, we do not find it unreasonable for the agency to conclude that [the protester] had not demonstrated that certain systemic problems had been corrected."

Evaluation Consistent with the Solicitation Factors

An agency's evaluation of proposals must be "reasonable and consistent with the stated evaluation criteria" set forth in the solicitation.[33] At times, this might simply be a matter of interpreting the terms of the solicitation. In *Lynwood Machine &*

Engineering, Inc., for example, the protester argued that the agency had acted improperly when it evaluated past performance information from projects completed more than two years before, while the solicitation had instructed offerors to provide references for projects completed within the past two years. GAO denied the protest, holding that "[a]lthough the RFQ requested references for projects completed within the last two years, it did not indicate that the evaluation of past performance would be based exclusively on such projects. . . . Accordingly, we do not think that it was inconsistent with the terms of the solicitation for the agency to have considered projects completed more than two years previously in evaluating Lynwood's past performance."[34]

Sometimes it is not clear under which particular evaluation criterion past performance information will be evaluated. GAO has held that agencies generally may consider an element of one evaluation criterion under one or more other evaluation criteria, as long as the "element is relevant and reasonably related to each criterion under which it is considered" and the practice does not "exaggerate the stated importance of any one evaluation criterion."[35] GAO approved this approach in *OSI Collection Services, Inc.,*[36] where the protester complained that the practice resulted in "double-counting" of periodic performance reports prepared by the agency during previous contract performance. The agency had considered the reports in evaluating the protester's past performance and then again when evaluating the past performance of the protester's key personnel. GAO found this approach reasonable, stating that "[i]t is obvious that the contributions made by key personnel to a firm's [performance reports] are relevant to the [agency's] consideration of their past performance."

GAO will also uphold awards resulting from an agency's reasonable efforts to deal with unexpected problems arising from the agency's intended approach for evaluating past performance information. In this case,[37] a solicitation for multiple indefinite delivery/indefinite quantity (ID/IQ) contracts provided that five references would be used for the past performance evaluation. However, for several of the offerors, fewer than five references responded to the agency's queries. More than five of the protester's references responded. As a result, the agency evaluated five of the protester's references at random, but for awardees with fewer than five references responding, it evaluated all responding references. The protester contended that the agency had failed to abide by the evaluation approach set out because it had used different numbers of references for different offerors.

GAO found this approach proper, holding that the agency's approach did not result in competitive prejudice to the protester because there was no indication that knowledge of the approach would have caused the protester to change its proposal to its advantage. GAO also noted that the agency had not relaxed the solicitation's requirements (offerors were still required to submit seven references) and did not eliminate the randomness inherent in the selection of evaluated references (which references responded, GAO reasoned, was random).

Reasonableness of Evaluation Methodology

Obviously, the evaluation methodology used to evaluate past performance must be reasonable, and GAO has sustained protests where it was not. In *American Development Corp.,*[38] the Army gathered past performance information on offerors from other agencies that had contracted with the offerors in the past. Under the Army's evaluation methodology, offerors received points simply for the number of "relevant" contracts they had performed. The protester argued that the evaluation methodology irrationally assigned the awardee points for having performed a "relevant" contract, whether or not the awardee's performance on the contract was good. GAO sustained the protest, finding the Army's methodology irrational: "In effect, the methodology chosen rewarded offerors which had held at least one contract relevant to the work to be performed under the RFP without consideration of the quality of the work performed under the contract."

Similarly, in *Green Valley Transportation, Inc.,*[39] the protester argued that the agency had conducted an improper past performance evaluation under a solicitation for freight transportation services. The agency had required offerors to submit copies of corrective measures they had taken in response to disciplinary actions and had collected various performance data on the offerors from the distribution center involved in past shipments. The agency then summarized the negative performance actions received by each offeror and determined that the protester's high number of such negative actions caused it to fail the requirements for the subfactor.

The protester contended that this methodology was unreasonable in that it failed to take into account the volume of shipments the offerors had moved while getting the negative performance actions. GAO held: "In our view, it was unreasonable for [the agency] to compare the absolute number of negative performance actions an offeror received, without considering that number in the context of the number of shipments the offeror had made over the relevant period." The protest was sustained.

The agency must still ensure that its best-value determination accords with FAR requirements not to penalize an offeror with no relevant past performance. In *National Aerospace Group, Inc.,*[40] the protester challenged an award to a higher-priced offeror that was based on the agency's determination that the higher offer represented the "best value" to the government. The award went to the higher offeror because its higher Automated Best Value Model (ABVM) score purportedly "represented a lesser risk of nonperformance" than the protester's neutral ABVM score. The contracting officer had offered no other rationale for her award decision. GAO sustained the protest because the contracting officer's decision "was tantamount to rejecting [the protester's] quotation based on its lack of past performance history."

A protester, however, cannot withhold relevant past performance information to force the agency to assign a neutral past performance information rating. In considering such a case, GAO stated:

> *Although FAR 15.305(a)(2)(iv)*[41] *requires an agency to assign a neutral rating where past performance information is "not available," here, the protester's proposal represented that its proposed subcontractors are engaged in projects that would illustrate their performance capability. The information thus was available, but MDA chose not to present the information in its proposal, in direct contravention of the terms of the RFP. In our view, an offeror cannot simply choose to withhold past performance information—and thereby obtain a neutral rating—where the solicitation expressly requires that the information be furnished, and where the information is readily available to the offeror.*

A different result occurred in *TEAM Support Services, Inc.*,[42] where the incumbent contractor's past performance rating was lowered because the contracting officer, who had been project officer on the previous contract and was the sole evaluator of the instant solicitation, stated that the protester's management was "uncooperative" in resolving disputes arising out of a government shutdown. GAO denied the protest and stated that the contracting officer's determination was reasonable because it had more to do with the protester's working relationship with the agency.

Use of Past Performance Information of Subcontractors, Affiliates, and Key Personnel

An agency's past performance evaluation "should take into account past performance information regarding predecessor companies, key personnel who have relevant experience, or subcontractors that will perform major or critical aspects of the requirement when such information is relevant to the instant acquisition."[43] Notwithstanding this rule, GAO has held in several cases that an agency is free to weigh the relevance of the performance history of such parties when evaluating an offeror's proposal. Indeed, not surprisingly, GAO has found the provision permissive, in that agencies may exclude such parties' past performance information altogether from an offeror's evaluation.[44]

While offerors may help their past performance by choosing an exceptional subcontractor, this tactic can get the offeror only so far. Agencies are free to determine the relevance of a proposed subcontractor's past performance, segregate the proposed subcontractor's past performance from that of the offeror, and rate the offeror's proposal based on a comparison of the prime contractor and subcontractor levels of effort.[45] An agency also may simply choose not to credit an offeror with the past performance of its subcontractor, especially if the subcontractor's effort on the contract will be minimal.[46]

The general rule is that a prime contractor will be held responsible for the performance of its subcontractors. Thus, agencies may downgrade an offeror's proposal because of problems its subcontractor experienced on a prior contract, even if the offeror had little or nothing to do with the problems aside from being prime contractor. For instance, in *Federal Environmental Services,*[47] the protester claimed that its past performance had been improperly evaluated under a procurement for hazardous waste removal and disposal services, based primarily on the protester's performance on an earlier contract with the same agency. Under that contract, the protester had delivered hazardous waste to its subcontractor, which then improperly disposed of the waste. The protester argued that the agency's past performance evaluation improperly punished it for the misdeeds of its subcontractor and claimed that it had done everything possible to control the subcontractor.

GAO denied the protest, finding reasonable the agency's conclusion that the matter indicated problems with the protester's earlier performance: "A prime contractor is responsible for the performance of its subcontractors. . . . In view of the seriousness of the subcontractor's misconduct here—a fact not in dispute—the agency had a reasonable basis to conclude that [the protester] had not properly monitored and supervised its subcontractor."

Because a prospective subcontractor's past performance may be considered along with the offeror's when determining a past performance rating, agencies must allow an offeror the opportunity to respond to unfavorable evaluations concerning its prospective subcontractor's past performance, at least under circumstances where the offeror would be allowed to respond to its own past performance information (such as where the subcontractor's past performance information could be explained to materially enhance the potential for award). In *Alliant Techsystems, Inc.,*[48] the agency downgraded the protester's past performance evaluation because of problems with its major subcontractor's past performance but did not raise the issue with the offeror during discussions. The agency claimed that the protester was aware of and could have addressed its subcontractor's past performance history during negotiations but did not. GAO rejected the agency's reasoning and sustained the protest:

> *[Protester's] knowledge that [subcontractor] had performance problems under the prior contract does not abrogate the agency's obligation to inform [protester] of its serious concerns regarding [subcontractor's] involvement in the [contractor's] "team." In this respect, an offeror could reasonably expect during discussions to be apprised of evaluated deficiencies in its subcontractors' past performance that significantly impact the offeror's evaluation standing.*

The FAR states that agencies should consider in their past performance evaluation "key personnel who have relevant experience." GAO has allowed agencies following this regulation practically to base an offeror's entire past performance rating upon the experience of a single individual. In *SDS International,*[49] the protester contended that it was unreasonable for the awardee, a recently formed firm with no prior experience, to receive a high rating on past performance. GAO disagreed, however, finding that the background and role of the awardee's vice president, summarized in the awardee's proposal, were sufficient to warrant the high rating: "Based on [the awardee's] vice president's extensive, unique, recent, and relevant experience, and in view of the degree of his involvement in managing this effort, we conclude that the SSET reasonably assigned the firm a high rating under the past performance evaluation subfactor."

Agencies generally have discretion as to whether to evaluate an offeror's affiliates for past performance purposes. The affiliates must, however, have some role in the procurement or the offeror's management structure.

In *ST Aerospace Engines Pte. Ltd.,*[50] the protester had been downgraded because of the poor past performance of its affiliated companies. Because there was no indication that the affiliates would be involved in contract performance, however, GAO found the evaluation of their past performance with that of the protester to be unreasonable. GAO set out the following standard for determining whether one company's performance should be attributed to its affiliates: "[T]he agency must consider not simply whether the two companies are affiliated, but the nature and extent of the relationship between the two—in particular, whether the workforce, management, facilities, or other resources of one may affect contract performance by the other." See also *Universal Building Maintenance, Inc.,*[51] (finding the agency had improperly given the awardee added past performance credit for an affiliate's performance without evaluating the relationship between the companies).

CONCLUSION

Government personnel must abide closely to the letter and intent of the FAR and interpretations by GAO. Just as important, contractors must take an informed and proactive role when their performance is evaluated and when past performance information is used in source selection. Contractors must also have some familiarity with past performance evaluation case law, to recognize mistreatment when it occurs and to understand recourses to remedy such situations.

* * *

Formalizing the use of past performance information represents a significant step toward emulating commercial practices in federal procurement. Government agencies that commit to following these new standards will gain a more efficient procurement process, select high-quality contractors, and treat all offerors equitably. Gaining these results, however, requires that agencies and contractors work together to ensure that contractor performance is evaluated periodically and past performance information is used appropriately in source selection.

NOTES

1. GAO decision in *OSI Collection Services, Inc.*, B-286597.3, June 12, 2001, CPD ¶18.
2. FAR 42.1503(b). "Agency evaluation of contractor performance prepared under this subpart shall be provided to the contractor as soon as practicable after completion of the evaluation. Contractors shall be given a minimum of 30 days to submit comments, rebutting statements or additional information."
3. FAR 42.1503(b). "... Agencies shall provide for review at a level above the contracting officer to consider disagreements between the parties regarding the evaluation."
4. FAR 15.305(a)(2)(ii). "The solicitation shall describe the approach for evaluating past performance, including evaluating offerors with no relevant performance history, and shall provide offerors an opportunity to identify past or current contracts (including Federal, State, and local government and private) for efforts similar to the Government requirement. The solicitation shall also authorize offerors to provide information on problems encountered on the identified contracts and the offeror's corrective action."
5. FAR 15.306(b). "*Communications with offerors before establishment of the competitive range.* Communications are exchanges, between the Government and offerors, after receipt of proposals, leading to establishment of the competitive range. If a competitive range is to be established, these communications—

   "(1) Shall be limited to the offerors described in paragraphs (b)(1)(i) and (b)(1)(ii) of this section and—

   "(i) Shall be held with offerors whose past performance information is the determining factor preventing them from being placed within the competitive range. Such communications shall address adverse past performance information to which an offeror has not had a prior opportunity to respond; and "(ii) May only be held with those offerors (other than offerors under paragraph (b)(1)(i) of this section) whose exclusion from, or inclusion in, the competitive range is uncertain; . . ."

6. FAR 15.306(e). "*Limits on exchanges.* Government personnel involved in the acquisition shall not engage in conduct that— . . . (4) Reveals the names of individuals providing reference about an offeror's past performance; . . ."
7. *OSI Collection Services, Inc.,* B-286597.3, June 12, 2001, CPD ¶18.
8. *Power Connector, Inc.,* B-286875.2, 2001 CPD ¶39.
9. *Lynwood Machine & Engineering, Inc.,* B-285696, 2001, CPD ¶113.
10. *Olympus Bldg. Services, Inc.,* B-282887, 99-2 CPD ¶49.
11. *Northeast MEP Services, Inc.,* B-285963.5, 2001, CPD ¶28.
12. *Walsh Distrib., Inc.,* B-281904, 99-1 CPD ¶92.
13. See *SCIENTECH, Inc.,* B-277805.2, 98-1 CPD ¶33 (protest sustained where agency failed to consider another contract with same agency for same services).
14. FAR 42.1503(e). "Agencies shall use the past performance information in PPIRS that is within three years (six for construction and architect-engineer contracts) of the completion of performance of the evaluated contact or order."
15. FAR 15.305(a)(2)(I). "Past performance information is one indicator of an offeror's ability to perform the contract successfully. The currency and relevance of the information, source of the information, context of the data, and general trends in contractor's performance shall be considered."
16. *Chemical Demilitarization Associates,* B-277700, 98-1 CPD ¶171.
17. *Cessna Aircraft Co.,* B-261953.5, 96-1 CPD ¶132.
18. *Dragon Services, Inc.,* B-255354, 94-1 CPD ¶151.
19. *OneSource Energy Services, Inc.,* B-283445, 2000, CPD ¶109.
20. *A.G. Cullen Construction, Inc.,* B-284049.2, Feb. 22, 2000, CPD ¶45.
21. Ibid.
22. *Lynwood Machine & Engineering, Inc.,* op. cit., ¶113.
23. FAR 15.306(b). "*Communications with offerors before establishment of the competitive range.* Communications are exchanges, between the Government and offerors, after receipt of proposals, leading to establishment of the competitive range. If a competitive range is to be established, these communications—

   "(1) Shall be limited to the offerors described in paragraphs (b)(1)(i) and (b)(1)(ii) of this section and—

   "(i) Shall be held with offerors whose past performance information is the determining factor preventing them from being placed within the competitive range. Such communications shall address adverse past performance information to which an offeror has not had a prior opportunity to respond; and

   "(ii) May only be held with those offerors (other than offerors under paragraph (b)(1)(i) of this section) whose exclusion from, or inclusion in, the competitive range is uncertain;

"(2) May be conducted to enhance Government understanding of proposals; allow reasonable interpretation of the proposal; or facilitate the Government's evaluation process. Such communications shall not be used to cure proposal deficiencies or material omissions, materially alter the technical or cost elements of the proposal, and/or otherwise revise the proposal. Such communications may be considered in rating proposals for the purpose of establishing the competitive range;

"(3) Are for the purpose of addressing issues that must be explored to determine whether a proposal should be placed in the competitive range. Such communications shall not provide an opportunity for the offeror to revise its proposal, but may address—

"(i) Ambiguities in the proposal or other concerns (e.g., perceived deficiencies, weaknesses, errors, omissions, or mistakes (14.407)); and

"(ii) Information relating to relevant past performance; and

"(4) Shall address adverse past performance information to which the offeror has not previously had an opportunity to comment."

24. *The Community Partnership LLC,* B-286844, 2001, CPD ¶38.
25. *Digital Systems Group, Inc.,* B-286931, 2001, CPD ¶50.
26. *CRAssociates, Inc.,* B-282705.2, 2000, CPD ¶63.
27. *Maytag Aircraft Corp.,* B-287589, 2001, CPD ¶121.
28. *NAHB Research Center, Inc.,* B-278876, 98-1 CPD ¶150.
29. *Daun-Ray Casuals, Inc.,* B-255217, 94-2 CPD ¶42.
30. *Lynwood Machine & Engineering, Inc.,* op. cit., ¶113.
31. *Charleston Marine Containers, Inc.,* B- 283393, 99-2 CPD ¶84.
32. *Engineered Air Systems, Inc.,* B-283011, 99-2 CPD ¶63.
33. *W R Systems, Ltd.,* B-287477, 2001, CPD ¶118.
34. *Lynwood Machine & Engineering, Inc.,* op. cit., ¶113).
35. *RAMCOR Services Group, Inc.,* B-276633, 98-1 CPD ¶121.
36. *OSI Collection Services, Inc.* op. cit., ¶18.
37. *NAHB Research Center, Inc.,* B-278876, 98-1, CPD ¶150.
38. *American Development Corp.,* B-251876.4, 93-2, CPD ¶49.
39. *Green Valley Transportation, Inc.,* B-285283, 2000, CPD ¶133.
40. *National Aerospace Group, Inc.,* B-281958, 99-1, CPD ¶82.
41. FAR 15.305(a)(2)(iv). "In the case of an offeror without a record of relevant past performance or for whom information on past performance is not available, the offeror may not be evaluated favorably or unfavorably on past performance."
42. *TEAM Support Services, Inc.,* B-279379.2, 98-1, CPD ¶167.
43. FAR 15.305(a)(2)(iii).
44. *Olympus Bldg. Services, Inc.,* B-282887, 99-2, CPD ¶49.
45. *Oceanometrics, Inc.,* B-278647.2, 98-1, CPD ¶159.
46. *Acepex Management Corp.,* B-279135.5, 98-2, CPD ¶128.
47. *Federal Environmental Services,* B-260289, 95-1, CPD ¶261.

48. *Alliant Techsystems, Inc.,* B-260215.4, 95-2, CPD ¶79.
49. *SDS International,* B-285822, 2000, CPD ¶167.
50. *ST Aerospace Engines Pte. Ltd.,* B-275725, 97-1, CPD ¶161.
51. *Universal Building Maintenance, Inc.,* B-282456, 99-2, CPD ¶32. (For an abridged version of the GAO decision, see Appendix B, Example 4.8.)

APPENDIX A

ABBREVIATIONS AND ACRONYMS

A&E	architect-engineer
ABVM	Automated Best Value Model
ACASS	Architect-Engineer Contract Administration Support System
ACBIS	Army Contracting Business Intelligence System
ACO	Administrative Contracting Officer
AFMC-ASC	Air Force Material Command-Aeronautical System Center
AFSPC-SMC	Air Force Space Command-Space and Missile Center
AMCOM	Aviation and Missile Command
BAFO	best and final offer
CCASS	Construction Contractor Appraisal Support System
CCE	Central Contractor Registry
C-E LCMC	Communications-Electronics Life Cycle Management Command
COC	Certificate of Competency
COR	contracting officer's representative
COTR	contracting officer's technical representative
CPAR	Contractor Performance Assessment Report
CPARS	Contractor Performance Assessment Records System
CPCS	Competitive Performance and Continuous Surveillance Evaluation
CPS	Contractor Performance System
DISA	Defense Information Systems Agency
DLA	Defense Logistics Agency
DoD	Department of Defense
DPSC	Defense Personnel Support Center
EBB	electronic bulletin board

FAC	Federal Acquisition Circular
FAR	Federal Acquisition Regulation
FDC	Federal Data Corporation
FPDS-NG	Federal Procurement Data System–Next Generation
FTSC	Fleet Technical Support Center (Navy)
GAO	Government Accountability Office
GFP	government-furnished property
GSA	General Services Administration
HUD	Housing and Urban Development
ID/IQ	indefinite delivery/indefinite quantity
IG	Inspector General
IGE	independent government estimate
ISR	Individual Subcontracting Report
MDA	Menendez-Donnel & Associates
MOCAS	Mechanization of Contract Administration System (Air Force)
NASA	National Aeronautics and Space Administration
NAVAIR	Naval Air Systems Command
NAVSEA	Naval Sea Systems Command
NIH	National Institutes of Health
OFPP	Office of Federal Procurement Policy
PAR	Performance Assessment Report
PCI	Power Connector, Inc.
PCO	procuring contracting officer
PDM	Product Demonstration Model Plan
PPAIS	Past Performance Automated Information System
PPDB	Past Performance Database
PPIMS	Past Performance Management System
PPIRS	Past Performance Information Retrieval System
PTO	Patent & Trademark Office
RFP	request for proposals
RFQ	request for quotes
RFO	request for offers

SBA	Small Business Administration
SDB	small disadvantaged business
SEB	source evaluation board
SOW	statement of work
SPA	small purchase agreement
SPI	Schedule Performance Index
SSET	source selection evaluation team
SSA	source selection authority
SSR	Summary Subcontracting Report
TCG	The Communities Group
TEC	technical evaluation committee
USACE	U.S. Army Corps of Engineers

APPENDIX B

GAO DECISIONS

Example 2.1: The Relative Importance of Past Performance Can Be Diluted by Adding Prior Experience

GAO Decision (abridged)

Matter of: Si-Nor, Inc.

File: B-282064; B-282064.2

Date: May 25, 1999

DIGEST

Determination that higher-priced proposal rated higher under past performance subfactor (compared to protester's) offered best value to government cannot be determined reasonable where price was approximately twice as important as past performance under solicitation's evaluation scheme, and documentation of tradeoff decision does not explain why agency considered awardee's evaluation advantage under past performance sufficient to offset protester's lower offered price.

DECISION

Offers were to be evaluated based on (1) past performance/experience and (2) price/cost, which were to be approximately equal in weight. Past performance and experience also were to be approximately equal in weight. Award was to be made on a best value basis. Past performance was to be assessed to determine offerors' relative capability and trustworthiness, and thus their relative reliability to perform the contract requirements, and experience was to be evaluated to assess offerors' experience in performing work on similar refuse collection and disposal services contracts.

Si-Nor challenges the source selection decision on the basis that the agency failed to document why any advantage reflected in Eagle's higher past performance rating warranted payment of an $858,636.80 premium. Si-Nor believes its lower evaluated price warranted a determination that its proposal represented the best value to the government.

Source selection officials in negotiated procurements have broad discretion in determining the manner and extent to which they will make use of the technical and price evaluation results. Price/technical tradeoffs may be made, and the extent to which one may be sacrificed for the other is governed only by the tests of rationality and consistency with the established evaluation criteria. In deciding between competing proposals, the propriety of such a tradeoff turns not on the difference in technical scores or ratings per se, but on whether the selection official's judgment concerning the significance of that difference was reasonable and adequately justified in light of the RFP evaluation scheme. In this regard, where a price/technical tradeoff is made, the source selection decision must be documented, and the documentation must include the rationale for any business judgments and tradeoffs made, including the benefits associated with additional costs.

Based on our review of the record, we conclude that the determination to award to Eagle was not adequately justified. The tradeoff rationale set forth in the new selection official's revised source selection decision stated as follows:

> I have determined [Eagle]'s proposal to be of better value than [Si-Nor]'s proposal. Both offerors received a low risk rating for experience. However, [Eagle] received an outstanding past performance rating based on their past performance record, meeting all contract requirements and exceeding some of the contract requirements, compared to the satisfactory rating given [Si-Nor]. . . . I believe that [Eagle]'s outstanding past performance outweighs the lower price offered by [Si-Nor], a difference of $858,636.80 for the total cost.

This determination—as well as the record as a whole—includes no explanation for the agency's conclusion as required by FAR § 15.308. While the record clearly sets forth the agency's conclusion that Eagle's past performance rating was worth an $858,636.80 price premium, it includes no documentation, evidence, or explanation of the benefits that the agency associated with Eagle's superior past performance rating which would outweigh the additional price. This lack of documentation is significant in light of the fact that price was to be essentially twice as important as past performance under the stated evaluation scheme.[1] Absent a more detailed rationale, there simply is no way to determine whether the agency in fact accorded price this substantially greater weight. Further, such a rationale would provide evidence that the second tradeoff was conducted using the price premium reflecting the [small disadvantaged business] SDB preference ($858,636.80), rather than (as the protester alleges) continuing to use the premium without the SDB preference ($55,668), which the agency used in the erroneous initial tradeoff.

We conclude that the record does not establish that the Air Force's tradeoff decision was reasonable, and sustain the protest on this basis.

NOTE

1. Since past performance/experience and price/cost were to be given approximately equal weight, each was worth approximately 50 percent of the overall rating; since, within past performance/experience, each of the two components was approximately equal, past performance was worth approximately 25 percent of the overall rating.

Example 2.2: Basing Evaluation on Contracts Most Relevant to Solicitation

GAO Decision (abridged)

Matter of: Power Connector, Inc.

File: B-286875; B-286875.2

Date: February 14, 2001

DIGEST

In evaluating past performance under solicitation for quantity of leather, agency reasonably disregarded non-leather supply contracts in its evaluation of the protester, and limited its evaluation to leather contracts, on the basis that leather contracts were the most relevant.

DECISION

Power Connector, Inc. (PCI) protests the award of a contract to Day Leather Corporation under request for quotations (RFQ) No. 6200000119, issued by the Federal Bureau of Prisons, UNICOR, for leather to be used in manufacturing work gloves. PCI argues that UNICOR should have rejected Day's quotation as materially unbalanced, and that it misevaluated PCI's past performance.

The solicitation provided for a best value award of a fixed-price, indefinite-quantity contract for a base year, with four 1-year option periods. The quotations were to be evaluated against three factors, listed in descending order of importance—past performance, compliance with technical specifications, and price; the past performance and technical factors combined were significantly more important than price. RFQ at 39. In order to establish compliance with the technical specifications, vendors were required to submit samples and lab test results for evaluation on a pass/fail basis. Regarding past performance, vendors were required to complete a business management questionnaire listing, among other things, from three to five references for previous similar contracts performed within the past three years. Prices were to be quoted on a per-foot basis for estimated quantities, with the evaluation to be based on the total extended prices for the base and option years. Four quotations, including PCI's and Day's, were received and found to comply with the technical specifications. Day's price ($9,720,000) was low, and PCI's ($9,975,000) second low. Agency Report (AR) at 3. Day was rated overall excellent for past performance based on three references for leather contracts (two excellent ratings, one good), and PCI was rated good based on three references for leather contracts (one excellent, two good ratings). The contracting officer selected Day for award, citing its superior past performance.

PCI maintains that Day's quotation should have been rejected as materially unbalanced because it quoted $1.36 per foot for the base year and $1.28 for each of the option years, despite the fact that the solicitation requests the same item for each year.

The concept of unbalanced pricing has only limited application in the context of a procurement under which the government's primary objective is the best overall value rather than the lowest price,...we apply the concept of unbalancing in such cases only where price constitutes the basis for the source selection. Here, although the award was ultimately made to the low-priced vendor, price was listed as the least important award factor, and the solicitation specifically provided that the technical and past performance factors were significantly more important than price. In addition, while in her source selection decision the contracting officer recognized that Day's price was low, it is clear that price was not the basis for her award decision. Rather, the source selection decision states, "In conclusion, it has been determined that award should be made to Day Leather Corporation due to the experience they have with the leather business." Since technical and past performance factors were more important than price, and since price did not dictate the award decision, the concept of unbalancing does not apply, and this argument could not provide a basis for sustaining the protest. We therefore do not address it further.

PCI listed four past performance references in its business management questionnaire, two for leather contracts and two for communications components contracts. After concluding that the communications components contracts were not similar to the leather supply requirement here, the contracting officer checked UNICOR's database and found that PCI had a current contract to supply leather to UNICOR. Since she viewed this contract as similar to the solicited requirement, she used it—instead of one of the communications components contracts—as PCI's third past performance reference. Based on the ratings for these three contracts—one excellent, two good—the contracting officer evaluated PCI as overall good for past performance. PCI challenges this rating, asserting that the contracting officer improperly failed to consider the two communications components contract references listed in its quotation; it concludes that, had she done so, PCI would have received all excellent references, would have been rated overall excellent for past performance, and would have been in line for the award.[1]

We review an agency's evaluation of vendors' submissions (such as the quotation at issue here) to ensure that it is fair, reasonable and consistent with the evaluation criteria stated in the solicitation. In evaluating past performance, an agency has discretion to determine the scope of the vendors' performance history to be considered, provided that it evaluates all submissions on the same basis and consistent with the solicitation. An agency properly may base its evaluation on contracts it believes are most relevant to the solicitation..., it has discretion to consider information other than that provided by the vendors, and need not consider all references a vendor submits.

UNICOR's actions fall within the above standard. The contracting officer sought to identify the most relevant contracts for purposes of assessing PCI's past performance and, in doing so, considered a relevant contract not listed in PCI's quotation and disregarded two listed contracts which were not similar to the current requirement. This was reasonable, and well within the agency's discretion. Moreover, although we think the logic of evaluating similar contracts to assess past performance is obvious, the RFQ requirement that firms provide references for "similar" contracts put PCI and the other vendors on notice that the agency wanted to evaluate similar contracts; thus, the agency's reliance on PCI's ongoing leather contract was fully consistent with the evaluation scheme.

PCI argues that UNICOR's failure to consider its two listed communications components contract references constituted disparate treatment, since the agency did consider a dissimilar contract (for fiberboard) in evaluating the past performance of another vendor (not the awardee). The agency acknowledges that it considered dissimilar contracts in evaluating that other vendor's past performance, but explains that it did so only because they were the only contracts the vendor listed, and a search indicated no other similar contracts. The contracting officer rated this vendor overall good for past performance because all three references rated the vendor good. Contracting Officer's Declaration at 5. However, she indicated on the evaluation form that the contracts were not for similar items, see Past Performance Evaluation, and also concluded in making the selection decision that, due to the vendor's lack of experience on similar contracts, an award to that firm would result in an unacceptable performance risk.

We find nothing unfair or otherwise improper in the contracting officer's actions. Her different approach to evaluating PCI and the other vendor reflected those firms' different circumstances, not improper disparate treatment. In evaluating both firms, the contracting officer considered similar contracts to the extent possible, consistent with the RFQ reference to "similar" contracts. Similar (leather supply) contracts, including the one she discovered in the agency's records, were available for PCI, so she considered those in PCI's evaluation. Since the other vendor had not performed leather supply contracts, she could not consider similar contracts to evaluate its past performance. Thus, she considered the firm's dissimilar contracts, and then penalized it in the evaluation by finding that the lack of past similar contracts made the performance risk too great to permit award to the firm. In our view, nothing in this record indicates that the treatment of PCI was unreasonable.[2]

PCI also asserts that two UNICOR employees—the chief of procurement and the general counsel—told PCI that it was appropriate to include the communications components contracts as past performance references for this solicitation.[3] Both employees deny discussing with PCI the references it intended to submit. Declarations of the Procurement Chief and General Counsel. In any case, however, PCI was not downgraded in the evaluation for listing these contracts and, moreover, this advice would not diminish the contracting officer's discretion to consider the most relevant contracts in evaluating PCI's past performance.

The protest is denied.

NOTES

1. PCI also argues that UNICOR should have engaged in clarifications or discussions with it on the issue of past performance. See Federal Acquisition Regulation § 15.306. However, UNICOR did not find PCI's past performance deficient or unclear in any way, and did not receive adverse past performance information that PCI had not had an opportunity to address. Under these circumstances, there was no requirement for discussions or clarifications with PCI.
2. PCI argues that the agency could not consider performance risk in the evaluation because it was not specified as an evaluation factor in the RFQ. However, risk is an element of quotation evaluation that may be considered even where it is not specifically listed as an evaluation factor.
3. PCI maintains that it appears from the record that two references for one of its listed prior contracts were not advised that they could rate PCI's performance excellent, and that their rating of PCI's past performance as good therefore did not accurately reflect the level of their satisfaction with its performance. However, the two references have stated that they knew the excellent rating was available, but chose to rate PCI good, and the contracting officer states that she informed all references of each possible rating, including excellent.

Example 3.1: Failure to Comply with RFP Instructions (#1)

GAO Decision (abridged)

Matter of: Menendez-Donnell & Associates

File: B-286599

Date: January 16, 2001

DIGEST

Agency reasonably found protester's proposal technically unacceptable under experience and past performance evaluation criterion, where record shows that protester failed to submit required detailed information showing that its proposed key subcontractors had previously performed contracts similar to the solicited effort; offerors have an affirmative duty to prepare an adequately written proposal.

DECISION

Proposals were to be evaluated on the basis of two technical considerations—experience and past performance of the prime contractor and key subcontractors on similar projects (the more important factor), and qualifications and past experience of key personnel.

Regarding the experience and past performance of the prime and subcontractors criterion, offerors were advised that a key subcontractor was one that would contribute 20 percent or more to project completion. In order to demonstrate experience and past performance, offerors were required to provide information on three prior similar contracts for the prime and each key subcontractor. Similarly, under the qualifications and past experience of key personnel criterion, offerors were required to provide information on three similar projects for each key employee to show that they were qualified to perform the requirement. The agency reserved the right to evaluate proposals and make award on the basis of initial offers, without conducting discussions.

Since an agency's evaluation is dependent upon the information furnished in a proposal, it is the offeror's burden to submit an adequately written proposal for the agency to evaluate, especially where, as here, the offeror is specifically on notice that the agency intends to make award based on initial proposals without discussions. An agency reasonably may reject a proposal for informational deficiencies that prevent the agency from fully evaluating the proposal.

We note initially that, since the record confirms that the prior contracts MDA listed to establish its past performance were not similar to the current requirement, MDA Proposal, Tab 2, at 1-3, the agency reasonably determined that MDA's prior contracts did not provide a basis for assessing the firm's past performance. However, it appears this aspect of MDA's past performance warranted a neutral, rather than an unacceptable, rating; under FAR § 15.305(a)(2)(iv), where an offeror does not have a record of relevant past performance, the offeror may not be evaluated either favorably or unfavorably. On the other hand, even if this is the case, and even if we also agreed with MDA that the agency should have clarified its experience or obtained additional information from its own records, as discussed below, GSA reasonably rated the proposal unacceptable based on MDA's failure to establish adequate experience and past performance for its subcontractors and key employees.

MDA's proposal generally refers to contracts which appear to be relevant and which were performed by MDA with its proposed subcontractors. However, detailed information necessary to assess the nature and relevance of those contracts was not included in the proposal. For example, with respect to the two primary asphalt subcontractors MDA proposed to use, the proposal states that MDA has ongoing projects with each contractor which are similar to the solicited requirement. However, the proposal omitted detailed information—such as, for example, the contract number, a contact point, and a description of the project—despite the express RFP requirement that such information be provided. RFP, Standard Form 1442, at 4.

To the extent MDA contends that GSA was required to assign a neutral rating to its proposal based on the absence of information relating to its key subcontractors, we disagree. Although FAR §15.305(a)(2)(iv) requires an agency to assign a neutral rating where past performance information is not "available," here, the protester's proposal represented that its proposed subcontractors are engaged in projects that would illustrate their performance capability. The information thus was available, but MDA chose not to present the information in its proposal, in direct contravention of the terms of the RFP. In our view, an offeror cannot simply choose to withhold past performance information—and thereby obtain a neutral rating—where the solicitation expressly requires that the information be furnished, and where the information is readily available to the offeror.

In any case, notwithstanding the evaluation under the experience and past performance factor, as noted, the agency also rated MDA's proposal unacceptable based on its determination that MDA's proposed key personnel lacked experience on projects similar to the solicited effort. MDA does not dispute the agency's conclusion, and we find nothing in the record that calls the evaluation in this regard into question.

The protest is denied.

Example 3.2: Failure to Comply with RFP Instructions (#2)

GAO Decision (abridged)

Matter of: Boland Well Systems, Inc.

File: B-287030

Date: March 7, 2001

DIGEST

Agency reasonably rated protester's past performance as "neutral with unknown confidence" where record shows that protester failed to submit in its proposal required detailed information showing that it had performed contracts relevant to the solicited effort.

DECISION

Boland Well Systems, Inc. protests the award of a contract to International Research and Development, Inc. (IRD) under request for proposals (RFP) No. F24604-01-D-0004, issued by the Department of the Air Force for the replacement of livestock gates at the Malmstrom Air Force Base missile complex in Montana. Boland asserts that the Air Force did not properly consider its past performance.

The RFP stated that the purpose of the performance risk assessment was to identify and review relevant present and past performance and then make an overall risk assessment of an offeror's ability to perform the effort. The agency reserved the right to award a contract to other than the offeror submitting the lowest evaluated price and to award to a higher priced offeror with a better performance risk rating. The RFP provided that price and performance risk were equal in weight and that one could be traded off against the other. The RFP required offerors to submit detailed past performance information to include aspects of the contract deemed relevant to the proposed effort; type of contract; and name, address, and telephone number for the program manager, administrative contracting officer, procuring contracting officer, and contract manager. The agency reserved the right to make award on the basis of initial proposals without conducting discussions.

Boland submitted the overall low price. Boland's past performance submission contained ten references. Past performance questionnaires were sent and four responses concerning Boland were received. While the ratings Boland received from its references ranged from satisfactory to very good, all of the responses involved contracts that were for landscaping projects and that were valued significantly less than the government estimate for this contract of $320,000. Since

Boland's prior contracts for landscaping work showed no relevance to the type of work—gate replacement—required by the solicitation, Boland's proposal received a rating of neutral/unknown confidence.

IRD submitted the second low price. Under the past performance factor, IRD's proposal received a rating of exceptional/high confidence. The past performance information submitted by IRD was for the "exact same type of work required by the solicitation." Pricing Memorandum at 3. Although Boland's total price was approximately $40,000 less than IRD's, the agency determined that IRD's proposal represented the best value to the government based on IRD's exceptional/high confidence past performance rating. Accordingly, the agency awarded the contract to IRD.

The record shows that the prior contracts listed by Boland were all landscaping projects. In our view, the agency reasonably concluded that the landscaping contracts were not relevant to the current requirement for gate replacements. Further, the agency reports that prior to award the cognizant agency official attempted to verify the company president's prior gate installation experience under a prior contract. The agency advises that the agency official could not find that individual's name in the employment records for contracts awarded by the base for gate installation.

In sum, Boland simply did not provide in its proposal or at any time during the conduct of the procurement evidence establishing that the company had relevant past performance. While the protester argues that the requirement is simple and that any construction worker could perform it, the solicitation specifically advised offerors that award would be based on the [performance price tradeoff] PPT technique and that a performance risk assessment would be performed to identify and review relevant present and past performance in order to make an overall risk assessment of an offeror's ability to perform the requirement. In accordance with the solicitation, the agency performed a performance/price tradeoff and determined that the higher-priced proposal of IRD, which had a better performance risk rating than the protester, represented the best value to the government. On this record, we have no basis to question the agency's evaluation of proposals or source selection decision.

The protest is denied.

Example 3.3: PPIRS Accessible to All Agencies

GAO Decision (abridged)

Matter of: Guam Shipyard

File: B-311321; B-311321.2

Date: June 9, 2008

DIGEST

Protest of agency's evaluation and award decision is denied where record shows they were reasonable and consistent with the terms of the solicitation and applicable procurement rules.

DECISION

The RFP, set aside for small businesses, anticipated the award of a fixed-price contract to the firm that submitted the technically acceptable proposal deemed to offer the best value to the agency considering two evaluation factors approximately equal in importance, price reasonableness and performance risk. The performance risk factor was [composed] of two subfactors also of approximately equal importance, past performance (including technical quality, schedule, and management) and price realism. The RFP advised that the evaluation of past performance would be subjective and based mainly on performance evaluations available in the agency's automated Past Performance Information Retrieval System (PPIRS), information obtained from the offeror's past performance references, and information available in local files. Each offeror was to submit past performance reference information for relevant contracts that the firm wanted to be considered. The RFP advised that the agency might not contact all of the references, and emphasized that the offeror was to ensure that references could be readily contacted, would be cooperative, and would provide performance information for evaluation.

Under the past performance subfactor, the firm's proposal was evaluated as marginal based on an unfavorable Contract Performance Assessment Report (CPAR) in the agency's automated PPIRS regarding the firm's recent performance of similar work for the agency. The CPAR was the only performance report available in the PPIRS, and the only past performance information considered by the evaluators for the firm since the contract reference Guam had provided for two other contracts failed to respond to the agency's email request for past performance information.

Guam protests the agency's evaluation of its past performance as marginal, contending that it has received accolades for performance of similar work in the past. The protester contends that if the agency had received information regarding its past performance from the reference Guam identified in its proposal, the information would have been favorable; in this regard, the protester questions the adequacy of the agency's attempt to contact the reference by email, since the agency has not demonstrated that the email message was in fact received by the reference. The protester also challenges the agency's reliance on the adverse CPAR regarding an ongoing Guam contract with the Navy for similar work. Guam has not refuted the substance of the performance problems described in that CPAR, either in its protest or when it had the opportunity to comment on the CPAR findings before the report became final in the PPIR.

In conducting a past performance evaluation, an agency has discretion to determine the scope of the offerors' performance histories to be considered, provided all proposals are evaluated on the same basis and consistent with the solicitation requirements. An agency is only required to use reasonable effort to contact an offeror's references, and is not required to make multiple attempts to contact a firm's past performance references.

Here, the agency points out that the past performance reference listed by the protester failed to respond to the agency's email inquiry for relevant survey information. [I]n light of the RFP's emphasis on the importance of the offeror providing reliable contact information (including, as was used here, email addresses) and ensuring cooperation from its references, we think the agency's email inquiry was an adequate effort to contact the reference; the failure of the reference to respond does not show that the agency's effort was inadequate (particularly in view of Guam's apparent failure to ensure, or, at a minimum, encourage its reference to cooperate) or that the past performance evaluation was improper.

[T]he agency, consistent with the terms of the RFP, considered a comprehensive, recent, and relevant CPAR that rated the firm's past performance as marginal and showed that Guam had problems with following procedures, safety issues, accidents, obtaining material, scheduling, manpower, and management. Guam had an earlier opportunity to respond to the information reported in the CPAR and, despite seeking an extension of time to do so, never refuted the CPAR, which then became a final report in the PPIRs and, in accordance with the terms of the RFP, was properly considered as part of the firm's past performance evaluation.

In light of the reasonableness of the performance risk assessment here, including the recent marginal past performance by the firm, we find no basis to question the agency's determination that the potential savings offered by Guam's very high risk proposal is not worth the increased risk to the government.

Example 4.1: Performance Problems Are Not Necessarily Adverse Past Performance

GAO Decision (abridged)

Matter of: The Communities Group

File: B-283147 (abridged)

Date: October 12, 1999

DIGEST

Protest that agency did not consider recent performance problems of subcontractor of awardee in evaluating past performance is denied where the problems were under investigation at time of past performance evaluation and record shows that the agency was favorably impressed by the subcontractor's prompt and appropriate response to the problems.

DECISION

The Communities Group (TCG) protests the award of a contract to Management Solutions of America, Inc. under RFP No. R-OPC-21303, issued by the Department of Housing and Urban Development (HUD), for real property inspections. TCG contends that HUD failed to conduct meaningful discussions and properly evaluate proposals.

We deny the protest.

...TCG contends that HUD, in rating Management Solutions' past performance, improperly failed to consider the negative past performance of the firm's subcontractor, MTB Investments, Inc., on a current HUD contract for similar services. TCG asserts that MTB, which had been proposed to perform a substantial portion of Management Solutions' contract, had to replace 20 of 100 inspectors for poor performance under a current HUD contract for similar services; that as a result of this performance the MTB had to reinspect approximately 89 sites; and that MTB's rejection rate was three to six times higher than TCG's under its current contract.

As with proposals in general, it is not the function of our Office to evaluate offerors' past performance de novo. Rather, we examine the agency's evaluation only to ensure that it was reasonable and consistent with the stated evaluation criteria and applicable statutes and regulations, since assessing the relative merit of competing offerors' past performance (and of their proposals overall) is primarily a matter of administrative discretion. A protester's mere disagreement with the agency's judgment does not establish that the evaluation was unreasonable.

HUD reports that MTB's past performance information was viewed favorably because the company had a significant amount of direct experience conducting HUD-certified inspections of HUD properties and that the performance problems alleged by the protester were not before the agency at the time past performance was evaluated because this matter was being investigated. Further, HUD advises that the protester's characterization of the alleged problems is inaccurate and that consideration of the matter would not have resulted in a negative past performance rating because MTB undertook prompt and appropriate remedial action. In this regard, HUD advises that it was discovered that a non-licensed individual was conducting inspections on properties using the credentials of a HUD-certified inspector employed by MTB, and that when apprised of the problem MTB took the prompt corrective action of reinspecting 83 properties, terminating the MTB employee involved, and reporting this matter to the relevant state authorities for appropriate disciplinary action.

We have reviewed the protester's allegations, as well as the agency's detailed response, and cannot say that Management Solutions' past performance rating was unreasonably high in light of MTB's past performance. As indicated, the incident had not been investigated when the past performance evaluation was done; in any event, the record indicates that TCG's version of MTB's problems is inaccurate and that HUD was favorably impressed with MTB's prompt and appropriate response when the problem was discovered. We note that under the technical evaluation plan employed to evaluate proposals under this RFP an offeror could still receive a high rating for past performance so long as problems identified during performance were handled to the satisfaction of the client.

The protest is denied.

Example 4.2: Clarifying Adverse Past Performance Information During Discussion

GAO Decision (abridged)

Matter of: Dynacs Engineering Company, Inc.

File: B-284234

Date: March 17, 2000

DIGEST

In evaluating awardee's past performance, procuring agency reasonably decided not to consider information that awardee had experienced transition problems in performing an ongoing contract, where awardee explained that performance problems in fact were not the result of its actions, and cognizant contracting officials had not actually assigned awardee a negative performance rating at the time of past performance evaluation.

DECISION

Dynacs Engineering Company, Inc. protests the award of a contract to Federal Data Corporation (FDC) under RFP No. 3-094978, issued by the National Aeronautics and Space Administration (NASA) for the development and operation of international space station facilities, and the development and performance of microgravity experiments. Dynacs protests that NASA misevaluated its and the awardee's proposals, held improper discussions with the awardee, and conducted an inadequate cost/price/technical tradeoff.[1]

We deny the protest.

The solicitation provided for proposals to be evaluated under three equal factors—mission suitability, cost/price and past performance…

The solicitation provided that the past performance of the offerors and any subcontractors and teaming partners would be assigned an adjectival rating of superior, satisfactory or unsatisfactory, based on their demonstrated accomplishment of work of similar magnitude, scope and complexity to the work required by the RFP. Dynacs argues that the agency, in assigning FDC a superior rating, unreasonably failed to consider negative past performance information regarding FDC's performance of an ongoing NASA contract at the Glenn Research Center (GRC). In this regard, during the first round of discussions, before offerors submitted FPR-1, the [source evaluation board] SEB learned that the contracting officer's representative (COR) administering that contract intended to give FDC a negative performance rating for its transition effort. COS, Jan. 7, 2000, at 7.

We review an agency's evaluation of an offeror's past performance only to ensure that it was reasonable and consistent with the stated evaluation criteria and applicable statutes and regulations, since assessing the relative merits of competing offerors' past performance (and of their proposals overall) is primarily a matter of administrative discretion. A protester's mere disagreement with the agency's judgment does not establish that the evaluation was unreasonable. The Communities Group, B-283147, Oct. 12, 1999, 99-2 CPD ¶ 101, at 5, 6.

The evaluation in this area was reasonable. After learning of the COR's potential negative rating, NASA asked FDC to respond to this information. FDC did so, both explaining its position and sending the SEB a copy of the response it had sent to the COR. According to FDC's response, the transition effort did not go well for reasons other than FDC's actions; FDC maintained that the follow-on contractor caused many of the problems. Letters from FDC to NASA (Sept. 10 and 13, 1999). Since the COR had not actually assigned FDC a negative final rating, the SEB considered the issue unresolved and did not use it to downgrade FDC in the past performance evaluation. COS, Jan. 7, 2000, at 8. We see nothing improper in the SEB's actions. Since the COR had not provided a final rating by the time the SEB was completing its past performance evaluation, and FDC provided a response in which it denied that it was responsible for the difficult transition, it was reasonable not to automatically attribute the problems to FDC. We think the SEB therefore reasonably could conclude that the information available did not support a finding of deficient past performance, and thus did not warrant downgrading FDC. See The Communities Group, supra.

The protest is denied.

NOTE

1. In its initial protest, Dynacs also asserted that the agency improperly penalized Dynacs twice for cost realism, failed to hold meaningful discussions with Dynacs, applied unstated evaluation criteria, and gave cost/price undue weight in the cost/price/technical tradeoff. The agency addressed each of these issues in its report, and Dynacs did not rebut the agency's arguments in its report comments. Accordingly, we consider these issues abandoned.

Example 4.3: Clarifying Adverse Past Performance Information Where Award Will Be Made Without Discussions

GAO Decision (abridged)

Matter of: A. G. Cullen Construction, Inc.

File: B-284049.2

Date: February 22, 2000

DIGEST

Where award is to be made without discussions, contracting officer must give an offeror an opportunity to clarify adverse past performance information to which the offeror has not previously had an opportunity to respond only where there clearly is a reason to question the validity of the past performance information; in the absence of a clear basis to question the past performance information, contracting officer has discretion, short of acting in bad faith, not to ask for clarifications.

DECISION

The RFP contemplated the award, without discussions, of a fixed-price construction contract to the offeror whose proposal represented the best value to the government.

Cullen argues that it should have received the award because it submitted the lowest-priced, technically acceptable proposal.

The solicitation here did not provide for selection of the lowest-priced, technically acceptable proposal; it provided for award to the offeror whose proposal represented the best value to the government based on a price/past performance tradeoff, with past performance significantly more importance than price. Thus, it was consistent with the RFP's evaluation scheme for the agency to select other than the lowest-priced proposal where it determined that another offeror's combination of past performance and price represented a better overall value to the government.

Here, we see nothing unreasonable or inconsistent with the evaluation criteria in the agency's determination that DiCicco's combination of past performance and price represented the best value to the government. The RFP provided that past performance would be significantly more important than price in the award decision, and DiCicco's proposal, which was only about 5 percent higher than Cullen's in price, received a higher rating than Cullen's under every past performance subfactor, as well as overall. Of particular significance to the contracting officer was DiCicco's exceptional rating under the timely performance subfactor, completion of the project on schedule being of paramount importance to the agency due to the fact the building was to remain occupied during the work. Given that past performance was to be significantly more important than price in the best value determination, that DiCicco received a better past performance rating than Cullen, and that the difference in price between the two offers was relatively small, we find no basis upon which to question the propriety of the agency's best value determination.

Cullen argues that it should have been given the opportunity to address the past performance information that the agency obtained from one of its references.

With regard specifically to clarifications concerning adverse past performance information to which the offeror has not previously had an opportunity to respond, we think that, for the exercise of discretion to be reasonable, the contracting officer must give the offeror an opportunity to respond where there clearly is a reason to question the validity of the past performance information, for example, where there are obvious inconsistencies between a reference's narrative comments and the actual ratings the reference gives the offeror. In the absence of such a clear basis to question the past performance information, we think that, short of acting in bad faith, the contracting officer reasonably may decide not to ask for clarifications.

Applying this standard here, we think that the contracting officer reasonably exercised his discretion in deciding not to communicate with Cullen regarding the adverse past performance information received from one of Cullen's references. There is nothing on the face of the reference that would create concerns about its validity. Given the permissive language of FAR § 15.306(a)(2), the fact that Cullen may wish to respond to the reference does not give rise to a requirement that the contracting officer give Cullen an opportunity to do so.

In any event, it is clear that Cullen was not prejudiced by the agency's decision not to ask for clarifications regarding the reference. As noted above, Cullen received an overall rating of very good, based on its ratings of very good in three of the subfactors, and satisfactory in the remaining two subfactors, including the one area—timely performance—in which it received the negative reference at issue. Even if its rating improved in that one area to the highest possible rating—exceptional—Cullen would still have scores of very good and satisfactory in the other four areas. Under these circumstances, we see no basis to conclude that Cullen's overall rating of very good would improve even if its rating in the one subfactor at issue were increased.

The protest is denied.

Example 4.4: If an Offeror Fails to Respond to Questions About Past Problems, You May Assume That the Problems Have Not Been Corrected

GAO Decision (abridged)

Matter of: Smith of Galeton Gloves, Inc.

File: B-271686

Date: July 24, 1996

DIGEST

Agency's evaluation of protester's past performance as marginally acceptable was reasonable where the record shows that the protester was delinquent on two contracts, and did not—in response to direct discussion questions—submit any evidence to explain these delinquencies.

DECISION

Under the past performance evaluation factor, the agency gave Nationwide's proposal an "acceptable" rating, which according to the RFP's definition meant that the "offeror's record of past performance demonstrates an . . . overall record of timely delivery." Although Nationwide completed one of the referenced contracts one month late, the remaining 11 had been completed on time or ahead of schedule. The agency's investigation also showed that the sole incident of delinquent contract performance occurred because, in compliance with the contract's warranty provision, Nationwide had been required to replace a small number of delivered gloves because of product defects. Because three other contracts for the same heavy duty glove had been successfully and timely performed without any quality or delinquency problem, the agency evaluators determined that, on balance, Nationwide's past performance record was acceptable.

In contrast, the agency rated Smith's proposal as "marginally acceptable" under the past performance factor. In its proposal, Smith had listed two contracts—neither of which could be considered by the agency since they did not fall within the prior two contract years, as required by the RFP. Nevertheless, the agency researched its own files and discovered two glove contracts Smith had performed for DPSC. Smith completed one of the contracts two years late. The agency evaluators also noted that minor quality problems occurred throughout Smith's performance of this contract. The second contract was completed 11 weeks late; although five of these weeks were deemed partially excusable as a result of a defective specification, the remaining six weeks were deemed inexcusable by DPSC since once the proper supplies to manufacture the gloves in accordance with the new specifications were delivered to Smith, it nonetheless delayed commencing production. As a result of these two delinquencies, and because no other contract references were provided, the agency determined—in accordance with the "marginally acceptable" rating definition set forth in the RFP—that Smith's "record of past performance demonstrate[d] a less than acceptable commitment to customer satisfaction and timely delivery."

On February 5, 1996, the contracting officer issued discussion letters to each offeror. Of significance to this protest, the contracting officer advised Smith that it had received a [product demonsration model] PDM rating of "acceptable" and that the missing identification and bar-code labels were deemed deficiencies in its offer. In the letter, the contracting officer advised Smith that to correct the label deficiencies, Smith could either submit a new PDM or certify that the firm would correct the deficiencies; the letter further apprised Smith that "by submitting a new PDM, your rating . . . for this factor may be upgraded or downgraded as necessary. By certifying that the above defects will be corrected, your present evaluation will not change."

Smith also was informed that it had received a "marginally acceptable" rating under the past performance technical factor; to remedy this deficiency, Smith was asked to "address the delinquency and quality problems experienced" on the two DPSC contracts, and to provide "past performance information for your commercial customers." Smith also was advised that the two contracts listed as references in its technical proposal could not be evaluated as they fall outside the RFP's two-year time frame.

Nationwide received a discussion letter similar to Smith's; as in the case of the protester, Nationwide was apprised of its PDM rating and advised that submitting a new PDM with corrected deficiencies could raise or lower its "acceptable" rating, while certifying correction of the label deficiency would not change the evaluation rating.

Both Nationwide and Smith submitted best and final offers (BAFO) by the February 8 BAFO due date. For its BAFO, Nationwide submitted a new PDM—with all the required labels; since Nationwide's PDM complied with every technical requirement, its PDM score was raised to highly acceptable, in accordance with the terms of the RFP. Nationwide's past performance rating remained unchanged—acceptable. Overall, Nationwide's proposal was rated acceptable.

Smith did not submit a new PDM; instead, as permitted by the agency's instructions, Smith provided a certification that the label deficiencies would be corrected during production. Consequently, its PDM rating of acceptable was not changed. Although the agency had invited Smith to address the identified contract delinquencies and/or submit additional reference information from commercial customers, Smith did not provide any additional information regarding the past performance factor in its BAFO. Therefore, Smith's proposal past performance rating remained unchanged as marginally acceptable. Overall, Smith's proposal was rated marginally acceptable.

The evaluation of technical proposals is primarily the responsibility of the contracting agency since the agency is responsible for defining its needs and the best method of accommodating them, and it must bear the burden of any difficulties resulting from a defective evaluation. It is not a function of our Office to reevaluate proposals; rather, we review the agency's evaluation of proposals only to ensure that it was fair, reasonable, and consistent with the evaluation criteria stated in the solicitation. Where a solicitation requires the evaluation of offerors' past performance, an agency has discretion to determine the scope of the offerors' performance histories to be considered, provided all proposals are evaluated on the same basis and consistent with the solicitation requirements. From our review of the record, there is no basis to object to the agency's evaluation of Smith's past performance.

First, while the RFP limited offerors to submitting past performance references for the preceding two years, the record shows that Smith disregarded these instructions and submitted two references for contracts performed prior to the two-year time limit set forth in the RFP. Next, although the agency identified and asked Smith to address its delinquent contract performance on the two DPSC contracts, Smith failed to provide any additional discussion or alternate contract references to alleviate the agency's concerns.

Given the agency's discussion letter, which clearly placed Smith on notice that the firm needed to furnish additional evidence to improve its past performance rating, and Smith's failure to respond—in any fashion—to the agency's past performance concerns, we think the agency reasonably found Smith's proposal marginally acceptable under the past performance factor.

Smith contends that it cannot be downgraded under the past performance factor without referral of the matter to the SBA for consideration under that agency's COC proceedings. Referral to the SBA is not required here. It is true that where an agency finds that a small business is nonresponsible, the agency is required to refer the matter to the SBA for consideration under the COC procedures. In a negotiated procurement, SBA referral is mandatory where the solicitation includes, as a matter to be evaluated on a pass/fail basis, a criterion that is traditionally a responsibility-type factor, and the contracting agency has determined that a small business's proposal should be rejected for failure to "pass" that criterion; this is so because the agency is viewed as having made a nonresponsibility determination notwithstanding its use of and reliance on a technical evaluation criterion.

The requirement for referral does not apply here. While the past performance criterion is a responsibility-type factor, it was not applied on a pass/fail basis. Rather, each proposal—including Smith's—was comparatively evaluated under this factor, and assigned a comparative adjectival rating. That means that the agency did not in essence make a responsibility determination, but simply integrated its relative assessment of past performance into its overall determination of which proposal was most advantageous to the government. In such circumstances, there was no need for referral to the SBA.

In sum, we conclude that the agency's evaluation of Smith's proposal as marginally acceptable under the past performance factor, and acceptable under the PDM factor, is unobjectionable. Further, we see no basis to question the agency's evaluation of Nationwide's proposal. Both Nationwide and Smith were given the same choice for remedying virtually identical PDM label defects. Nationwide—as a result of its decision to submit a new, fully compliant PDM—reasonably earned a highly acceptable rating, and fully demonstrated its commitment to providing a quality glove insert.

In contrast, Smith, instead of producing a new PDM, chose to certify that the label deficiencies would be remedied in the production stage—resulting in no change to its acceptable rating. With regard to past performance, Nationwide also demonstrated its technical superiority; a detailed list of 12 contracts was provided, demonstrating timely—and even expedited—compliance with all quality and delivery terms for 11 of the references. Smith, on the other hand, made no attempt to alleviate the agency's reasonable concerns about its performance under its two prior contracts.

Where, as here, a solicitation emphasizes that technical quality is more important than price, an agency may reasonably decide to award to a technically superior awardee for a slightly higher price premium. Given that the record supports the agency's conclusion that Nationwide's offer represented a superior demonstration of product quality and commitment to timely delivery, we see no basis to object to the agency's decision that Nationwide's offer represented the best value to the government and warranted payment of a 10-percent price premium.

Example 4.5: Filing of Contract Claims Is Not Poor Performance

GAO Decision (abridged)

Matter of: AmClyde Engineered Products Company, Inc.

File: B-282271; B-282271.2

Date: June 21, 1999

DIGEST

Agency reasonably evaluated the protester's proposal as acceptable, rather than outstanding, under the capability/relevant past performance subfactor, where the protester's proposal demonstrated extensive relevant experience but the agency received negative past performance information.

DECISION

AmClyde Engineered Products Company, Inc. protests the award of a contract to Samsung Heavy Industries Company, LTD . . . for the design and manufacture of portal cranes. AmClyde asserts that the proposals were misevaluated and the award selection was improper.

The Navy found that Samsung's proposal represented the best value. In doing so, the SSA concluded that there was very little difference between the proposals, although he ranked [DELETED] technical proposal first, AmClyde's second, and Samsung's third. The SSA noted that Samsung had no experience in building portal cranes for the Navy, but it had significant experience in the design and fabrication of container cranes, and all past performance references were complimentary. The Navy further noted that the pre-award visit confirmed that Samsung had significant experience designing and manufacturing portal cranes, and that it had the facilities, manpower, and demonstrated capabilities to successfully perform this work. With respect to AmClyde the Navy specifically noted that AmClyde had direct experience in the design of portal cranes for the Navy but that "[t]heir past performance history has been weak in customer satisfaction because of failure to meet milestone schedules, reliability problems, documentation inaccuracies and claims." Thus, after considering the merits of each proposal, the Navy found that the significant price advantage associated with Samsung's proposal was not offset by the technical advantages in the other proposals and that Samsung's proposal represented the best value.

Notwithstanding AmClyde's general disagreement with the negative comments concerning its past performance, we cannot conclude on this record that the Navy acted unreasonably in assigning AmClyde's proposal an acceptable, rather than an outstanding, rating, in the absence of a specific refutation of these comments by the protester.[1] [W]e note that at the hearing the Navy representative testified that one reference reported that it was unwilling to do business with AmClyde again because of its poor past performance.

AmClyde argues that the Navy should not have downgraded its proposal for making claims, since this is a mechanism that a contractor is entitled to pursue whenever there is a dispute on the contract and many of AmClyde's claims were meritorious. AmClyde also argues that it was improper for the Navy to cite claims history as justification for a lower rating because the Navy did not provide AmClyde the opportunity to address this concern during discussions. While it is true that the Navy did not mention any concerns regarding AmClyde's claims history with that firm during discussions, we find no basis to conclude that AmClyde would have been entitled to a materially better or an outstanding rating, even if it had been able to eliminate claims history as an area of concern, since the other aforementioned past performance problems still remain. Therefore, we find no basis to object to the agency's evaluation of AmClyde's proposal.[2]

NOTES

1. At the hearing conducted by our Office in connection with this protest, the Navy's representative testified that AmClyde's revised proposal following discussions did not adequately address the weaknesses in its past performance noted in the initial evaluation. While the protester now argues that it was unable to adequately address the Navy's concerns with its past performance because the Navy did not point to the weaknesses in its past performance with sufficient specificity, the protester should have been aware of this argument upon receipt of the agency report and therefore was required to raise this argument within 10 days of that date. However, except for its specific contention that the concerns about its claims history were not mentioned during discussions, AmClyde did not protest the adequacy of its discussions until its post-hearing comments. Therefore, this protest contention is dismissed as untimely and will not be considered.
2. While the claims apparently had no impact here, we agree with the protester that, absent some evidence of abuse of the process, agencies should not lower a firm's past performance evaluation based solely on its having filed claims. Contract claims, like bid protests, constitute remedies established by statute and regulation, and firms should not be prejudiced in competing for other contracts because of their reasonable pursuit of such remedies in the past.

Example 4.6: Evaluating Offerors with No Past Performance History (#1)

GAO Decision (abridged)

Matter of: Excalibur Systems, Inc.

File: B-272017

Date: July 12, 1996

DIGEST

Although the solicitation provided that an offeror's past quality performance was more important than price in determining the offeror representing the best value to the government, the agency nevertheless could properly award the contract to a lower-priced offeror with no past quality performance history where the solicitation also provided that price alone would be considered in evaluating first-time offerors or offerors for whom current past quality performance information was not available.

DECISION

Excalibur Systems, Inc. (ESI) protests the award of a contract to Condor Engineering, Inc. under RFP No. N00163-95-R-0044, issued by the Naval Air Warfare Center, Aircraft Division, Department of the Navy, for items for the Sensor System Improvement Program. ESI challenges the award to Condor, a lower-priced offeror.

We deny the protest.[1]

The RFP contemplated the award of a firm, fixed-price contract for basic and option quantities. The RFP stated that the procurement was subject to the Navy's Contractor Evaluation System Red/Yellow/Green (R/Y/G) Program which is used to assist contracting officials in determining the best value to the government, price, past quality performance, and other factors considered. Under this program, accumulated contractor quality performance data is used to classify a contractor's performance in terms of the degree of risk to the government of receiving poor-quality items. In this regard, an offeror's performance could be classified as either green/low risk, yellow/moderate risk, or red/high risk. First-time offerors or offerors for whom current, up-to-date quality performance history was unavailable are classified as "insufficient data" offerors.

The RFP also described the formula for determining the lowest-priced offeror. The RFP included a hypothetical example in which the formula was applied.

The RFP stated that although price would be significant in determining the successful offeror, past quality performance on the proposed item, as classified under the R/Y/G program, would be considered "essentially more important." In defining the individual R/Y/G classifications, the RFP provided that a green/low risk rating would be given greater weight or value in the evaluation than a red/high risk or yellow/moderate risk rating, and that a yellow rating would be given less weight or value than a green rating and greater weight or value than a red rating. The RFP further provided that offerors receiving insufficient data classifications "shall be evaluated solely on the basis of price [and that] [p]ast quality performance shall not be a consideration in their evaluation." (Emphasis in original.)

ESI, the incumbent contractor, and Condor submitted price proposals.[2] Both offerors received green/low risk past quality performance ratings. For this reason, the agency considered the offerors equal in terms of past quality performance. Since Condor's price was lower than ESI's price (by less than 1 percent), the agency awarded the contract to Condor.

ESI challenges the agency's assignment of a green/low risk rating to Condor for its past quality performance. ESI maintains that since Condor has never produced the required items, i.e., it is offering new items, it should have been assigned no more than an insufficient data rating. ESI further maintains that in light of its green/low risk rating for its past quality performance and the de minimis difference between its price and Condor's price, the agency should have awarded the contract to ESI.

The agency maintains that ESI was not prejudiced by Condor's green/low risk rating because even if Condor should have received an insufficient data classification, under the terms of the RFP the agency could not penalize Condor for the lack of a quality performance history and could properly make its best value determination based on a comparison of Condor's lower price vis-à-vis ESI's slightly higher price. In such circumstances, the agency states that it would still have selected Condor, the lower-priced offeror, for award.

In a best value procurement, price is not necessarily controlling in determining the offer that represents the best value to the government. Rather, that determination is made on the basis of whatever evaluation factors are set forth in the RFP, with the source selection official often required to make a cost/technical tradeoff to determine if one proposal's technical superiority is worth the higher cost that may be associated with that proposal. In this regard, price/past performance tradeoffs are permitted when such tradeoffs are consistent with the

RFP evaluation scheme. Dragon Servs., Inc., B-255354, Feb. 25, 1994, 94-1 CPD 151. Thus, where an RFP identifies past performance and price as the evaluation criteria and indicates that an offeror with good past performance can expect a higher rating than an offeror without such a record of performance, proposals must be evaluated on that basis, and ultimately the selection official must decide, if the offeror with the better past performance rating is not the low-cost offeror, whether the more costly offeror represents the best value to the government in light of the better past performance rating.

In general, we do not view RFP evaluation schemes that specify a "neutral" rating for vendors with no past performance record, see, e.g., Quality Fabricators, Inc., B-271431; B-271431.3, June 25, 1996, 96-2 CPD ¶ ; Caltech Serv. Corp., B-261044.4, Dec. 14, 1995, 95-2 CPD ¶ 285, as precluding this same type of source selection decision-making. That is, we think that the use of a neutral rating approach, to avoid penalizing a vendor without prior experience and thereby enhanc[ing] competition, does not preclude, in a best value procurement, a determination to award to a higher-priced offeror with a good past performance record over a lower-cost vendor with a neutral past performance rating.[3] Indeed such a determination is inherent in the concept of best value.

Here, however, the Navy explains that its evaluation scheme does not call for rewarding a vendor with good past performance over a vendor with no relevant past performance. Rather, the Navy further explains, its evaluation scheme is intended to differentiate between those with good past performance and those with differing degrees of less than good performance. In other words, the Navy's position is that under the RFP an offeror with a green rating is superior to an offeror with a red or yellow rating but not to an offeror with the neutral insufficient data rating.

We have no basis to disagree with the Navy. In fact, we have previously recognized that this very evaluation scheme contemplates that "a green rating [is] to be given greater weight in the evaluation only when compared to a red or a yellow rating," and that an offeror's green rating is "not to be given greater weight in the evaluation when compared to an offeror['s] . . . insufficient data rating," so that in the circumstances here the agency is to compare the competing proposals "based on price." Espey Mfg. & Elecs. Corp., B-254738.3, Mar. 8, 1994, 94-1 CPD ¶ 180.

Accordingly, we conclude that even if Condor's green rating is changed to an insufficient data rating the award decision would not change.

The protest is denied.

NOTES

1. This protest was resolved using an accelerated schedule. Bid Protest Regulations, 4 C.F.R. § 21.10(e) (1996). In addition, after reviewing various submissions from the protester and the agency, several conference calls were held at which time we advised the parties that we viewed two of the protester's issues as abandoned and two issues as having no merit. The substance of the conference calls partially dismissing the protest was confirmed in writing.
2. Technical proposals were not requested.
3. It does, however, preclude evaluation scoring that penalizes an offeror for receiving neutral ratings. See Inlingua Schools of Languages, B-229784, Apr. 5, 1988, 88-1 CPD ¶ 340.

Example 4.7: Evaluating Offerors with No Past Performance History (#2)

GAO Decision (abridged)

Matter of: Phillips Industries, Inc.

File: B-280645

Date: September 17, 1998

DIGEST

Agency selection of slightly higher-priced offeror with excellent performance history instead of lower-priced offeror with no performance history is reasonable and consistent with solicitation's evaluation scheme, which weighed past performance and price equally, and where the item was in backlog status, anticipated demand was high, and agency concluded that the awardee's established excellent record for timely delivery was worth the slightly higher price.

DECISION

Based on a comparative assessment of all prices offered, Amjay Chemicals [was] not the lowest offer received nor the highest scored, but [had] a very good ABVM score . . . . The low offers from Phillips Ind. & Landscapers Supply reveal that they have never furnished items to DSCR and therefore would be a great risk if an award were finalized with either of these firms considering that this item is already in a backorder situation.

Consistent with the ABVM Clause, [she] considered the presence of backorders and high demand for the item represented a higher than normal risk of non-performance. The lowest priced offerors, Phillips and [Landscapers Supply], had neutral performance ratings. The third lowest offeror, Amjay, had excellent performance history, rating a 97.8 out [of] 100 ABVM score. Yet, Amjay's price was only around 3% higher than Phillips and [Landscapers Supply]. She concluded that Amjay's price was worth the reduced risk of non-performance, in light of the high-demand for items already in a back-ordered inventory position. Thus, Amjay represented the best value to the Government.

We think the agency's decision to award to Amjay was reasonable and consistent with the RFP. Here, the RFP established that price and past performance would be the factors for award among the technically acceptable firms. The ABVM clause stated how past performance would be rated based on ABVM scores, that a lack of performance history would not disqualify a firm, but that, among other things, the offeror could be considered less favorably than an offeror with a favorable performance history. The clause further provided for a comparative assessment of offers and stated that "[w]here the offeror with the best performance history has not also offered the lowest price, the Government will determine the appropriate tradeoff of price for past performance." RFP, DSCR clause 52.215-9G05(f), at 13.

The RFP listed certain factors, including delivery schedule/inventory status, which could affect the tradeoff determination. Here, the contracting officer decided, given the high demand and the backlog status for the item, that award to a slightly higher-priced firm which had an excellent performance history was justified to ensure timely delivery and represented the best value to the government. This was entirely consistent with the RFP evaluation scheme and the discretion afforded the contracting officer in making the tradeoff decision.

[T]he use of a neutral rating approach, to avoid penalizing a vendor without prior experience and thereby enhance competition, does not preclude, in a best value procurement, a determination to award to a higher-priced offeror with a good past performance record over a lower-cost vendor with a neutral past performance rating. Indeed, such a determination is inherent in the concept of best value.

We share the protester's concern with the language in the selection decision documentation that Phillips and Landscapers Supply, vendors with no performance histories, pose a "performance risk" or a "great risk" for award. As the protester argues, a company like Phillips which may be new to government contracting should not be disqualified from award merely because it lacks a performance history.

As the agency recognizes, such an approach would be inconsistent with the FAR and the RFP. FAR § 15.305(a)(2)(iv) provides that, for past performance evaluations, in the case of an offeror without a record of relevant past performance or for whom information on past performance is not available, the offeror may not be evaluated favorably or unfavorably on past performance. The RFP ABVM clause also states that lack of performance history is not grounds for disqualification for award. RFP, DSCR clause, 52.215-9G05(d), at 13; CO Report, at 6-7.

Nonetheless, as explained above, the contracting officer's decision to award to the slightly higher-priced firm with an established excellent performance history, rather than a lower-priced vendor with no performance history with the agency, was permissible and reasonable.

We deny the protest.

Example 4.8: When Should One Company's Past Performance Be Attributed to Another?

GAO Decision (abridged)

Matter of: Universal Building Maintenance, Inc.

File: B-282456

Date: July 15, 1999

DIGEST

Agency improperly attributed past performance of parent company or its other subsidiaries to awardee where record does not establish that parent company or subsidiaries will be involved in the performance of the protested contract.

DECISION

The protester argues that the agency improperly evaluated Service Star USA, Inc.'s past performance by considering the contracts of Service Star's "affiliate," its parent company, Star Group International, Inc. The awardee received a consensus score of 2 for past performance based on individual scores of +1, +1, and 2. The score sheet for Service Star USA, Inc. contains the following comment: "Current + past exceeds criteria in similar performance + great reference checks."

The record shows, however, that Service Star USA, Inc. is performing only one of the five referenced contracts. In fact, although not made clear by the awardee in its written proposal, two of the five contracts listed were performed by Commercial Building Services, Inc., and two other contracts were performed by Service Star Building Cleaning, Inc., both of which are subsidiaries of Service Star International, Inc. One individual wholly owns Service Star USA, Inc., the above-named companies, and two other firms. The companies all perform commercial building services.

The protester argues that, based on the awardee's one contract, the awardee should have been given a 0 for failing to meet the standard for past performance. The agency responds that it properly considered the parent company's and its other subsidiaries' contracts in its evaluation of Service Star USA, Inc.'s performance. The agency cites FAR § 15.305 (a)(2)(iii) as the basis for its decision to consider these contracts. This provision provides in essence that a past performance evaluation "should [consider] information regarding predecessor companies, key personnel . . ., or subcontractors that will perform major or critical aspects of the requirement when such information is relevant." FAR §15.305(a)(2)(iii).

We have stated that in determining whether one company's performance should be attributed to another, an agency must consider the nature and extent of the relationship between the two companies—in particular, whether the workforce, management, facilities, or other resources of one may affect contract performance by the other. In this regard, while it would be inappropriate to consider a company's performance record where that record does not bear on the likelihood of successful performance by the offeror, it would be appropriate to consider a company's performance record where it will be involved in the contract effort or where it shares management with the offeror.

[T]he awardee's proposal does not establish this fact. We conclude that the agency did not reasonably evaluate the relationship of the companies for purposes of attributing the past performance of the parent company or its other subsidiaries to Service Star USA, Inc., and therefore could not consider four of the five contracts referenced by Service Star USA, Inc. in evaluating its past performance.

More specifically, there is no indication from the awardee's proposal that the parent company intends to use its workforce, management, facilities, or other resources in performing this contract. For example, GSA states that it relied in part on a corporate management chart in the awardee's technical proposal. The chart is not identified as Star Group International, Inc.'s management. We note that the narrative directly underneath the chart states that "Service Star is comprised of seasoned professionals."

Thus, it is not clear how the agency determined that this chart refers to the parent company's management. The chart certainly does not establish that the parent company's management or resources would be used for this contract. In fact, on the next page of the proposal is a specific organization chart for this contract. Although the president is the same for both companies (the awardee and its parent company), the director of operations and project manager are Service Star USA, Inc. personnel. More importantly, four of the contracts described under past performance, as noted above, were performed by two other companies that GSA does not even argue are involved in this contract, and Star Group International Inc., the "umbrella company," did not perform any of the contracts described in the awardee's proposal. Based on the record, we have no basis to conclude that any of these firms' past performance is relevant here.

The protest is sustained.

Example 4.9: Evaluating the Past Performance of Key Personnel

GAO Decision (abridged)

Matter of: SWR Inc.

File: B-286044.2; B-286044.3

Date: November 1, 2000

DIGEST

Past performance evaluation is unobjectionable where it was conducted in accordance with stated evaluation criteria and is supported by the record; protester's proposal was reasonably rated neutral under past performance factor where it showed no relevant prior performance by offeror and, although protester argues that the relevant experience of its proposed project manager should have been attributed to the protester, agency reasonably declined to do so where the individual was not currently employed by the protester, and the proposal did not contain a firm commitment by the individual to work for the protester.

DECISION

Several proposals were received and evaluated. Although all seven past performance references provided by SWR rated the firm exceptional or very good under each past performance subfactor, the agency found that the prior contracts were not similar in nature and scope to the RFP requirement, and therefore were not relevant; SWR's proposal thus was rated neutral overall for past performance. Pentad's proposal referenced three current food service contracts at defense installations, all of which were deemed relevant. For two of the contracts, Pentad's performance was rated exceptional, and for the third it was rated very good; this resulted in an overall exceptional rating under the past performance factor. Pentad's price, $1,829,979.81, was the lowest among four proposals rated exceptional; SWR's proposal was one of five rated neutral, and was the lowest-priced overall at $1,644,542.80. The source selection authority (SSA) compared Pentad's proposal to the one proposal rated satisfactory (which was the second lowest-priced overall at $1,649,817.90), and determined the premium was reasonable given the superior quality reflected in Pentad's exceptional past performance rating. Thus, Pentad's offer was determined to represent the best value to the government, and award was made to that firm. Following a debriefing, SWR filed this protest.

SWR objects to its neutral past performance rating. SWR acknowledges that it has no history of providing the identical services required here, but maintains that the agency was required—under the terms of the RFP and the Federal Acquisition Regulation (FAR)—to consider the experience of its proposed project manager, a key employee, who has worked in the same capacity for the incumbent contractor for three years. SWR concludes that, had the agency considered its project manager's past performance, SWR would have received a higher rating and, based on its lowest price, its proposal would have been determined the best value to the government.

SWR is correct—and the agency does not dispute—that the RFP indicated that the past performance evaluation would include key personnel. In this regard, the RFP stated under the heading "Past Performance Procedures," that "[i]nformation will also be considered regarding any significant subcontractors, and key personnel records." RFP attach. 5 at 2 (emphasis added). The RFP also referenced FAR § 15.305(a)(2), id. at 3, which states, in relevant part, that the agency should consider past performance information concerning "key personnel who have relevant experience ... when such information is relevant to the instant acquisition."

SWR's proposal indicated that the individual it was proposing as project manager was not a current SWR employee, but was employed as the project manager for the incumbent contractor. In order to establish that the individual intended to be employed by SWR, the firm included in its proposal a letter, purportedly from the individual.

The typed name of the project manager appears in the signature block, but the letter is unsigned. The letter is addressed to "To Whom this may concern," and there is no reference in the letter to SWR or any SWR employee.

The agency takes the position that the letter from the proposed individual did not reliably convey that she would, in fact, perform as project manager for SWR, and that it therefore reasonably did not attribute her experience to SWR. We agree. The possibility that, due to unforeseen circumstances, a proposed key individual may not be hired by the offeror, is an appropriate consideration for an agency in deciding whether the individual's experience should be imputed to the offeror for evaluation purposes. The letter included in SWR's proposal established no commitment on the part of the proposed individual to work for SWR and, indeed, did not even refer to SWR, and there was nothing else in the proposal indicating that SWR and the individual had even discussed specific employment terms. We think the agency reasonably could decline to impute the proposed individual's experience to SWR based on the absence of stronger evidence of an employment commitment, or other evidence indicating that the individual would in fact be employed by SWR.

The protest is denied.

Example 4.10: Evaluating the Past Performance of Subcontractors

GAO Decision (abridged)

Matter of: Battelle Memorial Institute

File: B-278673

Date: February 27, 1998

DIGEST

Since the prime contractor is ultimately responsible for successful performance of contract effort, past performance evaluation reasonably credited offeror who performed as prime contractor with relevant experience even though subcontractor on past contract was responsible for majority of technical work.

DECISION

Battelle Memorial Institute protests the award of a contract to DynPort LLC for development, licensure, and production of biological defense vaccines under RFP No. DAMD17-95-R-5020, issued by the Department of the Army, Joint Program Office for Biological Defense.

Battelle … argues that the agency failed to follow the evaluation criteria in its evaluation of the proposals. In this regard, it is not the function of our Office to evaluate proposals de novo. Rather, we will examine an agency's evaluation only to ensure that it was reasonable and consistent with the stated evaluation criteria and applicable statutes and regulations, since determining the relative merit of competing proposals is primarily a matter within the contracting agency's discretion. The protester's mere disagreement with the agency's judgment does not establish that an evaluation was unreasonable.

In evaluating past performance, the SSEB determined that both Battelle's and DynPort's proposals should be rated "green" with "moderate" risk. Battelle challenges this evaluation arguing that DynPort's rating should have been less favorable. In this regard, Battelle argues that the agency improperly gave DynPort credit for two contracts performed by its team member, Porton International. At the time these contracts were performed, Porton was teamed with [deleted] a firm which teamed with Battelle for this JVAP procurement. While Porton had claimed responsibility for developing and producing botulinum toxoids under both of these contracts, Battelle explains that [deleted] did all the development and production work while Porton was simply the marketing and distributing agency for products and services.

The record establishes that the agency's past performance evaluation was reasonable and in accordance with the stated evaluation criteria. DynPort's past performance information showed successful performance by itself and other team members on eight contracts involving AIDS, influenza, botulinum, and plague vaccines. The agency specifically noted that one of DynPort's subcontractors had successfully licensed a vaccine from clinical trials in only 14 months. Other than its assertions regarding Porton's contribution, Battelle has produced nothing to indicate that the agency's rating of [deleted] with [deleted] risk was an unreasonable evaluation.

With regard to its claims regarding Porton's work on two of the contracts, Battelle is essentially arguing that the only entity that may properly list a prior contract for purposes of a past performance evaluation is the concern which actually performed the work relevant to that covered in the solicitation. We disagree. The general rule is that a prime contractor under a government contract is responsible for the performance of its subcontractors. Further, subcontractors and joint venturers perform various portions of contracts and, accordingly, may obtain experience useful in predicting success in future contract performance. Where an offeror was involved as a subcontractor or joint venturer in performing work under a prior contract similar to work to be included under the instant contract, such experience may properly be considered in assessing that offeror's past performance. Porton, as prime contractor, was responsible for managing the performance of the two contracts at issue and the solicitation here calls for a significant management effort in directing the work of a number of subcontractors. On this record, there is no basis to question the agency's consideration of Porton's prior performance in the evaluation of the DynPort team's qualifications to perform the JVAP contract.

Based on the SSA's rationale, it is plain that cost was not the sole determinative factor. Rather, the decision was based on an integrated assessment of the relative technical/ management merit, past performance, and evaluated cost of the two proposals. As discussed above, there was nothing unreasonable or objectionable in the agency's evaluation. Thus, there is no basis for questioning the award determination due to alleged evaluation flaws. To the extent that cost may be considered to have become "determinative," where, as here, the selection authority reasonably concludes that the offers are essentially equal technically, cost may become determinative notwithstanding its being of lesser importance in the evaluation scheme. Accordingly, the determination to award to DynPort is unobjectionable.

The protest is denied.

Example 5.1: What Happens When Past Performance Questionnaires Are Not Returned?

GAO Decision (abridged)

Matter of: Advanced Data Concepts, Inc.

File: B-277801.4

Date: June 1, 1998

DIGEST

Argument that evaluation of past performance was unreasonable because none of the protester's properly-identified references returned the past performance questionnaire is denied where the agency followed the procedure identified in the solicitation of awarding a neutral rating for such unreturned references, and where there is no showing that the evaluators had some independent basis for knowing of the protester's allegedly excellent past performance, because, absent such a showing, there is no legal requirement that all past performance references be included in a valid review of past performance.

DECISION

Advanced Data Concepts, Inc. (ADC) protests the award of a contract to DynCorp EENSP, Inc., d/b/a DynMeridian by the Department of Energy (DOE), . . . ADC argues that DOE's evaluation of its proposal was unreasonable in the areas of personnel, past performance, and uncompensated overtime, and also contends that the agency failed to hold meaningful discussions with ADC and was biased in favor of the incumbent.

Offerors were advised that award would be made to the offeror whose proposal was considered most advantageous to the government. The RFP explained that the oral technical proposal would be more important than price in determining which proposal was most advantageous. The solicitation identified four technical evaluation criteria, each of which was [composed] of additional subcriteria. Although the RFP did not specifically identify the available points for the evaluation criteria, the criteria and the points used to evaluate them, are set forth below:[1]

Personnel Qualifications and Availability	333
Technical Approach	317
Past Performance	250
Organization and Management Capabilities	100
TOTAL	1,000

ADC argues that DOE's evaluation of its past performance was unreasonable because DOE assigned the company a neutral rating when none of the identified contact points for ADC's three references—two of whom are DOE contracting officers, while the third is a contracting officer for the Bonneville Power Administration—returned the past performance questionnaire sent them by the DOE contracting officer here. ADC argues that DOE's contracting officers should be required to return such requests for information, and contends that offerors should not bear the burden of an unfavorable evaluation when agency employees fail to perform their duties. DOE argues that the evaluation was reasonable because offerors were advised in advance that a neutral rating would result from unreturned questionnaires, and that the point score assigned for a neutral rating here was so high that ADC cannot reasonably claim to have been prejudiced.

DynMeridian identified three prior DOE contracts for review; ADC identified two prior DOE contracts, and one contract with the Bonneville Power Administration. The record shows that in each case, the contracting officer here prepared a letter and facsimile to the identified reference. The record further shows that all of DynMeridian's DOE references returned the past performance questionnaire, while neither ADC's DOE references, nor its Bonneville Power Administration reference, responded to the request for information.

DynMeridian received a total rating of [deleted] points. For ADC, however, since none of the references responded to the contracting officer's request for information, the [technical evaluation committee] TEC assigned a neutral rating to ADC's proposal. The TEC then converted the neutral rating to a point score by assigning ADC a rating of 8 under each of the five past performance sub-criteria, which translated to a total rating of [deleted].

ADC argues that the agency has violated the letter and spirit of FAR subpart 42.15 by failing to take steps to ensure that the references ADC identified in its offer—relating to two DOE contracts and one contract with the Bonneville Power Administration—returned the past performance questionnaires. DOE counters that the FAR provisions should not be interpreted to create rights for protesters where their references fail to respond to requests for information from a contracting officer.

Under the circumstances of this case, we need not decide whether DOE violated the FAR provisions at issue here because none of ADC's references fall within the requirements of the subpart. First, ADC admits that its Bonneville Power Administration reference falls outside the subpart because that organization is not covered by the FAR, and thus the requirement to share information, quoted above, does not apply. DOE also points out that the remaining two contracts referenced by ADC are not yet completed. Since interim past performance reports are voluntary, not mandatory, DOE contends, and we agree, that there was no requirement for it to have information related to these contracts.[2]

The remaining issue here is whether the agency evaluation was unreasonable because ADC was assigned a rating of neutral, in lieu of the actual ratings that could have been used had the DOE employees complied with the agency's request to provide past performance information. ADC argues that its past performance of DOE contracts was evaluated very favorably, and contends that the actual ratings would likely have exceeded the neutral ratings awarded by the agency.

Despite ADC's arguments to the contrary, there is no legal requirement that all past performance references be included in a valid review of past performance. For our Office to sustain a protest challenging the failure to obtain or consider a reference's assessment of past performance, a protester must show unusual factual circumstances that convert the failure to a significant inequity for the protester. The record here shows that the agency contacted each of ADC's references, and made at least an initial attempt to obtain the information properly identified by ADC in its proposal. When the agency did not receive responses, the agency followed the RFP-described procedure of assigning a neutral rating in this area. In addition, DOE translated its neutral rating to a favorable numerical score of 8 out of 10 available points. Thus, we cannot say that ADC was harmed in any significant way by the neutral rating. In short, without a showing that the DOE evaluators here should have been aware of the assessments that would have been received, and without some other showing that the agency's evaluation was unreasonable, we deny this protest ground.

In this procurement, the agency originally concluded that DynMeridian's higher-rated (970 points), higher-priced ($15.9 million) proposal represented a greater value to the government than ADC's lower-rated (644.9 points), lower-priced ($12.6 million) proposal. In its initial report, the agency reconfirmed its selection decision based on its concession that the ADC proposal would have received a rating of 665 points had the agency not used an erroneous weighting scheme. Despite our agreement with ADC in one other area—which we assume could raise ADC's score as high as 705 points—we cannot conclude that ADC was prejudiced here.

Our review of the Source Selection Statement reveals that the decision to select DynMeridian's higher-rated, higher-priced proposal was driven by the conclusion that DynMeridian's personnel qualifications significantly exceeded those of ADC. Specifically, the selection official focused on experience shortfalls for ADC's key personnel, and on areas of technical approach and understanding. None of these concerns is called into question by our findings here, and our findings do not suggest any significant change in the relative standing of these two offerors. Given these circumstances, and the significant remaining difference between the scores reasonably awarded these competing proposals, we cannot conclude that the limited errors identified in the conduct of this procurement support a reasonable finding that, but for the agency's actions, ADC would have had a substantial chance of receiving the award.

The protest is denied.

NOTES

1. Instead, the RFP explained that the criteria were listed in descending order of importance and provided that criteria 1 and 2 (each approximately equal) were each approximately weighted three (3) times the weight of criterion 4, and that criterion 3 was weighted two and a half (2.5) times the weight of criterion 4.
2. Although none of ADC's three contracts are technically within the requirements of FAR subpart 42.15, ADC correctly argues that agency personnel charged with the responsibility of answering past performance inquiries are required to provide such information when asked by the procuring office. See FAR § 42.1503(c). Since none of the DOE references named by ADC returned the procuring contracting officer's questionnaire—while all of DynMeridian's DOE references did so, giving rise to the claim of inequity here—DOE should consider whether measures to ensure compliance with the requirements of this regulation are necessary.

Example 5.2: Clarifying "Close at Hand"

GAO Decision (abridged)

Matter of: TRW, Inc.

File: B-282162; B-282162.2

Date: June 9, 1999

DIGEST

Agency's evaluation of the awardee's past performance was reasonable where the agency investigated and evaluated each of the contracts referenced in the awardee's proposal; other information regarding the awardee's allegedly deficient prior performance on subcontracts was not so "close at hand" that it had to be considered by the agency.

DECISION

TRW, Inc. argues that the agency's evaluation of Motorola's past performance and cost proposals was unreasonable.

The RFP stated that award would be made to the offeror submitting the proposal representing the best value to the government, considering management, technical, cost, and past performance evaluation criteria. The RFP stated that technical was more important than cost, that cost was more important than management, and that management was significantly more important than past performance.

The RFP informed offerors that the evaluation of past performance would involve the consideration of "the offeror's record of past and current performance to ascertain the probable ability to successfully perform the required effort of this solicitation." The RFP added that "[w]hile the Government may elect to consider data obtained from other sources, the burden of providing thorough and complete past performance information rests with the offeror."

While agencies generally need not evaluate all past performance references or those not reflected in the proposals, our Office has recognized that in certain limited circumstances an agency evaluating an offeror's past performance has an obligation (as opposed to the discretion) to consider "outside information" bearing on the offeror's past performance. Where we have charged an agency with responsibility for considering such outside information, the record has demonstrated that the information in question was "simply too close at hand to require offerors to shoulder the inequities that spring from an agency's failure to obtain, and consider, the information." Id.; see GTS Duratek, Inc., B-280511.2,

B-280511.3, Oct. 19, 1998, 98-2 CPD ¶ 130 at 14 (agency should have considered offeror's performance of a prior contract where the contract was discussed in the offeror's past performance proposal, was so relevant as to have served as the basis for the government estimate for the subject solicitation, and the contracting officer's technical representative for the contract was a member of the technical evaluation team for the subject solicitation); G. Marine Diesel, B-232619.3, Aug. 3, 1989, 89-2 CPD ¶ 101 at 4-6 (contracting officer that was personally aware of the awardee's continuing difficulties in performing a contract for services related to the subject solicitation, and considered the performance difficulties relevant to the extent that the contracting officer determined not to exercise the options in the contract awarded under the subject solicitation, erred in not considering the awardee's performance difficulties when determining whether the contract under the subject solicitation had been properly awarded); G. Marine Diesel; Phillyship, B-232619, B-232619.2, Jan. 27, 1989, 89-1 CPD ¶ 90 at 4-5 (agency should have considered awardee's prior experience under a directly relevant contract where the contract was referenced in the awardee's proposal and the agency personnel were familiar with the awardee's performance). However, the "close at hand" information in these cases generally concerned contracts for the same services with the same procuring activity, or at least information personally known to the evaluators. See Morrison Knudsen Corp., B-280261, Sept. 9, 1998, 98-2 CPD ¶ 63 at 5-6.

Here, the contracts on which Motorola's performance was allegedly unsatisfactory were between Motorola and TRW, with Motorola acting as a subcontractor and TRW as the prime contractor to the agency; they were not contracts between Motorola and the same procuring activity, such that the agency would necessarily have information concerning Motorola's prior performance close at hand. Additionally, the documentation provided by TRW in support of its contention regarding Motorola's performance on its subcontracts with TRW provides little support for TRW's claim. While the documents reflect that the contracts between TRW and Motorola were modified, there is only one document that reflects any concerns over the quality of the work performed. The concerns mentioned here appear to be relatively minor in nature and are not, with the exception of an affidavit submitted by a TRW employee, identified as attributable to work done by Motorola. In sum, the record does not demonstrate that there was outside information so "close at hand" regarding Motorola's prior performance that the agency either improperly ignored or erroneously failed to obtain.

The protest is denied.

Example 5.3: Past Performance Information Close at Hand

GAO Decision (abridged)

Matter of: International Business Systems, Inc.

File: B-275554

Date: March 3, 1997

DIGEST

Protest alleging that agency's evaluation of past performance was unreasonable is sustained where the technical evaluation scheme envisioned a price/past performance tradeoff among technically acceptable proposals to determine the best value to the government, and where the agency failed to consider the past performance of the protester on a contract involving the same agency, the same services, and the same contracting officer because an individual in the agency did not complete and return the past performance evaluation materials.

DECISION

International Business Systems, Inc. (IBSI) argues that the agency's evaluation of past performance was unreasonable, and that DNA's proposal was noncompliant with certain technical requirements in the solicitation.

The RFP anticipated award of a fixed-price contract to the offeror whose proposal was determined most advantageous to the government. One of IBSI's challenges in its initial protest was that DNA's excellent past performance rating was unreasonable given that DNA did not have direct experience as a prime contractor furnishing and installing telephone systems. In response to this assertion, the contracting officer (CO) decided "to take corrective action" by reevaluating the past performance of DNA and IBSI. In essence, the CO opted to cull from her past performance review any reference involving a contract for other than furnishing and installing telephone systems, and any reference for which the offeror was not the prime contractor.

In reevaluating DNA's proposal, the contracting officer decided that none of DNA's references was directly applicable to furnishing and installing telephone systems. Under the terms of the RFP, offerors were advised that if they lacked past experience relating to this requirement, the proposal would "not be evaluated favorably or unfavorably on these factors." Thus, the CO awarded DNA's proposal a "neutral" rating under the past performance factor.

In reevaluating IBSI's proposal, the contracting officer identified two references directly applicable to this solicitation—both involving installation of telephone systems at VA hospitals. However, the CO based her review on only one of the references. The CO explained that the second reference—involving the installation of a similar telephone system at the VA Medical Center in Brockton/West Roxbury, Massachusetts—was not considered because the individual within the agency responsible for completing the form did not do so. Using the one completed relevant reference, the CO concluded that IBSI's past performance should be rated "good."

In comparing the neutral rating of DNA and the good rating of IBSI, the CO concluded that the two offerors were essentially equal in the area of past performance. Thus, the agency report explains that DNA would continue to be the awardee given its lower price.

IBSI's challenge to the past performance evaluation is that the agency could not reasonably ignore IBSI's past performance on the Brockton/West Roxbury contract when that contract involved the same agency, the same CO, and virtually the same services as here. IBSI further argues that this result is untenable when other evidence—i.e., the CO's letter to the SBA—demonstrates the CO's first-hand knowledge of IBSI's past performance of this work. Thus, IBSI argues that the inclusion of the Brockton/West Roxbury experience would have enhanced its standing in the area of past performance, and would have made less likely a finding that the two offerors were equal in this area. We agree.

We start our review with the evaluation approach outlined in the agency report. As described above, the conclusion that IBSI and DNA were essentially equal under the past performance factor, leading to a selection decision based on price, was based on an evaluation of one relevant reference for IBSI and no relevant references for DNA. Thus, the contracting officer compared a rating of "good" with a rating of "neutral" to reach her conclusion that the offerors were essentially equal. In the abstract, we have no basis to disagree with this conclusion.

Our disagreement with the agency springs from its overly mechanical application of its procedures for evaluating past performance. While the VA is correct in its view that there is no legal requirement that all past performance references be included in a valid review of past performance, some information is simply too close at hand to require offerors to shoulder the inequities that spring from an agency's failure to obtain, and consider, the information.

Example 5.4: An Evaluator's Personal Knowledge May Be Used

GAO Decision: (abridged)

Matter of: Omega World Travel, Inc.

File: B-271262.2

Date: July 25, 1996

DIGEST

Protest against downgrading of protester's past performance based on evaluators' personal knowledge of complaints about protester's performance under incumbent contract is denied, where the evaluation judgments were documented in sufficient detail by internal agency memorandum and surveys of agency travelers to show reasonableness of evaluation.

DECISION

Omega World Travel, Inc., protests the award of a contract to WorldTravel Partners (WTP) under request for offers (RFO) issued by the Patent & Trademark Office (PTO) for travel management services. Omega maintains that its proposal improperly was downgraded under past performance based on the undocumented personal knowledge of the evaluators. This allegation is based on narrative comments contained in the evaluation score sheets for two of the three evaluators, which state "info provided was responsive, but personal experience resulted in lower score" and "see [Solicitor of PTO's] memo" under weaknesses. The protester complains that, because the personal experience and Solicitor's memorandum referred to in the narrative comments were not included in the contemporaneous evaluation record, and the third evaluator made no narrative comment under weaknesses in this area, the evaluation was inadequately supported. In contrast to the evaluation score sheets, the protester cites a response to a reference check questionnaire (provided by the agency to references at random) which rated the firm "good" (under a rating scale of good, satisfactory, and unsatisfactory).

The agency explains that the evaluators' personal knowledge of Omega's past performance was based on numerous documented and undocumented complaints from PTO travelers. The record also includes responses to surveys (in preprinted questionnaire form entitled "travel evaluations," and referred to by the agency as "quality control surveys") from 16 PTO travelers who used Omega's travel services from the fall of 1992 to the fall of 1994; they are identified by the traveler's name and/or travel order number. Additionally, the agency has submitted post-protest declarations from the evaluators explaining the basis for their personal knowledge of the quality of Omega's service and the basis for their downgrading the firm's proposal, which include the above-described documented complaints, as well as other undocumented complaints.

An evaluator's personal knowledge of an offeror may be properly considered in a past performance evaluation. More specifically, where the solicitation provides for references to be used in the evaluation, as here, the agency may consider the unsatisfactory past performance of an offeror under a recent contract with the agency, thus, in effect, furnishing its own reference. In an evaluation which takes into account the agency's own knowledge of offerors, the fundamental requirement that evaluation judgments be documented in sufficient detail to show that they are reasonable and not arbitrary still must be met.

The evaluation of Omega's past performance was reasonable based on the evaluation record, as supplemented by the internal PTO memoranda and surveys of PTO travelers, as well as the post-protest declarations by the evaluators. First, contrary to the protester's primary contention, the fact that the extrinsic evidence of Omega's past performance relied on by the evaluators (i.e., the internal PTO memoranda and surveys of PTO travelers) was not physically included in or attached to the evaluation score sheets does not render them invalid as sources of information available to the evaluators, since the record, when read as a whole, shows that the evaluators relied on this evidence, the evidence was submitted into the protest record, and it clearly supports the reasonableness of the evaluation. In this regard, while we accord more weight to contemporaneous documents in determining whether an evaluation was reasonable, our review is based on all information in the record, including documentation prepared in response to the protest contentions. The evaluators' declarations, which are not disputed by the protester, in two instances indicate reliance on the internal PTO memoranda and surveys of PTO travelers—one of the evaluators states, she "read" the memorandum from PTO's Solicitor; another evaluator states, she was "in receipt" of the memorandum written to the Associate Commissioner of PTO (which the agency explains was the previously described memorandum from PTO's Assistant Secretary and Commissioner) and surveys of PTO travelers; and all three evaluators state they were aware of undocumented complaints about the quality of Omega's performance.

Based on these numerous documented complaints about Omega's past performance, which were the basis of the personal knowledge of two of the evaluators and which are undisputed by the protester, we have no basis to question the downgrading of Omega's proposal under past performance. (We note that, while the third evaluator's score sheet did not include any specific narrative comments under weaknesses, it is clear from her declaration that she was aware of the same kinds of complaints that appeared in the documented complaints.

Example 5.5: An Agency's Perception of Poor Past Performance Prevails When Supported by Sufficient Evidence

GAO Decision (abridged)

Matter of: Quality Fabricators, Inc.

File: B-271431; B-271431.3

Date: June 25, 1996

DIGEST

Exclusion of the protester's proposal from the competitive range was reasonable where, based on the evaluation of its past performance, which included late deliveries, quality deficiency reports concerning manufacturing defects, and a refusal or inability to manufacture some of the same items under a previous contract, the agency reasonably concluded that the firm had no reasonable chance for award.

DECISION

Quality Fabricators, Inc. (QFI) protests the exclusion of its proposal from the competitive range under RFP No. N00140-96-R-D110, issued by the Department of the Navy for various types of lockers for the Navy's habitability program.

The contracting officer noted that she considered three quality deficiency reports on a [QFI/]Hampton Roads contract for the same or similar lockers as called for here. The contracting officer noted that an official of [the Navy's Fleet Technical Support Center] FTSC characterized Hampton Roads as a poor performer whose performance included problems of delivery and quality as well as an undesirable record of customer satisfaction. Based on this reassessment, the contracting officer affirmed the marginal past performance rating assigned to QFI.

The contracting officer also reviewed the information on which Tri-Way's past performance rating was based and noted that the FTSC data base included information on 898 requisitions for Tri-Way; of that 898, the data base indicated 93 requisitions more than 30 days late. The contracting officer stated that she reviewed those 93 requisitions and found 31 with deliveries actually more than 30 days late, with an average delinquency of only 31.9 days. These 31 delinquencies represented only 115 items. The contracting officer also noted that a report from FTSC rated Tri-Way as a highly satisfactory performer; that four other contracting officers rated Tri-Way as an outstanding performer; and that there have been no quality deficiency reports for manufacturing defects on Tri-Way's products. According to the contracting officer, based on the reassessment, there was no reason to change the exceptional past performance rating on Tri-Way and no reason to include QFI's proposal in the competitive range.

The Federal Acquisition Regulation (FAR) provides that the competitive range must include all proposals that have a reasonable chance of being selected for award and that any doubt as to whether a proposal is in the competitive range should be resolved by inclusion. FAR sec. 15.609(a) (FAC 90-31). While the determination of whether a proposal is in the competitive range is principally a matter within the reasonable exercise of discretion of the procuring agency, we closely scrutinize any evaluation that results in only one proposal being included in the competitive range, in view of the importance of achieving full and open competition in government procurement.

An agency's evaluation of past performance may be based upon the procuring agency's reasonable perception of inadequate prior performance, regardless of whether the contractor disputes the agency's interpretation of the facts. This record affords us no basis upon which to object to the Navy's conclusion regarding QFI/Hampton Roads' past performance—that it produced some items of poor quality under prior contracts and could not, or would not, manufacture certain items which are the subject of this solicitation. While QFI offers explanations and interpretations of the record that provide a more favorable picture of its performance history than drawn by the agency, this does not alter the fact that there was sufficient evidence for the agency to conclude that the firm had a series of performance problems under its prior contracts.

We also conclude that QFI's proposal was reasonably excluded from the competitive range. Under the solicitation, past performance was considered significantly more important than price and the agency was permitted to award to other than the lowest-priced offeror. Under this evaluation scheme, which placed paramount importance on past performance, it was a reasonable exercise of the agency's discretion to decide that a firm with an exceptional performance history (based on very favorable references and no deficiency reports) and a relatively low price would be the only firm with a reasonable chance for award when all other offerors had significantly higher prices and/or less attractive performance histories. This is particularly true since the agency's assessment of Tri-Way's past performance as exceptional is unchallenged. Since the agency reasonably concluded that QFI had no reasonable chance for award, the exclusion of its proposal from the competitive range is not legally objectionable.

Example 6.1: Determining the Best of the Best

GAO Decision (abridged)

Matter of: Airwork Limited-Vinnell Corporation (A Joint Venture)

File: B-285247; B-285247.2

Date: August 8, 2000

DIGEST

Protest by incumbent against agency's past performance evaluation, in which both protester and awardee were rated excellent/high confidence, is denied where protester has not shown how, given awardee's highly-rated relevant past performance, protester's additional, relevant past performance would contribute to better satisfying agency's stated needs so as to warrant a significantly higher rating under the past performance factor.

DECISION

Airwork Limited-Vinnell Corporation (A Joint Venture) (AWV) protests the Department of the Air Force's award of a contract to DynCorp Technical Services, Inc., under RFP No. F44650-99-R0007, for War Reserve Materiel (WRM) services in Southwest Asia. AWV, the incumbent contractor, challenges the evaluation of DynCorp's past performance.

Award was to be made to the responsible offeror whose proposal conformed to the solicitation requirements and represented the best value to the government. The solicitation provided for proposals to be evaluated based on the following four evaluation factors: (1) mission capability (with subfactors for program management/organization structure; receive/ship, store and outload; maintain, repair and reconstitute; and quality control); (2) proposal risk; (3) past performance; and (4) price/cost. The solicitation stated that "[t]he first three factors are equal in value and when combined are significantly more important than the fourth factor," that is, price/cost.

DynCorp was rated exceptional/high confidence under past performance, the same adjectival rating given AWV, and the evaluated most probable cost of DynCorp's proposal ($[DELETED]) was the lowest among the proposals. As a result, the source selection authority determined that DynCorp's proposal offered the best value to the government and award was made to DynCorp on April 20, 2000. After receiving a debriefing, AWV filed this protest with our Office.

AWV challenges the evaluation of past performance. In this regard, the solicitation provided for evaluation of both the quality and relevance of an offeror's past performance. Specifically, past performance was to be "evaluated as a measure of the Government's confidence in the offeror's ability to successfully perform based on previous and current contract efforts and offeror's effectiveness in performing similar contracts"; a rating of either exceptional/high confidence, very good/significant confidence, satisfactory/confidence, neutral/unknown confidence, marginal/little confidence, or unsatisfactory/no confidence was to be assigned. According to the solicitation, "[t]he recency and relevancy of past performance information is critical to the Government's evaluation." The RFP required offerors to submit past performance references for the last eight current and completed "contract efforts similar to the Government's [Southwest Asia] Prepositioned WRM"; "explain what aspects of the contract are deemed relevant to the proposed [Southwest Asia] Prepositioned WRM effort"; and specifically "address contracts for the same or similar services and explain similarity of services, considering such areas as: the nature and complexity of the service involved, contract environment, contract type, and location of work to be performed."

The Air Force assigned a rating of exceptional/high confidence to DynCorp based upon numerous exceptional and very good ratings (as well as favorable narrative comments) in questionnaires returned by DynCorp's past performance references for a number of contracts. These contract efforts included: (1) the transition phase to assuming responsibility, under the Department of the Army's Prepositioned Stocks Afloat Program (APS-3), for maintaining Army prepositioned stocks in an operational status at Charleston, South Carolina and aboard ships that store and transport Army war reserve assets; (2) aircraft operations maintenance and logistics support for Department of State (DOS) anti-narcotics enforcement operations in Central and South America; (3) aircraft maintenance, modification and logistics support for the National Aeronautics and Space Administration; and (4) contractor maintenance services and engineering technical services in support of Kuwait Air Force F/A-18 aircraft.

The Air Force's evaluation under the past performance factor noted that the majority of DynCorp's contracts seem to emphasize aircraft maintenance. However, even though they are aircraft maintenance contracts there are many similar efforts that are relevant to the WRM requirement. These efforts range from efficient organization structures, to maintenance efforts on vehicles and AGE, to operating major supply/inventory systems. In addition, DynCorp had one contract that is very relevant, an Army contract for "maintenance of Army prepositioned stocks afloat." Although the government rater gave DynCorp high marks, this contract is still in its infancy stage. When the team inquired why such good ratings were given for a new contract, the government rater indicated the transition stage was exceptional. . . .

AWV generally asserts that it possesses vastly more relevant experience than DynCorp, such that the agency could not reasonably assign the same past performance rating to both offerors. In addition, AWV specifically claims that the agency improperly ignored two cure notices issued to DynCorp under its APS-3 contract.

We find that the Air Force reasonably rated DynCorp's past performance as exceptional/high confidence. As noted above, DynCorp received numerous excellent and very good ratings from its past performance references, and the Air Force determined that aspects of DynCorp's performance under these contracts were directly relevant to the contract requirements here. For example, according to the agency, DynCorp's contracts demonstrated its ability to successfully manage contracts in fluid environments in foreign countries, utilize large inventory control systems, manage parts supply and accountability, perform operations at dispersed locations, adhere to government maintenance directives, and perform at the quality levels required on the WRM contract.

In this regard, the agency reports that DynCorp demonstrated the ability to meet program requirements in a fluid environment in foreign countries under its DOS contract for aircraft operations maintenance and logistics support for anti-narcotics enforcement operations in Central and South America; according to the agency, this ability is relevant to performing the WRM contract requirements in the highly fluid political and military environment which the WRM contractor must deal with. The agency reports that DynCorp also demonstrated under the DOS contract an ability to manage large inventory control systems with high levels of accuracy and to conduct operations at dispersed, remote locations. Further, according to the agency, DynCorp demonstrated under its Kuwaiti F/A-18 aircraft contract the ability to manage parts supply and accountability, as well as control sand intrusion, salt corrosion and the impact of high heat in the same region as the WRM contract is to be performed.

We find no basis for objecting to the agency's evaluation of DynCorp's proposal in this area. The agency rated DynCorp based on the considerations identified in the RFP for the past performance factor, and the rationale for its conclusions is well documented. There is nothing inherently unreasonable in its conclusion that DynCorp's performance of different aspects of various types of contracts—similar to aspects of the current contract—warranted the highest possible rating.

We recognize that, as asserted by AWV, that company possesses extensive, relevant experience. For example, AWV is not only the incumbent Air Force

WRM contractor in Southwest Asia; it has also provided base operations and maintenance services for Air Force bases in Turkey; training, logistics and related support to the Saudi Arabian National Guard; and personnel support services for United States personnel in Egypt. However, AWV received the highest possible rating under this factor, reflecting the high quality and relevance of its past performance, and the agency was not obligated to reduce the rating reasonably assigned to DynCorp even if, as AWV contends, AWV's past performance was even better. Agencies are not required to give evaluation credit for proposal features it determines will not contribute in a meaningful manner to better satisfying the agency's needs. Here, given DynCorp's highly-rated relevant past performance, it is unclear how AWV's additional, relevant past performance would contribute to better satisfying the agency's stated needs so as to warrant a significantly higher rating under the past performance factor. In any event, in view of DynCorp's higher rating under two of the four mission capability evaluation subfactors and AWV's higher evaluated cost, there is no basis for concluding that a marginally higher rating for AWV under the past performance factor would affect the outcome here.

Our Office has recognized that in certain limited circumstances an agency evaluating an offeror's past performance has an obligation (as opposed to the discretion) to consider outside information bearing on the offeror's past performance, as where the information in question was simply too close at hand to require offerors to shoulder the inequities that spring from an agency's failure to obtain, and consider, the information. However, the "close at hand" information in these cases concerned contracts for the same services with the same procuring activity, or at least information personally known to the evaluators. There has been no showing that such circumstances are present here.

The record includes statements from agency evaluators and source selection officials indicating that they either did not read [DELETED]'s FPR cover letter or did not understand it to refer to DynCorp, and stating that, in any case, they were unaware of the cure notices until after award. AWV has pointed to no evidence establishing that the contracting officials in fact knew of the cure notices and, moreover, the evidence on which the argument is founded consists solely of a statement that was submitted with a competitor's proposal and that neither identified DynCorp by name nor referred to cure notices. Thus, although an agency generally may not ignore negative past performance information of which it is aware, see G. Marine Diesel, supra, the record here does not establish that contracting officials were on notice of potential problems in DynCorp's performance of the APS-3 contract such that they were required to investigate further.

The protest is denied.

Example 6.2: Past Performance/Price Tradeoffs

GAO Decision (abridged)

Matter of: H.F. Henderson Industries

File: B-275017

Date: January 17, 1997

DIGEST

Agency selection of higher priced offeror with a low performance risk rating instead of the lower priced offeror with a reasonably based moderate performance risk rating based on prior contract delinquencies was reasonable and consistent with the solicitation's evaluation scheme, which weighted past performance and price equally, where timely delivery was imperative.

DECISION

The RFP advised that the best value award decision would be based on a trade-off between performance risk and price, with performance risk and price being equally weighted. Proposals were to be assigned a performance risk rating of either low, moderate, high, or not applicable. Award was to be made to the lowest-priced offeror if it received a low performance risk rating, but award could be made to other than the lowest priced offeror if that offeror received other than a low performance risk rating.

Eleven proposals were submitted. Henderson submitted the lowest-priced offer of $7.8 million, but received a moderate performance risk rating due to reported late (delinquent) deliveries under some current and prior contracts. Datacom submitted the next lowest-priced offer of $9.2 million with a low performance risk rating based upon consistent early or timely performance under its contracts. Based on its detailed review of each offeror's past performance record, the Air Force determined that Datacom's higher-priced offer represented the best value because its past performance indicated that it was more likely that the government would receive timely delivery, as compared to Henderson's past performance which indicated a moderate risk that timely deliveries may not be made.

In a best value procurement, price is not necessarily controlling in determining the offer that represents the best value to the government. Rather, that determination is made on the basis of whatever evaluation factors are set forth in the RFP, with the source selection official often required to make a cost/technical tradeoff to determine if one proposal's technical superiority is worth the higher cost that may be associated with that proposal. In this regard, price/past performance tradeoffs are permitted when such tradeoffs are consistent with the RFP evaluation scheme.

Thus, where, as here, an RFP identifies past performance and price as the evaluation criteria and indicates that an offeror with good past performance can expect a higher rating than an offeror without such a record of performance, proposals must be evaluated on that basis, and ultimately the selection official must decide whether or not a higher-priced offeror with the better past performance rating represents the best value to the government.

Henderson argues that its moderate performance risk rating was unreasonable because some of the information that the Air Force relied upon was misleading. One contract, identified from MOCAS documents, is assertedly being held in a delinquent status until the government recoups an overpayment of progress payments; another, identified from CPARS documents, had late deliveries which Henderson attributes to defective government technical drawings as evidenced by the equitable adjustment it obtained under that contract; and a third, also identified from CPARS documents as delinquent, is assertedly so dissimilar from this RFP work that it should not have been considered.

[T]he Air Force reports, and the record confirms, that Henderson is delinquent on 4 of 13 other open contracts. In contrast, Datacom's performance record indicated that it met or exceeded all contract requirements and had no delinquencies or delays, which supported its low performance risk rating. The Air Force judged that Henderson's demonstrably spotty present and past performance record, particularly its delinquent deliveries, evidenced that there was a risk that Henderson may not make timely deliveries if it was awarded this contract. While Henderson disagrees with its past performance assessment, it has not demonstrated that its moderate performance risk rating was unwarranted.

In making the performance/price tradeoff, the Air Force found that the price premium associated with making award to Datacom, instead of Henderson, was justified, given Datacom's low performance risk, based on its consistent timely and early contract deliveries, as compared to Henderson's moderate performance risk, which evidenced a greater potential for untimely deliveries under this contract. The Air Force explained that it was imperative that the kits be delivered on schedule, and that award to a higher-priced offeror with a low performance risk was warranted in these circumstances because of the potential for additional costs to the government due to slips in delivery of these kits and the detrimental impact that delays would have on the mission-essential fleet upgrade. While Henderson disagrees, we find nothing unreasonable in this determination, which is consistent with the RFP evaluation scheme.

Example 6.3: Using Past Performance to Evaluate New Firms or Firms with No Performance History—Making Price/Past Performance Tradeoffs

GAO Decision (abridged)

Matter of: National Aerospace Group, Inc.

File: B-281958; B-281959

Date: May 10, 1999

DIGEST

Placement of an order at a significant price premium for the sole reason that the vendor quoting a lower price has no prior performance history in supplying the item being procured was unreasonable, where determination was not made in accordance with the stated evaluation scheme.

DECISION

RFQ-A426 sought prices for metal sheets with a specified dimension for delivery within 120 days after the date of order. The agency evaluated vendors under the Automated Best Value Model (ABVM). Tara had an ABVM score of 95.4. National, which was a relatively new supplier, was given a rating of 999.9 because it lacked a performance history for this item. Under the ABVM procedures, a supplier with no performance history is assigned a rating of 999.9, which is referred to in the record as a neutral rating.

The award justification document, signed and dated on January 20, 1999, was a preprinted form, which permitted the contracting officer to select one of a variety of reasons for the award. Here, in pertinent part, the contracting officer completed the form as follows: "Lower priced offer(s) not selected because: . . . Other score(s) not a true indicator of performance because score(s) based on too few contract line items."

[T]he contracting officer states that, "[e]ssentially, [she] determined that Tara, who had a composite ABVM score of 95.4 represented a lesser risk of nonperformance than did [National] who had a neutral rating of 999.9 because it is a relatively new supplier."

National argues that it was improperly penalized without any justification for a lack of previous performance history. National asserts that the agency's selection decision violates the ABVM notice provision which provides, in pertinent part, that "[a]n ABVM score does not determine an offeror's award eligibility, or technical acceptability," and that "[n]ew offeror status will not be grounds for disqualification for award."

[T]he FAR requires that the contracting officer evaluate quotations "on the basis established in the solicitation" and support "the award decision if other than price-related factors were considered in selecting the supplier." Here, we conclude that the selection decision was flawed because it is inadequately supported and was not based on the criteria announced in the [small purchase agreement] SPA.

In a recent case involving [Defense Logistics Agency's] DLA's use of ABVM scoring, we concluded that the use of a neutral rating approach to avoid penalizing a vendor without prior experience does not preclude a determination to award to a higher-priced firm with a good past performance record over a lower priced vendor with a neutral past performance rating. Indeed, such a determination is inherent in the concept of best value. Nonetheless, we expressed concern that the vendor without a performance history not be disqualified from award merely because it lacked a performance history; we pointed out that such an approach would be inconsistent with the FAR and the DLA ABVM clause. As DLA recognized in that case, FAR § 15.305(a)(2) provides that in the case of an offeror without a record of relevant past performance or for whom information on past performance is not available, the offeror may not be evaluated favorably or unfavorably on past performance. The ABVM clause states that lack of performance history is not grounds for disqualification for award.

There is nothing in the record to show that the contracting officer performed a comparative assessment of the vendors. The contracting officer merely checked a box on a form indicating that National was not selected because its 999.9 ABVM score was based on insufficient information and, therefore, was not a true indicator of its capabilities. Nor is there any indication that the contracting officer performed a tradeoff that considered the significant price premium in ordering from Tara, or that the contracting officer considered in her decision that National quoted a significantly shorter delivery time and confirmed that the metal sheets were in stock. Unlike in Phillips, there is no indication here that the item was in backlog or high demand status or that timely delivery was critical and worth the price premium to avoid the risk of using a vendor with no performance history. We conclude that the contracting officer failed to make a meaningful best value determination consistent with the SPA to justify paying a significant premium to Tara. As a result, DLA's decision was tantamount to rejecting National's quotation based on its lack of past performance history, which is inconsistent with 41 U.S.C. § 405(j)(2), FAR § 15.305(a)(2), and the clauses which implement the ABVM program, as discussed in the Phillips decision.

We therefore sustain National's protest of the order to Tara under RFQ-A426.

Example 6.4: When Evaluating Past Performance, the Comparative Assessment of Complexity Cannot Be Superficial

GAO Decision (abridged)

Matter of: PMT Services, Inc.

File: B-270538.2

Date: April 1, 1996

DIGEST

PMT Services, Inc. protests the award of a contract to Moheat Environmental Services, Inc. under RFP No. SP4400-95-R-0016, issued by the Defense Reutilization and Marketing Service (DRMS), Defense Logistics Agency, for hazardous waste disposal services at DRMS offices in San Antonio and Fort Hood, Texas, and surrounding locations. PMT challenges the agency's evaluation of its past performance and the source selection decision.

DECISION

Agency's technical evaluation of an offeror's past performance of hazardous waste disposal contracts under the solicitation's past performance evaluation factor and selection of a substantially higher-price proposal for award is unreasonable where the agency did not meaningfully consider the complexity of the protester's prior contracts vis-à-vis the complexity of the contract to be awarded.

While contract size may be relevant to contract complexity, evaluating "complexity" of contract requirements based on size alone, without considering such other indicators of complexity may not yield a meaningful conclusion about an offeror's probability of future success. An increase in the amount of waste to be disposed of under a contract, for example, or the number of pick-up locations are factors to be considered, but it does not follow that the complexity of the requirement has increased merely because of increases under these factors. In other words, if a contractor that has successfully disposed of 200,000 or 600,000 pounds of specific waste—as PMT has done under two prior contracts—now must dispose of 2 million pounds of waste, it may simply have to make more pick-ups using the same procedures and similar resources. On the other hand, the contractor may have to do considerably more, such as develop new procedures for handling hazardous waste with which it has no experience, provide more trucks and drivers, and coordinate the additional resources committed to the effort. The point to be made on the record is that one cannot simply say that because the size of the contract has increased, its complexity has also increased.

There has been absolutely no showing on this record that what is primarily a two-location requirement is more complex than the one-location requirement PMT previously serviced. In this regard the agency's evaluation did not identify any types of waste, handling procedures, staffing requirements, or quantity and management resources which could make this RFP work meaningfully more complex than that performed under the Tooele contract. In sum, on this record, we cannot say that an agency's reliance on the size and number of waste generation locations reflects a reasonable analysis of PMT's prior contracts and, in the absence of a meaningful distinction in the complexity of this work as compared to PMT's previous work, that the agency's evaluation of PMT's past performance as "marginal" is reasonably based.

Although the SSA discounted the number of waste generation locations in increasing Moheat's past performance rating, the record shows that the SSA did not similarly consider the immateriality of those locations to PMT's rating. To the contrary, PMT's lack of experience with multiple locations under a single contract was a specific concern stated by the SSA in his selection decision.

The SSA selected Moheat for award after determining that the evaluated difference in the firms' past performance justified a more than one million dollar (49 percent) price premium. This tradeoff decision, however, is based upon an inadequate evaluation of PMT's past performance. Until there is a proper assessment of PMT's past performance, the SSA cannot reasonably determine whether Moheat's past performance is worth the 49 percent price premium.

We recommend that DRMS reevaluate proposals and make a new source selection decision consistent with this decision. If DRMS selects an offeror other than Moheat for award, it should terminate the contract to Moheat and make award to that other offeror. We also recommend that the protester be reimbursed its costs of filing and pursuing its protest, including reasonable attorneys' fees. Bid Protest Regulations, § 21.8(d)(1), 60 Fed. Reg. 40,737, 40,743 (Aug. 10, 1995) (to be codified at 4 C.F.R. § 21.8). The protester should submit its certified claim for costs to the contracting agency within 90 days of receiving this decision. Bid Protest Regulations, § 21.8(f)(1).

The protest is sustained.

Example 6.5: Past Performance/Price Tradeoffs Must Be Fully Documented

GAO Decision (abridged)

Matter of: Si-Nor, Inc.

File: B-282064; B-282064.2

Date: May 25, 1999

DIGEST

Determination that higher-priced proposal rated higher under past performance subfactor (compared to protester's) offered best value to government cannot be determined reasonable where price was approximately twice as important as past performance under solicitation's evaluation scheme, and documentation of tradeoff decision does not explain why agency considered awardee's evaluation advantage under past performance sufficient to offset protester's lower offered price.

DECISION

Si-Nor, Inc. protests the Department of the Air Force's award of a contract to U.S. Eagle, Inc. under RFP No. F64605-98-R0032, for refuse collection and disposal services at Hickam Air Force Base, Hawaii.

We sustain the protest.

The RFP contemplated award of a fixed-price requirements contract for an eight-month base period, with four one-year options. No technical proposals were required, but each offeror was required to submit financial references and at least three past performance references for service contracts exceeding $100,000 in revenues annually on which it had performed as prime contractor during the period November 1, 1995, through October 31, 1998.

Offers were to be evaluated based on (1) past performance/experience and (2) price/cost, which were to be approximately equal in weight. Past performance and experience also were to be approximately equal in weight. Agency Report, Tab 7, Decision Document, Feb. 24, 1999, at 1st unnumbered page, and Decision Document (original), at 1st unnumbered page. Award was to be made on a best value basis. Past performance was to be assessed to determine offerors' relative capability and trustworthiness, and thus their relative reliability to perform the contract requirements, and experience was to be evaluated to assess offerors' experience in performing work on similar refuse collection and disposal services contracts.

Five offers were received. Based on the evaluation, the source selection official determined that Eagle's proposal represented the best value to the government. Although Si-Nor's evaluated price ($7,974,020) was slightly lower than Eagle's ($8,029,688), and both proposals were rated low risk for experience, Si-Nor's proposal was rated only satisfactory for past performance, while Eagle's was rated outstanding. In comparing Eagle's proposal to Si-Nor's, the selection official stated as follows:

> I have determined [Eagle]'s proposal to be of better value than [Si-Nor]'s proposal. [Eagle] received an outstanding past performance rating compared to the satisfactory rating given [Si-Nor]. [Eagle]'s quality control and business relations, in particular, received laudatory comments from customers. I believe that [Eagle]'s outstanding past performance outweighs the lower price offered by [Si-Nor], a difference of $7,944 (Basic Period).

Upon learning of the resulting award to Eagle, Si-Nor first filed an agency-level protest, and then later filed a protest with our Office, arguing in part that the agency improperly had failed to apply a small disadvantaged business (SDB) evaluation adjustment to prices. The agency agreed, concluding that Federal Acquisition Regulation clause 52.219-23, which provides for addition of an evaluation factor to all non-SDB offers for evaluation purposes, erroneously had been omitted from the RFP. The agency then reevaluated prices, applying a 10-percent factor to the prices of offers from non-SDBs (that is, all offers other than Si-Nor's, since Si-Nor was the only SDB offeror). This increased Eagle's evaluated price to $8,832,656.80, and increased the difference between its and Si-Nor's total price from $55,668 to $858,636.80. However, a new selection official determined that Eagle's proposal still represented the best value to the agency in light of its outstanding performance.

Si-Nor challenges the source selection decision on the basis that the agency failed to document why any advantage reflected in Eagle's higher past performance rating warranted payment of an $858,636.80 premium. Si-Nor believes its lower evaluated price warranted a determination that its proposal represented the best value to the government.[1]

Source selection officials in negotiated procurements have broad discretion in determining the manner and extent to which they will make use of the technical and price evaluation results. Price/technical tradeoffs may be made, and the extent to which one may be sacrificed for the other is governed only by the tests of rationality and consistency with the established evaluation criteria. In deciding between competing proposals, the propriety of such a tradeoff turns not on the difference in technical scores or ratings per se, but on whether the selection official's judgment concerning the significance of that difference was reasonable and adequately justified in light of the RFP evaluation scheme. In this regard, where a price/technical tradeoff is made, the source selection decision must be documented, and the documentation must include the rationale for any business judgments and tradeoffs made, including the benefits associated with additional costs. Federal Acquisition Regulation § 15.308; Opti-Lite Optical, B-281693, Mar. 22, 1999, 99-1 CPD ¶ 61 at 5.

Based on our review of the record, we conclude that the determination to award to Eagle was not adequately justified. The tradeoff rationale set forth in the new selection official's revised source selection decision stated as follows:

> I have determined [Eagle]'s proposal to be of better value than [Si-Nor]'s proposal. Both offerors received a low risk rating for experience. However, [Eagle] received an outstanding past performance rating based on their past performance record, meeting all contract requirements and exceeding some of the contract requirements, compared to the satisfactory rating given [Si-Nor]. . . . I believe that [Eagle]'s outstanding past performance outweighs the lower price offered by [Si-Nor], a difference of $858,636.80 for the total cost.

This determination—as well as the record as a whole—includes no explanation for the agency's conclusion as required by FAR § 15.308. While the record clearly sets forth the agency's conclusion that Eagle's past performance rating was worth an $858,636.80 price premium, it includes no documentation, evidence or explanation of the benefits that the agency associated with Eagle's superior past performance rating which would outweigh the additional price. This lack of documentation is significant in light of the fact that price was to be essentially twice as important as past performance under the stated evaluation scheme.[2] Absent a more detailed rationale, there simply is no way to determine whether the agency in fact accorded price this substantially greater weight. Further, such a rationale would provide evidence that the second tradeoff was conducted using the price premium reflecting the SDB preference ($858,636.80), rather than (as the protester alleges) continuing to use the premium without the SDB preference ($55,668), which the agency used in the erroneous initial tradeoff.

We conclude that the record does not establish that the Air Force's tradeoff decision was reasonable, and sustain the protest on this basis. By letter of today to the Secretary, we are recommending that the agency perform and document a proper tradeoff analysis. If the Air Force determines that Eagle's proposal does not represent the best value to the government under the stated evaluation factors, the agency should terminate Eagle's contract for the convenience of the government and make award to Si-Nor. In addition, we recommend that the protester be reimbursed its costs of filing and pursuing the protest. 4 C.F.R. § 21.8(d)(1) (1998). The protester should submit its certified claim, detailing the time expended and costs incurred, directly to the contracting agency within 60 days of receiving this decision. 4 C.F.R. § 21.8(f)(1).

The protest is sustained.

NOTES

1. Si-Nor also argues that Eagle's proposal should have been rated moderate (rather than low) risk under the experience subfactor because Eagle has not had prior contracts in the waste disposal field of a scope similar to that under the contract here. The risk ratings are unobjectionable. The RFP requested information on contracts over $100,000, thus indicating that such contracts could be considered relevant, and Eagle's proposal cited its performance of refuse disposal contracts at military and naval installations with approximate annual values of $600,000, $304,000, and $185,072. (For the contract at issue in this protest, Eagle's proposed price was $1,397,384 for the eight-month base period and $1,658,076 for the first option year.) Although Si-Nor's proposal referenced a number of contracts with higher annual values ($900,000, 850,000, $800,000, and $625,000), as well as some smaller contracts ($488,172, $300,000, $259,620, $209,676, $86,808, and $80,000), these values also were well below the value of the contract here. Si-Nor's argument thus provides no basis for questioning the risk ratings.
2. Since past performance/experience and price/cost were to be given approximately equal weight, each was worth approximately 50 percent of the overall rating; since, within past performance/experience, each of the two components was approximately equal, past performance was worth approximately 25 percent of the overall rating.

APPENDIX C

PAST PERFORMANCE INFORMATION FORM

Instructions: Use this form to identify each current and past contract similar to the RFP requirement.

1. **Contract Identification:**

    A. Contracting party (name, address, email, and telephone number) ____________

    ____

    ____

    ____

    ____

    B. Contract number ____________________________

    C. Type of contract. Fixed price ☐ Cost reimbursement ☐ Negotiated ☐
    Sealed bid ☐ Other (explain) ____________________

    D. Date of award / /

    E. Completion date / /

2. **Size** (contract dollar value): $

3. **Scope** (summary statement of work): ____________________

    ____

    ____

    ____

    ____

    ____

    ____

4. **Complexity:** Difficult ☐ or Routine ☐

5. **Contact Information** (name, telephone number and email address of one or more of the contracting party's procurement officials or other references):

INDEX

K

L

M

N

Q

R

S

T

U

Complement Your Federal Contracting Library with These Additional Resources from

MANAGEMENTCONCEPTS

Understanding Government Contract Source Selection

Margaret G. Rumbaugh

From planning to protest and all the steps in between, this is the one reference government professionals and commercial contractors will want to have close at hand. The book details each step in the source selection process. Examples drawn from current case law clearly illustrate what can go wrong in the process and offer insights on how to avoid the pitfalls in the future.

ISBN 978-1-56726-273-5 ■ Product Code B735 ■ 509 pages

Federal Acquisition: Key Issues and Guidance

Paula B. Compton

This book is an essential guide to understanding and working within the complex world of federal government contracting. It offers brief but comprehensive explanations of the major phases and essential tasks in the contracting process. Written in a clear and easy-to-understand style, this resource provides the perfect foundation for building a thorough understanding of federal contracting.

ISBN 978-1-56726-248-3 ■ Product Code B483 ■ 292 pages

Federal Contracting Answer Book, 2nd Edition

Terrence M. O'Connor and Mary Ann P. Wangemann

Anyone involved in government contracting — whether a contractor or a federal contracting professional — knows how tough it is to learn the contracting process and stay on top of the ever-changing rules, regulations, and details. This book provides clear, succinct answers to questions on all aspects of federal government contracting, particularly procedures and regulations. The straightforward, practical approach allows for quick and easy access to critical information, while providing valuable insights into the changing landscape of federal government contracting.

ISBN 978-1-56726-245-2 ■ Product Code B452 ■ 558 pages

Guide to Contract Pricing: Cost and Price Analysis for Contractors, Subcontractors, and Government Agencies, 5th Edition

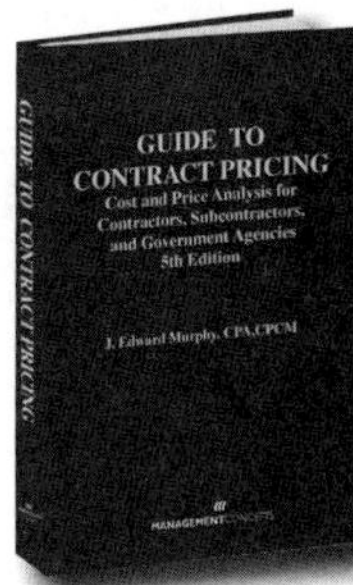

Editor J. Edward Murphy, CPA, CPCM

This master reference — in its fifth edition — contains everything you need to know about government pricing rules and regulations in one easy-to-use volume. *Guide to Contract Pricing* explains how the government conducts business and walks you through every step of the contracting process. This fully updated edition includes a new chapter on the role of auditors in contract pricing as well as five new detailed appendices. A CD-ROM provides sample forms, templates, and tools to facilitate the cost and price analysis process.

ISBN 978-1-56726-241-4 ■ Product Code B414 ■ 254 pages

The COR/COTR Answer Book, Second Edition

Bob Boyd

Today, many CORs, COTRs, and other members of the acquisition team are taking on additional responsibilities from their contracting officers—including overseeing and monitoring contracts. If you are facing these new challenges, your knowledge of contracting issues is critical to your success. This book provides the practical guidance you need to ensure each contract's successful completion. Written in an easy-to-use Q&A style, this comprehensive guide includes answers to 460 common questions on how to monitor and oversee contracts.

ISBN 978-1-56726-215-5 ■ Product Code B155 ■ 405 pages